# MARKS OF DISTINCTION:
# AMERICAN EXCEPTIONALISM REVISITED

# THE DOLPHIN

*General Editor:*
*Dominic Rainsford*

32

# MARKS OF DISTINCTION: AMERICAN EXCEPTIONALISM REVISITED

*Edited by*
*Dale Carter*

AARHUS UNIVERSITY PRESS

Printed in Denmark by Narayana Press
ISBN 87 7288 383 9
ISSN 0106 4487

AARHUS UNIVERSITY PRESS
Langelandsgade 177
DK–8200 Aarhus N, Denmark
Fax (+45) 8942 5380
www.unipress.dk

73 Lime Walk
Headington, Oxford OX3 7AD
Fax (+44) 1865 750 079

Box 511
Oakville, Conn. 06779
Fax (+1) 860 945 9468

*Editorial address:*
THE DOLPHIN
Department of English
University of Aarhus
DK–8000 Aarhus C, Denmark
Fax (+45) 8942 6540

This volume is published with financial support from the Aarhus
University Research Foundation and the Danish Research Council for
the Humanities.

Cover design: Jørgen Sparre
Cover photography: Inger Hunnerup Dalsgaard

# Contents

## Institutions                                                    *165*

## Laws                                                            *229*

## Returns                                                         *283*

# Acknowledgements

In my acknowledgments to a previous volume in this series, *Cracking the Ike Age: Aspects of Fifties America* (1992), I expressed my thanks to those who had helped bring that collection into the world for remaining cool and efficient in spite of 'my flexible deadline editing system.' Regrettably though unintentionally, that system in the intervening years has become yet more flexible. I would therefore like to thank, first, the contributors to *Marks of Distinction*: not only for their tolerance of the editor's unnerving blend of serial agitation and inertia but also for their patience during this book's protracted journey from its origins to its present, much-expanded form.

In the course of that journey, both book and editor have become indebted to various other individuals and institutions, and I am happy now to thank them too, in some cases for their multiple contributions. I am grateful to David E. Nye of Southern Denmark University, Odense, for initially suggesting that the seminar proceedings deserved to find published form, and to Mick Gidley of the University of Leeds in England for offering subsequent encouragement and advice about potential expansion of the volume and eventual publication. I am also grateful to Michael Kammen of Cornell University and the Editors of *American Quarterly*, and to Joyce Appleby of UCLA and the Editors of the *Journal of American History*, for permission to reproduce their contributions to this volume, both of which have appeared previously in the respective journals. I would like to extend the same gratitude to the Executive Committee of the Nordic Association for American Studies and the Editorial Board of *American Studies in Scandinavia*, whose members kindly granted permission to reproduce those articles which originally appeared in a special issue of the journal, devoted to American Exceptionalism. I would like to thank, too, the University of Aarhus Research Fund, the Danish Research Council for the Humanities, and the Department of English, University of Aarhus, for financial support which has made publication of this volume possible;

as well as the staff at Aarhus University Press for helping transport *Marks of Distinction* beyond its long-running virtual stage. Many thanks are due, moreover, to Dominic Rainsford, General Editor of *The Dolphin* series and Head of the Department of English, for his bureaucratic and technical assistance in bringing the book closer to publication, and for his scholarly and financial wizardry in bringing funding closer to the book.

Last but not least, I am grateful to Inger Dalsgaard for the collection's front cover illustration. Highlighting Grand Central's classical design against the former Pan-Am building's international style, the photograph not only juxtaposes two familiar architectural symbols (ironically) of American national identity. In locating Hermes – agent of good-fortune, protector of traders and god of the marketplace in some versions; storm-bringer, thief and courier of the dead in others – between the technologies of railroad and high-rise and their associated temporal and spatial conquests, it also problematizes myths of national purpose. At once endorsing one of John Kouwenhoven's responses to his celebrated inquiry into 'what's "American" about America?' the photograph from another angle questions his premises.[1] For if some of the nation's distinctive cultural contours can indeed be identified, as Kouwenhoven believed, on the Manhattan skyline, then on that selfsame skyline any such marks of distinction may simultaneously dissolve; in the very act of expressing themselves, indeed, aspects of American Exceptionalism may paradoxically undermine their claims.

Dale Carter

### Notes

1. John Kouwenhoven, 'What's "American" About America,' in Kouwenhoven, *The Beer Can By The Highway* (Garden City, NY: Doubleday, 1961), 43–50.

# Departures

# Introduction: The Death and Life of an Exceptional Concept

*Dale Carter*

The end of American exceptionalism has long been anticipated or proclaimed. As early as 1949 Harold Laski was writing in *The American Democracy* that 'no one now takes seriously the legend of a special American destiny.' Just over a quarter of a century later, defeat in Vietnam and the Watergate scandal prompted Daniel Bell to argue that the associated erosion of the nation's physical power and its claims to moral superiority had by the mid–1970s reduced American exceptionalism to little more than constitutional formalities.[1] Another twenty-five years on and at the turn of Henry Luce's 'American Century,' John Carlos Rowe advocated a 'more internationalist and comparative' American Studies: one capable of challenging those 'nationalist paradigms and assumptions' traditionally organized around the concept of exceptionalism, from 'narrow definitions of national character' to 'the assumption that the nation-state [is] the proper unit of analysis for understanding American experience.'[2] Both the map and the territory, it seems, have been and should be remodelled.

Yet like one of its more enduring fellow travellers, American liberalism, the concept of American exceptionalism has proven a great survivor. No sooner proclaimed dead and buried in one place, it reappears, alive and kicking, in the next: apparently prepared, in the wake of the Cold War and the associated reconceptualization of the United States as the world's only superpower, to continue its odyssey across the nation's material and imaginary landscapes well into the new millennium.[3] During the past decade or so, the scholarly landscape in particular has witnessed a renewal of interest in this most enduring of ideas. In 1991, Byron Shafer edited a selection of papers by distinguished

*Marks of Distinction: American Exceptionalism Revisited*, ed. Dale Carter,
*The Dolphin* 32, pp. 11–23. © 2001 by Aarhus University Press, Denmark.
ISBN 87 7288 383 9; ISSN 0106 4487.

social scientists from a Nuffield College conference under the title *Is America Different? A New Look at American Exceptionalism*. Three years later, David Adams and Cornelius van Minnen co-edited *Reflections on American Exceptionalism*, the proceedings of the inaugural European Historians of the United States conference held in 1993 at the Roosevelt Study Center, Middleburg, Holland. In 1996, Seymour Martin Lipset added to his Nuffield College keynote address a full-length study, *American Exceptionalism: A Double-Edged Sword*, and this volume was followed two years later by Deborah Madsen's critical review of the concept's cultural and historical contours, *American Exceptionalism.*[4] During the 1990s academic journals also carried a number of significant essays on the topic, ranging from Joyce Appleby's 1992 presidential address before the Organization of American Historians to Michael Kammen's 1993 *American Quarterly* reassessment of the debate in the light of the previous twenty years' scholarly enquiry. Complementing these prominent conferences and publications have been numerous other meetings, articles and reviews, including the seminar on 'Aspects of American Exceptionalism' held at the American Studies Center, University of Aarhus, in February 1996, at which the following collection of papers on the topic began to take shape.[5]

Those engaged in re-evaluating the origins, nature, meaning, scope, strengths and limitations of exceptionalism in recent years have reached little agreement on the issues. As Michael Kammen writes in his review of the literature, with which this collection closes, a 'striking feature of the latest contributions [to the debate] is that they differ so radically among themselves' – even when assessing identical evidence or arguments. Where Kammen claims that Byron Shafer's *Is America Different?* collection 'reaffirms the notion' of American exceptionalism, for example, the editor himself argues that the conference proceedings offer 'tremendously varied responses' to the question of exceptionalism's fate: 'it never was; it once was, but is no more; new versions have substituted for old; it continues on, unchanged in its essence.'[6] None of this should come as a surprise, perhaps. Given the nature of the concept itself, the diverse disciplinary roots of those scholars attracted to it, the variety of analytical tools and theoretical assumptions brought to bear upon it, and the range of data drawn on in the process, such disagreements are to be expected. What may be more surprising, at least at first glance, is that the concept of American exceptionalism has continued to be of scholarly concern at all. For the fifteen to twenty year period over which Michael Kammen cast his attention in 1993 has been one in which developments within and beyond the academic world appears in a number of ways to have brought into question, revealed the shortcomings of, and perhaps even thoroughly undermined, exceptionalism in all its diverse forms.

Many of the developments associated with the social, political, cultural and intellectual transformations of the 1960s and beyond have been registered within and informed American historical, literary and cultural scholarship.[7] Both Lawrence Veysey writing in *American Quarterly* and *Reviews in American History* in 1979, and Joyce Appleby in her 1992 OAH address, for example, refer to the ways in which new departures in American historical studies have challenged beliefs in the nation's distinctiveness. To Veysey, the rise of social history brought with it a growing emphasis upon comparative, and particularly cross-national, research, and a corresponding 'questioning of previously unexamined assumptions about American uniqueness.' Appleby, meanwhile, pointed to the ways in which a new generation of social historians had since the late 1960s challenged the individualist, ahistorical and universalist biases she saw underpinning American exceptionalism's 'grand narrative.' Closely associated with the rise of social history, the adoption of multicultural perspectives within and beyond the academic world has also challenged exceptionalist paradigms. Appleby told OAH members of how the new 'multicultural history of the United States' had begun to salvage the nation's original diversity by recovering and expanding the public memory – a memory belonging, not least, to those immigrants, African-Americans, Native Americans and women whose identities had since the early nineteenth century been overshadowed by an exceptionalism that was less a manifestation of nature's laws than a racial-, ethnic- and gender-specific cultural construct.[8] Writing in *American Quarterly* in 1990, Elizabeth Fox-Genovese sounded similar themes when evaluating the contribution of feminist and African-American scholarship to the reconstruction of American literary and cultural history. Given the ways in which American culture had successfully 'promote[d] the ideal of American exceptionalism' only by 'exclud[ing] those who do not fit' its circumscribed notions of national identity, Fox-Genovese asked of herself and her readers 'whether we can appropriately speak of a unified culture at all.' The following year, the publishers of Philip Fisher's anthology of *Representations* essays *The New American Studies* answered confidently that its contents 'deal[t] a fatal blow to the idea of a unified American culture.'[9]

Less frequently acknowledged, but of particular significance in preparing the ground for some of the challenges to exceptionalism cited above, has been the impact of New Left historiography. The approach of the New Left towards American exceptionalism has been a complicated one, as Michael Kammen points out. Even as it lamented or denied common features of the exceptionalist creed, notably the latter's faith in a fundamental American benevolence, so as a political and social movement the New Left embodied qualities often associated with exceptionalism, such as a preference for self-reliance and personal insight over state control or class consciousness, and a belief in the quasi-mystical recuperative powers of the American landscape. To a fraction of the New Left, at least, all of the nation's self-evident shortcomings simply made it uniquely evil.[10] Within the narrower confines of the academic world, too, the New Left's concern for certain familiar exceptionalist staples was evident. To the influential diplomatic historian William Appleman Williams, for example, the influence of the frontier was as crucial and pervasive in ideological terms as it was to Frederick Jackson Turner during the Progressive era and those he influenced thereafter. Yet a preoccupation with some of the touchstones of exceptionalism scarcely constituted a subscription to the faith itself. Following in the footsteps of his revisionist predecessor, Charles Beard, Williams analysed the significance of the frontier in American history in order to explain why in his view it had to be transcended. Americans could not begin, he quoted Walter Lippmann approvingly, until they had learned to abandon the belief 'that utopia is in the old American frontier.' Along with that belief would go, he implied, the debilitating conviction at the heart of all exceptionalist creeds: that the United States was not like other lands. To this extent, Williams was not only recovering a marginalized past, like Appleby's social historians; he was encouraging and enabling Americans to acknowledge that they *had* a past, as opposed to an historical mythology.[11]

One part of the nation's past Williams attempted to confront his fellow citizens with was, of course, its imperial past, not least for the light it might throw on its imperial present, from the shores of Castro's Cuba to the battlefields of South Vietnam. And any account of the discrediting of exceptionalism would obviously be incomplete without reference to the effects of the South East Asian conflict on American self-confidence and perhaps even self-definition. It is certainly possible to interpret US involvement in Vietnam as revealing – or even deriving from – certain distinctive American cultural traits, and thereby to find in the conflict further evidence of exceptionalism's enduring influence.[12] A more common reading, however, has identified in the war an erosion or loss of public belief in once-distinctive national traits, from military invincibility to moral innocence. Moreover, whatever the nature and extent of Vietnam's impact on exceptionalism, the war has been only one of a number of events, processes and developments whose combined effects over the past thirty years have challenged exceptionalism's appeal. The fact that journalists and other commentators have felt driven, and been able, to proclaim the nation's loss of innocence on so many occasions in recent years – whether in connection with the assassination of the Kennedy brothers and Martin Luther King, Jr. or with the Watergate, Irangate or Monica Lewinsky scandals – might suggest that a belief in this particular feature of American exceptionalism has proven difficult to eradicate. Yet whatever effects may be attributed to individual events, broader long-term economic, social, political ·and technological transformations have increasingly called into question beliefs in the fundamentally distinctive nature of the United States. As Giles Gunn remarks in *The Culture of Criticism and the Criticism of Culture* (1987): 'To take but one example of modern restructuring, the multinational corporation has so fundamentally revised the meaning of national boundaries, not to say social differences, that it has become essentially pointless to talk any longer about cultural purity or ... cultural uniqueness.'[13] In his contribution to this collection, Tom Byers speculates along similar lines about 'exceptionalist ideology in an age of ... economic globalization.' One of the points of departure of Eric Guthey's contribution, meanwhile, is that the 'the globalizing and decentralizing tendencies' associated with the recent development of new technologies now 'threaten to dissolve the usefulness of the nation state and further confuse and fragment the already-problematic notion of an American national identity itself.'

By calling into question the significance of both the nation-state and associated concepts of national identity, Gunn and Guthey could easily be interpreted as challenging not only the *raison d'être* of American exceptionalism but also one of the assumptions upon which American Studies as a scholarly movement developed from the 1930s onwards. Something similar might be said of Peter Bardaglio's contribution, which among other things notes the ways in which exceptionalist logics have written the American south out of the national norm, incorporated African-Americans as at best marginal figures, and correspondingly distorted our understanding of US history. Not surprisingly, perhaps, many critics in recent years have spoken of the close connections between exceptionalist beliefs and the American Studies agenda, at least during the latter's earlier phases. That agenda, it has been argued, can only be understood if related to the growth of American political, economic, social and cultural power from the 1930s – and particularly World War Two – onwards. In tandem with the growth of American influence and the deepening of the Cold War during the late 1940s and 1950s, critics claim, there developed a 'consensus history' which helped make of American Studies something of a handmaiden of power by prompting it to ask not whether but *why* the United States was so different. Such associations may have been exaggerated and simplified, but they were by no means groundless.[14] Even if the connections were more tenuous than some critics suggested, moreover, the existence of such a relationship suggests that signs of decline or diffusion in one realm may have implications for the other. A common way of reading the history of American Studies has been to identify a chronological arc, reaching up from the pioneering works of Perry Miller and F. O. Matthiessen in the 1930s to the climactic expressions of the so-called 'myth and symbol school' in the 1950s and 1960s – after which a mixture of disciplinary fragmentation, intellectual disillusion and institutional attrition left American Studies, in Giles Gunn's words, 'in considerable trouble.' A less Spenglerian version of the discipline's trajectory might stress the ways in which American Studies has repeatedly rejuvenated itself by drawing what was once marginal into its centre: most recently via the development of a 'post-national' American Studies that, in John Carlos Rowe's words, 'is critical of US hegemony and the constructedness of both national myths and national borders.' In either case, however, if the fate of American Studies and of American exceptionalism are at all related, the implications for the latter are self-evident.[15]

Whatever the nature of the relationship (and in his contribution to this anthology James Mendelsohn suggests that American Studies now adopts a predominantly critical stance), exceptionalism – or at least belief in it, which may be one and the same thing – endures.[16] Many of those historic, social, cultural, political and other features often cited as causes of distinctiveness – from the impact of the frontier and slavery to the influence of immigration and ethnicity; from the supposed lack of a feudal past to the consequences of high living standards – continue to exercise the thoughts of students of American life. As many of the contributors to Byron Shafer's *Is America Different?* and much of the scholarly work reviewed in Michael Kammen's survey of the literature confirm, it *is* difficult to ignore the wide range of evidence documenting the many distinctions between the United

States and, say, Europe, which have endured to this day – though whether such *differences* by themselves constitute a case for *distinctiveness* is another matter. Significantly, perhaps, while interpretations and agendas have moved on a good deal since the days of Frederick Jackson Turner, Louis Hartz and David Potter, the sense of distinctiveness they shared has not entirely vanished, even among more recent generations of Americanists. In his introduction to *The New American Studies*, for example, Philip Fisher writes of 'a set of underlying ... national facts around which all identities are shaped and with which the many rhetorics of our culture are engaged.' The former, he goes on, include a 'troubled utopian core of enterprise, freedom, and democratic culture.'[17] Just as definitions of evidence change and intellectual tools, concepts and agendas undergo transformation, in other words, so traditional gestalts survive. In an era during which concerns for borders, fragmentations and differences have grown in prominence, it should not be completely surprising that exceptionalism's logic of differentiation endures.

Possible explanations for that endurance are numerous. One might have to do with the very protean nature of exceptionalism, definitions of which have been as difficult to agree upon as estimates of its sources or longevity. (In this regard, exceptionalism and liberalism have a good deal in common.) Not only do, for example, Seymour Martin Lipset and Deborah Madsen in their surveys document the concept in rather different ways (in oversimplified terms, the former emphasizing social and political indices, the latter cultural and religious); as Michael Kammen points out, historians and social scientists over the past half century have changed places in their understanding and assessment of exceptionalism rather than finding common ground.[18] A second explanation, closely related to the first, might entail innovations in its scholarly treatment. As much as they have challenged it, changing intellectual trends, innovative research methods and new disciplines may also have played a part in modernizing and reinvigorating exceptionalism. The so-called 'linguistic turn,' the diffusion of techniques first developed in literary criticism, and the study of social history and popular culture, for example, have not simply challenged facile claims concerning, say, 'the American mind.' They have also identified or articulated previously unrecognized features of what might be considered distinctively 'American.'

A number of the papers that follow certainly fit one or more of these characterizations. In relation to common practices and identities, Helle Porsdam's contribution, for example, emphasizes the ways in which, in the United States more so than anywhere else, a common faith in law continues to unite those on opposite sides of social, political and racial barriers. David Nye's essay on American culture and technology, meanwhile, concludes that 'Americans of different ethnic and racial backgrounds usually resemble each other more than they do people from their nations of origin.' With reference to national distinctiveness, John Halsey and Bruce Leslie's paper suggests that while American higher educational models and logics have in recent years been adopted in other countries such as Great Britain, and have thus been rendered less distinctive, they have for much of the nation's history constituted an exception to the European norm. Exploring the cultural intersections of exceptionalism and the Anglo-American 'special relationship,' Inger Dalsgaard's contribution finds in the nation's early engagements with technology a series of distinctive characteristics, but emphasizes that whatever exceptionalism was read into them by contemporary British observers owed as much to what might be called – to extrapolate from Hayden White – the tropics and politics of post-imperial discourse as it did to Republican *amour propre*.[19] Jody Pennington's chapter, finally, argues that what he calls 'the unique system of judicial review' continues to distinguish the American political and legal systems from their European counterparts. None of these authors subscribes to or restores an uncontested exceptionalist faith; all make clear, however, that the concept at the very least still retains heuristic uses.

A third, though by no means final, explanation might involve less scholarly than popular concerns. In a 1991 critique of exceptionalist thought, Ian Tyrell acknowledged the continuing presence of the concept of exceptionalism within one of the most often-cited indices of public beliefs, attitudes, values and needs: popular culture. Stephen Fender put it in a slightly different way in a 1993 article when he wrote that 'Americans are different because they think they are, or wish to be, and the wish has always been mother and father to the fact.'[20] As almost all of the following papers point out, regardless of the shifting contours of academic debate, the American public continue for a variety of reasons to subscribe to a belief in the nation's distinctiveness.

Beyond this point, the papers collected together here pursue a variety of approaches to, and adopt a range of positions in relation to, the common topic. The collection has as its point of departure Joyce Appleby's 1992 critique of, and call for a move beyond, exceptionalism. It then presents a thematically organized series of papers which not only address aspects of exceptionalism but also respond in various ways to Professor Appleby's arguments. The majority of the papers grouped under the headings 'Cultures' and 'Technologies' were presented at the 'Aspects of American Exceptionalism' seminar at the University of Aarhus in February 1996, at which Appleby's *Journal of American History* article provided the common frame of reference. The next four (grouped under the headings 'Institutions' and 'Laws') were written in the wake of, and as often as not by other participants in, the seminar, and were for the most part also inspired by Appleby's piece. A few of these papers endorse and build on her arguments; others revise or qualify them; still others challenge directly their assumptions or implications. The collection concludes with Michael Kammen's 1993 review of the literature on exceptionalism: a survey which recognizes the limits of the concept and its sometimes pernicious uses and consequences, but which also demonstrates the returns to be derived from its analysis and thereby its continuing value as an object of scholarly attention. As Kammen's piece makes plain, whatever explanations are put forward – for its origins or endurance, for its nature and meaning, for the legitimacy or otherwise of the concept – reports of 'the end of American exceptionalism' (to cite the title of Daniel Bell's 1975 essay) still appear to be exaggerated. *Marks of*

*Distinction* constitutes a further contribution to a lively and ongoing debate.

## Notes

1. Laski quoted in William R. Brock, 'Americanism,' *The United States: A Companion to American Studies*, ed. Dennis Welland, 2nd ed. (London: Methuen, 1987), 88; Daniel Bell, 'The End of American Exceptionalism,' *The Public Interest*, 41 (1975): 193–224.
2. John Carlos Rowe, 'Introduction,' *Post-Nationalist American Studies*, ed. John Carlos Rowe (Berkeley: University of California Press, 2000), 3–5. The literature on 'post-national' or 'post-nationalist American Studies' has flourished in recent years. Key texts include Jane C. Desmond and Virginia R. Dominguez, 'Resituating American Studies in a Critical Internationalism,' *American Quarterly*, 48 (1996): 475–90; Paul Giles, 'Virtual Americas: The Internationalization of American Studies and the Ideology of Exchange,' *American Quarterly*, 50 (1998): 523–47; Paul Giles, 'Reconstructing American Studies: Transnational Paradoxes, Comparative Perspectives,' *Journal of American Studies*, 28 (1994): 335–58; Mary Kelley, 'Taking Stands: American Studies at Century's End,' *American Quarterly*, 52 (2000): 1–22; Paul Lauter, 'The Literatures of America – a Comparative Discipline,' in Lauter, *Canons and Contexts* (New York: Oxford University Press, 1991); and *Criticism in the Borderlands*, ed. Hector Calderon and Jose David Saldivar (Durham, NC: Duke University Press, 1991).
3. For an historical account of American liberalism's persistence, see James Young, *Reconsidering American Liberalism: The Troubled Odyssey of the Liberal Idea* (Boulder, CO: Westview Press, 1995).
4. *Is America Different? A New Look at American Exceptionalism*, ed. Byron Shafer (Oxford: Clarendon, 1991); *Reflections on American Exceptionalism*, ed. David K. Adams and Cornelius A. van Minnen (Keele: Keele University Press, 1994); Seymour Martin Lipset, *American Exceptionalism: A Double-Edged Sword* (New York: Norton, 1996); Deborah L. Madsen, *American Exceptionalism* (Edinburgh: Edinburgh University Press, 1998).
5. Joyce Appleby, 'Recovering America's Historic Diversity: Beyond Exceptionalism,' *Journal of American History*, 79 (1992): 419–31; Michael Kammen, 'The Problem of American Exceptionalism: A Reconsideration,' *American Quarterly*, 45 (1993): 1–43. Other recent notable contributions to the debate have included Ian Tyrell, 'American Exceptionalism in an Age of International History,' *American Historical Review*, 96 (1991): 1031–72. The 1995 French Association for American Studies annual conference also addressed the question of American exceptionalism. For a full review of the literature, see Kammen.
6. Kammen, 1; Byron Shafer, 'What is the American Way? Four Themes in Search of Their Incarnation,' *Is America Different?*, ed. Shafer, 223.

7. For a good overview, see 'A Round Table: What Has Changed and Not Changed in American Historical Practice?', *Journal of American History*, 76 (1989): 393 ff.

8. Lawrence Veysey, 'The Autonomy of American History Reconsidered,' *American Quarterly*, 31 (1979): 455–77; Lawrence Veysey, 'The "New" Social History in the Context of American Historical Writing,' *Reviews in American History*, 7 (1979): 9; Appleby, 427–31.

9. Elizabeth Fox-Genovese, 'Between Individualism and Fragmentation: American Culture and the New Literary Studies of Race and Gender,' *American Quarterly*, 42 (1990): 7–34; *The New American Studies: Essays from Representations*, ed. Philip Fisher (Berkeley: University of California Press, 1991), back cover.

10. Kammen, 16. On the New Left and the American pastoral, see Leo Marx, 'Pastoralism in America,' *Ideology and Classic American Literature*, ed. Sacvan Bercovitch and Myra Jehlen (New York: Cambridge University Press, 1988), 61–66. The broader literature on the New Left is now extensive. For reviews, see Maurice Isserman, 'The Not-so-Dark and Bloody Ground: New Works on the 1960s,' *American Historical Review*, (1989): 990–1010; Winifred Breines, 'Whose New Left?' *Journal of American History* (September, 1988): 528–45.

11. William Appleman Williams, *The Contours of American History* (1966; New York: New Viewpoints, 1973), 479. Along with *Contours*, originally published in 1961, Williams's most influential studies included *The Tragedy of American Diplomacy* (Cleveland, OH: World Publishing, 1959). On the work of Williams and New Left historiography more broadly, see A. A. M. van der Linden, *A Revolt Against Liberalism* (Amsterdam: Rodopi, 1996); *Redefining the Past*, ed. Lloyd Gardner (Corvallis: Oregon State University Press, 1986), Part 1.

12. The subtitle of Loren Baritz's *Backfire: A History of How American Culture Led Us into Vietnam and Made Us Fight the Way We Did* (New York: William Morrow, 1985) gives a sense of the possibilities. Chapter 1 of Baritz's book adds further detail.

13. Giles Gunn, *The Culture of Criticism and the Criticism of Culture* (New York: Oxford University Press, 1987), 150.

14. On what might be called the 'incorporation of American Studies' and the ways in which during its earlier phases it may have served as an instrument of cultural diplomacy, see Gene Wise, '"Paradigm Dramas" in American Studies: A Cultural and Institutional History,' *American Quarterly*, 31 (1979): 308–12; Patrick Brantlinger, *Crusoe's Footprints: Cultural Studies in Britain and America* (New York: Routledge, 1990), 26–33; Rowe, 4–5. The tendentious nature of such characterizations is demonstrated by Linda Kerber, 'Diversity and the Transformation of American Studies,' *American Quarterly*, 41 (1989): 415–31; and Elaine Tyler May, 'The Radical Roots of American Studies,' *American Quarterly*, 48 (1996): 179–200.

15. Gunn, 147; Rowe, 3. One frequently-cited survey of the development of American Studies is Gene Wise, '"Paradigm Dramas" in American Studies.' It should be added, though, that Wise's portrait of the discipline since the 1960s speaks more in terms of diffusion than decline. On the margin/centre metaphor, see Michael Cowan, 'Boundary as Center: Inventing an American Studies Culture,' *Prospects*, 12 (1987): 1–20.

16. Stephen Fender emphasizes that in order to 'describe the American difference ... we must begin by recognizing that what we are discussing is not an actual difference but the idea of one.' See Fender, 'The American Difference,' *Modern American Culture*, ed. Mick Gidley (London: Routledge, 1989), 7, 20.

17. Philip Fisher, 'Introduction: the New American Studies,' *New American Studies*, ed. Fisher, xiv.

18. Kammen, 2.

19. Hayden White, *Tropics of Discourse. Essays in Cultural Criticism* (Baltimore: Johns Hopkins University Press, 1978).

20. Fender, 20.

# Recovering America's Historic Diversity: Beyond Exceptionalism[1]

*Joyce Appleby*

Before America became a nation it was a phenomenon. In the reform-minded salons of Paris, at commemorative gatherings of London's non-conformists, among emergent working class radicals, the struggle for independence undertaken by thirteen of Britain's North American colonies was given ideological shape and weight and infused with magnetic force. 'They are the hope of the human race, they may well become its model,' Anne Robert Turgot told Richard Price and Denis Diderot proclaimed the newly United States an asylum from fanaticism and tyranny 'for all the peoples of Europe.' Thomas Jefferson's young secretary, William Short, who remained in Paris after Jefferson returned home to become Secretary of State, elaborated on this asylum theme when he compared Americans to a group of prisoners who have broken out of 'a common gaol' and are being watched by their fellow inmates with 'an anxious eye' to see if escape is possible. Summarizing these European reactions, the French historian Bernard Faye concluded that 'Not a book on America was printed between 1775 and 1790 but ended with a sort of homily,' a fact which prompted another historian, Durand Echeverria, to depict Europeans creating for themselves a 'Mirage in the West.' We could call this America an Enlightenment version – or perversion – of Pandora's box, filled with all the social cravings from a restless European spirit which once freed were scattered to the four winds leaving behind only doubt.[2]

From these sophisticated reflections about a colonial rebellion 3,000 miles away came American exceptionalism, a concept that began in high-spirited conversations and ended as an uncontested assumptions structuring the political consciousness of the

*Marks of Distinction: American Exceptionalism Revisited*, ed. Dale Carter, *The Dolphin* 32, pp. 24–42. © 2001 by Aarhus University Press, Denmark. ISBN 87 7288 383 9; ISSN 0106 4487.

American people. Exceptional does not mean different. All nations are different; and almost all national sentiments exploit those differences. Exceptionalism does more; it projects onto a nation – in this case a cluster of newly-independent states – qualities that are envied because they represent deliverance from a common lot. There are no exceptions without well-understood generalizations or norms in contrast to which the exception commands attention. The United States became a political prodigy in reference to a consensus shared by continental *philosophes*, English Dissenters, and radical pamphleteers. These Europeans celebrated American anomalies because they gave proof that reform was possible, that, to use Short's metaphor, the escaping prisoners would sustain the hopes of those left behind. But even if European draftsman sketched the lineaments of this exceptional new nation, the picture found its enduring appeal in the United States because it offered eighteenth-century Americans a collective identity before they had any other basis for spiritual unity. Pushed into prominence in the contentious politics of the 1790s, exceptionalism formed the core concept of popular political rhetoric. Turgot's 'hope of the human race' was then transmogrified into a peculiar destiny; what had been contingent and adventitious in the colonial past acquired purpose and momentum. A grand narrative was adumbrated and those events which had preceded the Declaration of Independence were reinterpreted as preparations of it. 1776 marked both a culmination and a beginning.

Exceptionalism, in this analysis, is America's peculiar form of Eurocentrism. In the nation's critical first decades, it provided a way to explain the United States's connection to Europe within a story about its geographic and political disconnection. But today, exceptionalism raises formidable obstacles to appreciating America's original and authentic diversity. This evening I would like first to discuss how exceptionalism – what I have designated as our peculiar form of Eurocentrism – created a national identity for the revolutionary generation and then examine how that identity foreclosed other ways of interpreting the meaning of the United States. It is to that foreclosure two centuries ago that we should now look in order to diagnose our present discomfort with calls for a multicultural understanding of America. During the past quarter century historical scholarship has begun to free our imagination from the impress of that venerable tale about a singular national destiny. The rich implications of this new work invite us to move beyond the polemics of multiculturalism to its rewarding possibilities. In order to recover America's historic diversity, however, we will need to examine the intellectual wraps that have hidden it from us.

America, in the minds of its attentive European observers of the eighteenth century was exceptional because its healthy, young, hard-working population had won a revolutionary prize of an empty continent upon which to settle its free-born progeny. America was exceptional because the familiar predators of ordinary folk – the extorting tax collector, the overbearing nobleman, the persecuting priest, the extravagant ruler – had failed to make the voyage across the Atlantic. Natural abundance, inhabitants schooled in tolerance, historic exemption from Old World social evils: these were the materials with which the European reform imagination worked to create the exceptional United States.

Elisabeth d'Houdetot expressed American exceptionalism with fine Gallic clarity in a letter to Jefferson. Writing in 1790 when the violent career of the French Revolution had barely begun, she noted that 'the characteristic difference between your revolution and ours is that having nothing to destroy, you had nothing to injure, and labouring for a people, few in number, incorrupted, and extended over a large tract of country, you have avoided all the inconvenience of a situation, contrary in every respect. Every step in your revolution was perhaps the effect of virtue, while ours are often faults, and sometimes crimes.'[3] Here is a depiction of American exceptionalism in its pristine form.

But think what is missing from this rather patronizing description of America's 'contrary situation.' There is no hint of the daily, perfunctory brutality of a slave institution that incorporated mandatory physical abuse of men, women and children into the laws of a majority of the newly-united states. Nor did awareness of the systematic ejection and extermination of the indigenous population mar Madam d'Houdetot's benign depiction of 'a people, few in number, incorrupted, and extended over a large tract of country.' We might explain her failure to discuss these acts of oppressions from a nation dedicated to liberty and equality on the grounds that acquaintances rarely take the occasion of a friendly letter to abrade each other's sensibilities. But I think these lacunae signify more than politeness. Madame d'Houdetot's conceptual optic nerve could not pick up the color of black and red because already Europeans had learned to make the other invisible. And the citizens of the United States followed their lead. Accepting a role in the new script about an age of revolutions, many Americans extended the category of invisible others to those who failed to play their part in the high drama of progress. Increasingly white Americans came to view the founding of a free and equal people as their calling in the world and as they did so their collective remembrance of the diverse purposes animating colonial settlements atrophied.

Necessity mothered this ideological invention because Americans in 1776 had to create the sense of nationhood which other countries inherited. The United States's nationhood – its juridical standing – preceded the formation of a national ideology and this peculiar inversion of sentiment and status led to a quest for national identity. Americans had not only not lived long in their land, but the land they lived in belonged to other people. Indeed much of it still remained part of the ancestral domain of Amerindians.

Fighting a war for independence had not unified Americans. Rather it created the problem of nationalism – that imperative to hang together once the practical tasks of fighting a common foe and securing a peace treaty no longer exerted centripetal pressure. The commonalities that did exist among the rebellious colonies – those of language, law and institutional history – all pointed in the wrong direction, backwards to the past, towards Britain, their erstwhile enemy. Ordinary Americans had political identities but they were separate, parochial ones, attached to the vibrant traditions of their own locale. We tend to forget the tensile strength of regional ties, how full of resonating symbols and tactile reminders of a shared past the diverse colonial cultures were.

The desire for a closer union, moreover, had not been widely felt, but rather reflected the aspirations of a group of men who were already nationalist in their thinking and cosmopolitan in their outlook. From these leaders came the noisy complaints in the 1780s about state factions and the Cassandra-like predictions of political fragmentation. The Constitution they championed provided new institutions for national governance, but its very success in removing power from local majorities worked against the forming of a popular, patriotic culture. Neither the Constitutional debates nor the state ratifying conventions produced the stuff of culture in appeals to cherished sentiments and references to visceral convictions. The case for 'a more perfect union' was made in a lawyerly fashion by nationalist leaders, most of them lawyers. Outside of their circles, there were abroad in the land few common sentiments, fewer shared assumptions operating at the intimate level of human experience, and a paucity of national symbols recognizable from Georgia to Maine.

There was the Declaration of Independence with its charged statement of high moral purpose, but its thrilling affirmation of inalienable rights proved far more divisive than unifying in the 1780s and 90s. The flagrant contradiction between slavery and the principle of equality led to the first emancipation movement as one after another of the Northern states abolished slavery in the waning years of the eighteenth century. With these remarkable acts the old surveyors' line which Messrs. Mason and Dixon has established as the boundary between Maryland and Pennsylvania became the symbolic division between freedom and slavery. This in itself was an ominous development at a time when so few sentimental ties existed to pull Americans into a national union.

The return of prosperity after the post-revolutionary depression also strengthened confidence in the republican experiment, but the conversion of American exceptionalism into a unifying ideology did not take place until the mid-1790s. Then a critical juncture in domestic politics converged with a momentous tidal

shift in European affairs. Convinced of the elitist intentions of the
government he was serving as Secretary of State, Jefferson in
league with James Madison set out to alert the body of politically
inert voters about the undemocratic tendencies of the Washington
administration. This effort began just as news of the execution of
Louis XVI reached the United States. Quite unexpectedly the
proclamation of the French Republic called forth a new cohort of
American radicals, most of them too young to have engaged in
the protests against the British. They took up the French cause as
their own, finding in the destructive fury of 1793 a confirmation
of the portentousness of the moment. The demise of the French
royal family turned Europe's great continental monarchy into a
republic, giving ominous substance to the concept of a revolutionary era and a new dispensation for mankind. Here was a
narrative that could lift the American War for Independence out
of its British frame of reference and turn it into the first act in a
universal drama of political liberation. The French embrace of
newness, moreover, suggested that the novelties of American
society were anticipations of things to come rather than egregious
examples of raw provincialism. The United States could be
harbinger, pathbreaker and model. Many ordinary white male
citizens used American exceptionalism to hitch their wagonful of
social demands to the rising star of modern revolution. Profoundly alienated from aristocratic European culture, they could
relate to this new European vision of a world-transforming
future. The fight against Great Britain that conservatives were
happy to account a mere war of independence, the new democratic radicals hailed as the first revolution in a revolutionary
era.

   The French Republic roused political passions in the United
States in part because it coincided with the Federalists' determined effort to recapture the homage of their social inferiors
through the workings of an energetic central government. The
Federalists' defense of conservative wisdom was forthright
enough. They made it clear that democracy stopped on election
day, defending the decorum, formality, even the secrecy, of the
Washington administration as necessary for effective governing.

Although the Federalists endorsed meritocracy, they stressed qualifications for public office rarely possessed by ordinary men. Theirs would be a sponsored mobility for those who understood the simple prudence of history and common sense. Alas instead of attentive listeners, the public had turned teacher. The Federalists' hopes for deference dissolved into a round of public demonstrations in support of republican France's military victories. Political clubs formed in flagrant imitation of the Jacobins, and a dozen Republican newspapers started into existence for the sole purpose of attacking the government.

George Washington's experience illuminates the new situation. Willing in 1794 to expend a part of his considerable political capital to denounce the republican clubs as 'certain self-created societies,' his voice carried no further than the circles of officialdom surrounding him in Philadelphia. Outside a different logic prevailed. As one radical writer drolly reflected, 'had the British succeeded in impressing our minds with a firm belief in the infamy of self creation, we should never have been free and independent.'[4]

During these same years, America had entered into a period of great commercial prosperity which promoted the construction of roads, the extension of postal services and the founding of newspapers in country towns. A dense new communication network amplified the resonance of partisan disputes. The control over information and opinions once exercised exclusively by an elite had been wrested away by the articulate critics of that elite. The tactical advantages that had accrued to an upper class small enough for concerted action were overpowered by the mobilization of the popular will through print campaigns. By 1800 the democratic majority in the United States had found their voice, their cause and their strategy for prevailing at the polls.

This dramatic reconfiguration of social influence precipitated a withdrawal from politics by Federalist families, leaving the issue of national purpose for others to define. Deeply offended by the crass self-assertion of common folk, many conservatives turned their educated refinement into an end in itself, strengthening their ties with the English world that shared their values.

The rambunctious politics of the 1790s brought disillusionment to America's first cultural nationalists, men whose nationalist fervor had been nourished by fantasies of American greatness in areas already marked out by the high civilization of metropolitan Europe.[5] They had expected that the free institutions of America would promote literature, science and scholarship, not noisy confrontations and egalitarian bombast. For them the outburst of revolutionary passion from uneducated men had proven the conservatives right: when the pot boils the scum rises. The abandonment of national politics by these Federalists reflected more than a change of personnel; it was the defeat of a venerable concept of authority. Responsibility for creating a national identity passed down the social ladder.

America's undistinguished citizens – the ones who voted the Federalists out of office – sought affirmation of their values in the celebration of what was distinctively American: its institutional innovations, its levelling spirit; above all, its expanded scope for action for ordinary people. To them the idea of American exceptionalism had enormous appeal, for it played to their strengths. Taking up land in the national domain could become a movement for spreading democratic institutions across the continent. Exceptionalism established a reciprocity between American abundance and high moral purposes. It infused the independence and hardiness of America's farming families with civic value, generating patriotic images that could resonate widely without evoking the curse of slavery. The fourth of July rhetoric of the hoi polloi made clear that American exceptionalism freed them from the elite's embrace of European gentility. To be genteel, one had to accept cultural domination as the price to pay for admission in polite society. For ordinary Americans the country's greatness emerged in a lustier set of ideals: open opportunity, an unfettered spirit of inquiry, destruction of privilege, personal independence – the qualities reform-minded Europeans had already plucked out from the tapestry of American society at the time of the Revolution.

In this analysis I am distinguishing political independence from national identity, the latter dependent upon the wide circulation of compelling ideas to create that imagined community which forms a nation. During the nineteenth-century, ordinary white Americans ignored the actual insignificance of their political existence and propelled their republic discursively into the vanguard of the march of progress. The propagandists of American democracy breached the geographic isolation of their country by universalizing what was peculiar to Americans: their endorsement of natural rights, their drive for personal independence, their celebration of democracy. What might be construed elsewhere as uninterestingly plebeian was elevated by the national imagination to a new goal for mankind. America was the only nation, Richard Hofstadter once wryly commented, that began with perfection and aspired to progress. And American history was written to explain how this could be.[6]

Most of what really happened in the colonial past was ignored because it fit so ill with the narrative of exceptionalism. The colonial settlements had to be presented as the foundations for the independent nation to come, an interpretation similar in logic to interpreting our own times in terms of the aspirations of those who will live in the 22nd century. Embarrassing facts abounded in the colonial past. Everywhere one looked one found profoundly different concerns engaging the attention of women and men. The exotic cultures of Africans and Native Americans could not be incorporated into American history, for these people's very claims to have culture would have subverted the story of progress. The self-conscious crafters of American identity took great pride in freedom of religion, but the major religious figures of the colonial era, the Puritans of New England, openly embraced orthodoxy – banishing dissidents, whipping Baptists, even executing four Quakers. 'Tolerance stinks in God's nostrils,' Puritan Nathaniel Ward announced. And so it went with free speech. Congress composed a Bill of Rights guaranteeing free speech, but colonial legislators had been much more likely to jail their critics than to protect their speech. And then of course there was the elaboration of slave codes by colonial legislators. How were those laws to be integrated into the teleology of a peculiarly free people?

All that vibrated with particular meaning in early America was homogenized into elements of a national heritage for heirs as yet unborn. What the colonial period had to offer were a few heroes like Roger Williams and Benjamin Franklin, ancestors worthy of their descendents, and some memorable scenes. A deep forgetting fell over the 20,000 Puritans who came to America to build a city on the hill for the edification of their European brethren. Instead, the inspiring tableau of dozens of humble Pilgrims sitting down to dinner with Pawtuxet Indians in mutual respect and general thanksgiving came to stand in for the whole gallery of disputatious colonists. Patriotic writers set out to explain how autonomous individuals – virtually all male – endowed with a uniform drive for self-improvement and the universal capacity to act independently – had filled the American landscape with farms, schools. factories, courthouses, churches and assembly halls.

We should not take lightly this accomplishment. Reorienting American social values to the twin poles of liberty and equality was a breathtakingly ambitious moral project, because it required rooting out the pervasive colonial residues of hierarchy and privilege. True heirs of European culture, the American colonists had perpetuated the invidious distinction between the talented few and the vulgar many, making status an important feature of all their institutional arrangements. Democratizing social values became the task of the country's history books. Through them, a depiction of self-activating, productive nation-builders was articulated to replace the venerable theory of natural subordination. As John Stephens had rhapsodized in 1787, Americans would have the honor of teaching mankind the important lessons 'that man is actually capable of governing himself.'[7]

Now two centuries later, this grand narrative stands in the way of a different understanding of our past, one that foregrounds those experiences that were earlier cast into the shadows. The arguments developed long ago for the radicals' attack on aristocratic pretensions have left a residue of assumptions that impair our capacity to respond to the multicultural agenda. Three insistent themes of American exceptionalism need to be examined, each with its own conceptual entailments: the clean slate with its implicit rejection of the past; the autonomy of the individual with its accompanying disparagement of dependency; and the concept of a uniform human nature with its ascription of universality to particular social traits.

Let's look first at the autonomous individual. The United States in 1800 was poised on the eve of a great evangelical movement, but this successful repietizing of American society did not strengthen religious institutions. Like Jeffersonian republicans, American Protestants forgot the past, indifferent alike to the historic church and its traditions. The proliferation of denominations advertised the freedom of religion even as it made necessary that wall of separation between church and state. By the early decades of the nineteenth century, American churches like its male citizens, had been individualized and endowed with rights to life, liberty and the pursuit of private truths. Meanwhile nature had come to dominate the social imagination of Americans: the nature, that is, that Bacon, Newton and Locke had made orderly, comprehensive and knowable. Beneath the myriad of surface variety and detail, the natural philosophers had discovered regularities and uniformities of lawlike certainty. Here was a new kind of authority, one that assigned moral worth to those human arrangements that conformed to the objective and irresistible laws of cause and effect. However, to detach society from the domain of politics and study it as a manifestation of nature, was to alter dramatically the character of social inquiry. With reality as the dispenser of rewards and punishments, a different kind of freedom could be conceived, one which consisted of liberation from artificial arrangements. 'What is?' replaced 'What ought to be?' as the dominant moral question posed by nature and what Jefferson called 'nature's God.'

These inferences from the new sciences, familiar to all students of the Enlightenment, had a special conceptual career in the United States. What could only be entertained as theory in Europe could be accepted by sensible Americans as a description of how things actually were. Carriers of an essential human nature, men and women could shed the irrelevant accretions of time and wipe clean the social inscriptions of outworn usages. To speak the language of sociology, an undersocialized concept of man emerged to take the place of that older European figure who had brought the complex tools of civilization to the wilderness. By construing their own liberty as liberation from historic institutions, the enthusiasts of democracy made the United States the pilot society for the world. It was not Americans, but all men, who sought freedom from past oppression. The presumed universality of their values turned them into empirical propositions about human nature.

A philosophy that taught that nature disclosed the moral ends of human life and then read nature as having endowed each man with a right to pursue his own happiness comported well with the actual biases of most Americans. Their natural rights doctrine was both normative and prescriptive. Factually, it taught that all men are the same; philosophically, that all men should have equal rights; but practically only those men who met the liberty-loving, self-improving ideal were freely admitted to the category 'all men.' When circumstance, failure, disinclination or racial origins raised barriers to taking one's place as a progressive individual, this was read as empirical proof of a failure of fitness. Over time, this language of uniformity turned differences into deviations. Discursively those people who failed to embody established norms became deviants. And if they were denied their rights, it was nature that authored the denial. We can see these assumptions operating most powerfully in relation to minorities and women, but these are but the most conspicuous applications of a principle which confounded a theory of nature for nature itself.

The idea of a clean slate helped create the illusion of a frontier emptied of human inhabitants, a virginal continent awaiting the arrival of potent males, an image which drew a veil over the violent encounters which actually paced the westward trek of Americans. It also denied the force of history, for it is past actions that clutter up the metaphorical slate. The clean slate suggests most powerfully a freedom of choice: the freedom to be the designer of one's own life unaided or impeded by others. Yet there have always been severe limits to this kind of choice in the

United States. Clean slates are denied those people whose color or sex has already been assigned a value at birth. Thinking that we create our own identities highlights volition and autonomy and minimizes the categorical force of race and gender in shaping our social existence. Identities partake of a complex two-way relationship between ourselves and others in which the messages we send out are frequently returned, unopened. The metaphor of the clean slate promotes more than a rejection of the past; it perpetuates the fantasy that we can uncouple ourselves from a genetic inheritance or from our society's cultural coding. Multicultural histories contest these comfortable illusions about choice and autonomy and force us to attend to those life stories that point to different truths.

Twenty-five years ago a new generation of scholars – many of them in this room – began ferreting out fugitive facts in the American past. Equipped with computer skills, fresh questions and excellent eyes, they poured over the records of births, marriages, and deaths; they examined probate inventories, land titles, slave purchases, city plats, employment rolls, and tax assessments. From these recondite sources, they ingeniously mapped the patterns of living and dying, marriage and mobility, opportunity and outcome in an earlier America, giving voice at last to those men and women who had been muffled by the celebration of American exceptionalism. Digging away in the public archives, these historians brought to light the tales of frustration and disappointment that had been buried under the monolithic myth of American success. Here too they found the group dependency – that clannishness born of cruel necessity – that nineteenth-century Americans had found so threatening in the 'wretched refuse' from Europe's teeming shores.

The undersocialized concept of man of earlier histories ran head long into the oversocialized concept of men and women whom the new histories turned into repositories of social data. But there was more than an armory for ideological warfare in this new social research. There was also life: Irish, Italian, Jewish immigrants successively occupying and recoding neighborhood cultures; pioneer women spilling the grief of separation into their prairie diaries; freed slaves miraculously reconstituting their dispersed families at the end of the Civil War; Polish housewives juggling their New World opportunities with their husbands' definitions of propriety. Black Americans so long hidden under the blanket rubric of slaves came alive when we met them as the persistent protectors of their indigenous customs or as bold self-liberators (a rather striking contrast to the label, runaway slave).

A cohort of social historians – many of them the children and grandchildren of immigrants, some the great grandchildren of slaves – turned their dissertation-writing tasks into a movement of memory recovery. Like the Boston Brahmins who formed the caste of gentlemen historians in the nineteenth century, they too found their ancestors in the American past, but they found them in most unlikely places for historical personages: shop floors, slave quarters, drawing rooms, relocation centers, temperance meetings, barrios, sodhouses, rice fields, tent communities.

With social scientific hypotheses to test, scholars could afford to lavish months, even years, calculating the changing proportion of tenant and farmer-owned acreage in selected counties of Iowa or determining the relative fertility of black women in Jamaica, Barbados and Virginia. Investigating the behavior of groups, often with only names to count, social historians reported their findings as patterns, structures, models and processes, using norms, modes and standard deviations to make their points. The importance of the systematic had finally been flushed out of America's historical records. At last we could see a system – or more ominously, the system – categorizing the worth of individuals, controlling access to opportunity, distributing the nation's cultural and economic goods. Social history lifted from obscurity those who had been left behind, excluded, disinherited from the American heritage. It also demonstrated how the functioning of impersonal systems influenced personal lives and challenged the plausibility of human uniformity, a clean slate, and the autonomous individual.

It would be hard to exaggerate the dissonance between history recounted through the doings of the individual – the American Adam – and history reconstructed with the modular

units of group experience. Whether the subject was the charter
families of Germantown, Pennsylvania, the enslaved Ibos of
South Carolina, the Dust Bowl migrants of Oklahoma or the
political leaders of the Progressive era, the story played differently when the actors were approached as members of a group
with discernible group destinies. That old familiar tale of the
pioneer man alone with his family, or Protestant man alone with
his God, or the rights-bearing man alone with his conscience only
made sense when one was confident that the individual's virtues
were a natural endowment rather than the product of character-
molding processes of socialization. Different assumptions criti-
cally effect the moral of one's story. When historians depicted
autonomous individuals as being in charge of events, blame for
failure could be laid at their feet. When the role of society was
made conspicuous, it became harder not to assign responsibility
for who got what to the institutional arrangements that patterned
opportunity.

The conviction that society got to the individual first and
stamped her or him with a group identity raised a number of
troubling questions about the older belief in universal human
traits. Qualities that had been assumed to be natural began to look
as though they might possibly be social in origin. The insistence
of younger scholars that the experience of women be taken
seriously also gave a rude jolt to the presentation as universal of
standards that were merely male. Research on women's lives
revealed differences which threw into sharp relief the gender-
specificity of our social ideals. Perhaps nothing made clearer the
exercise of authority in historical scholarship than the exclusive
focus upon male interests and achievements.

History like literature speaks directly to our curiosity about
human experience, but we need concrete details before we can
enter into an imaginative encounter with the past. Philip Greven
told us that fathers in Andover, Massachusetts delayed their sons'
marrying by barring their access to land.[8] A few statistics about
wills, ages at marriage, land conveyances and we could fill in the
social reality of parental control and filial submission. The effect
of this new capacity to vivify the characteristics of countless

mundane lives is moral. It sparks a human connection. There is an enormous difference, for instance, between knowing that there were slave quarters and being able to gaze at a floor plan and calculate living space. What the history of ordinary life delivers is the shock of recognition: my kind is humankind.

These changes in historical scholarship set off more than a rage of anti-whiggery. At times, it seemed as though recovering the past of ordinary women and men had produced more history than we could consume. We were – and still are – snowed under by an avalanche of information: much of it inassimilable into a coherent national narrative. But that older, lamented coherence had actually come from the European concept of American exceptionalism rather than wide-ranging empirical research. It depended upon an induced amnesia and a depiction of the present as always straining towards a destined end. Some critics now see multiculturalism as a threat to the national unity that the older history cemented. Others claim it sacrifices historical knowledge to the achievement of political ends. They do not recognize that the conventional narrative about a new nation conceived in liberty and dedicated to the proposition that all men are created equal – even when affirmed by the eloquence of a Lincoln – is itself a cultural artefact

Concepts and theories, of course, deliberately obscure the multiplicity of details in real situations in order to highlight significant relationships. But this involves deciding in advance which human lives and whose social enactments will be counted as significant. And this is an act of authority, not research design. Specifically, the idea of American exceptionalism projected onto the United States a future more significant than its past, encouraging a neglect of the historic diversity of the United States in deference to an imagined time when progressive, cumulative, irreversible processes of change would have worn away the variety in human experience.

Closely examined, the objectivity of science is suspect for historians too. Impartiality involves a logic of identity which denies and represses difference.[9] Every one of the determinative dichotomies of our culture – masculine and feminine, WASP and

ethnic, black and white, normal–deviant, heterosexual–homosex-
ual – has drawn strength from the suppression of the knowledge
of the other. Yet when the suppressed particular has been raised
to structured consciousness – as in the histories of the diverse
groups that compose the United States – knowledge of the non-
conforming cases forces out the question, what exactly is there in
the other that must be devalued? If deviations actually give
evidence of the plentitude of human possibilities, whose purposes
are served by employing a language of uniformity and standardization? Without minimizing the real, enviable freedoms that we
Americans enjoy, it is not amiss to consider the oppression
exercised by an omnipresent cultural model which has carried
with it so many mixed messages about the freedom to be different.

   Our sense of worth, of well-being, even our sanity depends
upon our remembering. But alas our sense of worth, our well-
being, our sanity also depend upon our forgetting. Remembering
and forgetting determine the history we tell. I read a recent
editorial on the various national histories of the Second World
War which concluded with this aphorism: 'Remember your
sufferings, forget your crimes, and you make war. Forget your
sufferings, remember your crimes, and you make peace.'[10]
Nothing is that simple, but those provocative lines point to the
historian's inescapable role as moralist. What we attend to in the
past will form that restructured memory that we call history, the
reservoir of knowledge about human experience that informs our
ideas about suffering and crimes, virtues and vices, recordable
accomplishments and unworthy happenings. No scientifically-
based, objective model exists to guide our curiosity. It is we and
the cultural milieu in which we think that determine historical
significance.

   It's important to note that multiculturalism does not share the
postmodernist stance. Its passions are political; its assumptions
empirical; its conception of identities visceral. There is no doubting that history is something that happened and that those
happenings have left their mark within our collective consciousness. History for multiculturalists is not a succession of dissolving

texts, but a tense tangle of past actions that have reshaped the landscape, distributed the nation's wealth, established boundaries, engendered prejudices, and unleashed energies. To look at those aspects of the American past that do not fit into a one-sidedly celebratory account of the nation's origins will require more, not less, rigorous standards of proof, a greater commitment to research, and a superior capacity for analytical persuasion. This does not mean that ideological partisanship – that scholarly equivalent of original sin – will disappear, but rather that the tension between what we as partisans in life wish to believe and what a rigorous and searching examination of evidence forces us to accept is nakedly exposed. Contention is inseparable from creating knowledge. It is not contention we should try to avoid, but discourses that attempt to suppress contention.

As the torrent of statements about multiculturalism so noisily proves, knowledge is power. History exercises that power by awakening curiosity, stretching imaginations, deepening appreciation and complicating one's sense of the possible. We find writing the multicultural history of the United States difficult because we have never rooted our present in our past. Rather we have used the past as a springboard for vaulting into a future which promises liberation from the past, a future of novelties: new nationalisms, new deals, new frontiers, new world orders. Perhaps we can think of multiculturalism as an invitation to look at what has always been there: a cluttered slate of interdependent and highly diverse people shaped by the consequences of five centuries of interaction in the New World. *E pluribus unum* is an ideal; it is not a description of American life in any period. Free of this restricting ideological imperative, we can now set out to recover the historic diversity in our past.

## Notes

1. This paper was originally published in the *Journal of American History*, 79 (1992): 419–31, and is reproduced here by kind permission of the author, the editor of the journal and the Organization of American Historians.

2.  Durand Echeverria, *Mirage in the West: A History of the French Image of American Society to 1815* (Princeton: Princeton University Press, 1957), 69; William Short to Colonel William Grayson, June 21, 1787, box 2, Short Papers (Manuscript Division, Library of Congress); Bernard Fäy, *The Revolutionary Spirit in France and America*, trans. Ramon Guthrie (New York: Harcourt, Brace, 1927), 194.

3.  Elisabeth d'Houdetot to Thomas Jefferson, 3 September 1790, in *Les Amitiés américaines de Madame d'Houdetot, d'après sa correspondance inédite aux Benjamin franklin et Thomas Jefferson*, ed. Gilbert Chinard (Paris: Champion, 1924), 56. Elisabeth Françoise Sophie, comtesse d'Houdetot, befriended both Franklin and Jefferson when they were in Paris.

4.  *Philadelphia Independent Gazetteer*, 28 January 1795.

5.  Joseph J. Ellis, *After the Revolution: Profiles of Early American Culture* (New York: Norton, 1979), 29–33.

6.  Benedict Anderson, *Imagined Communities: Reflections on the Origin and Spread of Nationalism* (London: Verso, 1983), 15. I have borrowed Anderson's phrase. I am indebted to Professor J. R. Pole for his recollection of Richard Hofstadter's remark.

7.  [John Stevens], *Observations on Government, Including Some Animadversions on Mr. Adams's Defence of the Constitutions of Government of the United States of America and on Mr. De Lolme's Constitution of England* (New York, 1787), 14.

8.  Philip J. Greven, Jr., *Four Generations: Population, Land, and Family in Colonial Andover, Massachusetts* (Ithaca, NY: Cornell University Press, 1970).

9.  Iris Marion Young, 'Impartiality and the Civic Public: Some Implications of Feminist Critiques of Moral and Political Theory,' *Feminism as Critique: On the Politics of Gender*, ed. Seyla Benhabib and Drucilla Cornell, (Minneapolis: University of Minnesota Press, 1987), 57–76.

10. *Los Angeles Times*, 29 January 1992, B6.

# Cultures

# A City Upon a Hill: American Literature and the Ideology of Exceptionalism

*Thomas B. Byers*

This essay offers an overview of the relation between exceptionalism and American literature, with a focus on how this ideology has shaped both the production and reception of America's literary texts. It suggests, in particular, that exceptionalism bears a relation to the literature that is at once constraining and generative. The assumption that grounds the argument, and that is already evident both in the title and my opening sentence, is that exceptionalism is, precisely, an ideological formation. I say 'precisely' with some irony, because both 'exceptionalism' and 'ideology' are among the more slippery terms in contemporary scholarly discourse. Hence it may be useful to specify at the outset how the two terms are used here.

By 'exceptionalism' I mean a way of thinking that, in Joyce Appleby's words, 'projects onto a nation ... qualities that are envied because they represent deliverance from a common lot.'[1] In America's case, it does even more than that. It imagines the nation as both the surpassing of the past and the hope of the future – as Walt Whitman does in the following passages. At the end of 'Song of the Redwood-Tree,' apostrophizing the 'lands of the western shore,' he says,

I see in you certain to come, the promise of thousands of years, till now
    deferred,
[...]

The new society at last, proportionate to Nature,
[...]

Fresh come, to a new world indeed, yet long prepared,
I see the genius of the modern, child of the real and ideal,

*Marks of Distinction: American Exceptionalism Revisited*, ed. Dale Carter, *The Dolphin* 32, pp. 45–68. © 2001 by Aarhus University Press, Denmark. ISBN 87 7288 383 9; ISSN 0106 4487.

Clearing the ground for broad humanity, the true America,
heir of the past so grand,
To build a grander future.[2]

American exceptionalism is a doubly teleological vision, in which
all of history prior to the formation of the Euro-American 'New
World' was pointed toward this formation as a goal, and in which
that 'New World' is not simply a place, but a mission.

This definition of exceptionalism stands in opposition to that
offered by Seymour Martin Lipset in his recent book, *American
Exceptionalism: A Double-Edged Sword*, where the term refers
simply to 'the ways in which the United States varies from the
rest of the world.'[3] I align myself instead with Appleby, who
argues that 'Exceptional does not mean different. All nations are
different; and almost all national sentiments exploit those differences.'[4] To exploit them is simply part of the formation of a
national identity and self-consciousness – as concomitantly, are
the identification and study of a national literary tradition.[5] But
American exceptionalism is not only the claim that America is
different, but that it is unique, one of a (superior) kind – and
generally that that kind carries with it a unique moral value and
responsibility.

By this definition, there are certain ways in which America is
clearly different that in fact run contrary to exceptionalism as a
faith. Perhaps the most obvious is our history with regard to
slavery and race. In recent years exceptionalism as faith has
undergone a revival in American political discourse; certainly it
was one of the staples of Ronald Reagan's appeal to the American
people. At the same time we have had the highest rates of murder
and incarceration of any developed nation, and we are clearly
distinct among the wealthy nations in gaps between rich and
poor, in percentage of children living in poverty, and in our lack
of a national health system. But these are not the sorts of distinctive attributes that count in terms of the political uses of
exceptionalism.

Rather, exceptionalism is an *ism*, an ideology that selectively
defines the attributes of the nation in order to justify and celebrate

it. If, indeed, as Lipset says, 'The United States ... has defined its raison d'être ideologically,' exceptionalism is a name for both the content and the process of that self-definition. Lipset quotes Richard Hofstadter as noting that, 'It has been our fate as a nation not to have ideologies, but to be one.'[6] Exceptionalism is at once the ideology that we are, and the fact that, as a nation, we are an ideology (rather than simply, for instance, a political entity or a place with a history). The literary implications and manifestations of all of this are discussed in more detail below.

What, then, is 'ideology'? On the one hand, in traditional Marxist usage the term denominates a form of 'false consciousness' (Engels uses this phrase in his 1893 Letter to Mehring).[7] If Appleby referred to exceptionalism as an ideology, I suspect it would be in this sense. On the other hand, 'ideology' is often used more broadly, in a way that its proponents would claim (and I would generally agree) to be more theoretically sophisticated. This seems to be the sense in which Myra Jehlen uses it in defining the subject of her *American Incarnation:*

[W]hen the European settlers saw themselves as quickening a virgin land, the modern spirit completed its genesis by becoming flesh in the body of the American continent. The *ideology* of this incarnation as it fulfilled Europe's ideal liberalism, and as it is represented, appropriately incarnate, in the form and matter of American writing, is my central concern in this book.[8]

Jehlen later defines this ideology as '[c]onstituting what one thinks and talks *with* rather than *about* ... [r]eaching down to levels of consciousness that are themselves mute – never told but retold inside consciously constructed arguments.' The task of reading this 'ground itself, lying below the cited grounds of thought' is one of 'trying to see the limits of a language, and therefore to see what it denies as well as what it asserts.' It 'involves saying what the writer has *not* said.'[9]

This view goes back to Louis Althusser's notion of ideology as inescapable, as the very condition of thought, as what he calls 'a representation of the imaginary relationship of individuals to their real conditions of existence.'[10] We never stand outside ideology (though we may stand outside particular ideologies). Ideologies are not (or not primarily) the contents of thought; rather, they are its conditioning structures and figures. And they are not merely limiting (though they are that); they are also, and importantly, productive. Much has already been said by many writers, and something more will be said here, about how exceptionalism is limiting. But I also want to suggest how it is productive; and particularly how it is so – often in somewhat unpredictable ways – for American literature.

Still, despite his enrichment of our understanding of the term, Althusser ultimately cannot dispense (nor can I) with a certain kind of reinscription of the old idea of ideology as false con-sciousness. For him it takes the form of his reliance on the opposition between the imaginary and the real ('a representation of an imaginary relation to real conditions'), an opposition tinged in his discourse with Jacques Lacan's reinvention of those terms, but one that still carries with it strong traces of the notion of a reality from which ideology departs. A later move in his essay, in which he posits 'science' (as in 'scientific socialism') as ideology's other, has the same effect of aligning ideology with falsehood.[11]

The point of this rather extended reflection is finally this: when I speak of exceptionalism as an ideology, I both do and do not mean that it is a 'false consciousness.' There are ways, I will argue, in which, at least in its mainstream versions, it is patently false, both because of what it actively claims and because of what it silently excludes. On the other hand, the recognition of those patent falsehoods may still come under the sign, or in the context, of exceptionalism as a conditioning mode of consciousness, as a representation of individuals' imaginary relation to real condi-tions. Those, for instance, who criticize the mainstream notion of America as the cradle of democracy by pointing out the nation's failures, injustices, and founding inequities with regard to race or class are, on the one hand, exposing the falsehood of popular exceptionalism – particularly the falsehood of the notion that America is the 'land of the free.' But on the other hand, at least in the case of canonical American writers – and/or of readers who interpret canonically (that is, according to the canons of

Americanness in writing) – this critique itself pretty much invariably takes place within the framework of exceptionalism as a mode of thought.

There are certain identifiable real conditions to which exceptionalism represents an imaginary response. They have to do with the fact that the USA was both the first nation whose hegemonic ideologies and institutions were more or less uncontestedly bourgeois, and the first major one to become 'post-colonial' in the contemporary senses of that term. It was the former condition, allegedly guaranteed by the expanse of available 'unowned' land, that made America seem the land of open opportunity and the place where the individual (white) man could perhaps, to paraphrase Ralph Waldo Emerson's transcendentalist imperative, build his own world.[12] It was a combination of the two factors (our status as both bourgeois and post-colonial) that made America seem the world's hope for the future, for in becoming post-colonial we had also thrown off the burden of oligarchy.

But exceptionalism was, nonetheless, not only an imaginary response, but a highly problematic one, particularly in two regards. First, there was an obvious contradiction between the ideology of exceptionalism and the material reality of a nation in which all were clearly not in fact equal. The white man's 'own world' was built in significant part by the labor of Black men and women he owned, and the ostensibly free and classless opportunity allegedly guaranteed by open land was (or quickly became) more imaginary than real, and in any case depended upon the erasure of the Amerindians and their prior claims to that land.

A second, and related, way in which the promise of American exceptionalism was highly problematic was in its going beyond the political to the mystical, beyond history to destiny. Three things must be said about this strain of exceptionalism at the outset. First, it should be taken as a proof and a reminder that imaginary formations do have real material effects: the notion of 'manifest destiny' was not merely an apology, but an energizing force, for American imperialism. Second, this sort of exceptionalism has done far more harm than good; the genocidal effects of the doctrine of manifest destiny alone demonstrate this, even

without invoking such other ugly aspects as the connection between exceptionalism and the eugenics movement of the early
part of this century. Third, though no positive effects of such
exceptionalism outweigh the negatives, it has also been positively
productive – not only in literature as an inspiration for Whitman's
democratic poetics, but also in other spheres for social critics such
as Martin Luther King, who returned to the notion of America as
a potential promised land in eloquent and politically progressive
ways.

In terms of the cultural work it has performed, the metaphysi-
cal extension of exceptionalism may have been in large part a
response to the fact that the United States was the first major post-
colonial nation. Among the effects of this were that the new
nation had no models for the development it had undertaken, and
that it still had links of enormous tensile strength with the
imperial power that it thought it had thrown off. In this light
mystical exceptionalism can be seen as a sort of overcompensa-
tion – a hyperbolic attempt to establish our difference from the
metropolis. And its persistence as a symptom indicates that
America really did not get over Europe for a very long time
(indeed, it is only in the postmodern climate of the utter forgetting of the past that we may be said to have done so: if one has no
memory at all the question of origins ceases to matter). For one
example of the persistence into modernity and modernism of our
colonial past and our mystical compensation, and of how these
things have been generative of American literature, consider
William Carlos Williams's obsessive attempts to repudiate T. S.
Eliot's old-world notion of the tradition, efforts that extend from
*Spring and All* through *Paterson* and one of the greatest of exceptionalist texts, *In the American Grain,* and all the way into 'The
Desert Music.' Williams's powerful emphasis on the particularity
and curative strength of the local ground gains its intensity in
large part from the desire to repudiate our subordination to
European culture.

In general, the traditional canon of our literature constantly
manifests and reacts to exceptionalist ideology, for two major
reasons. The first is simply that exceptionalism has been an

integral part of the way many American authors, like Americans in general (particularly but by no means exclusively white Americans), have imaged their nation to themselves. The second is, as Nina Baym's essay on 'Melodramas of Beset Manhood' suggests, that exceptionalism has historically been one of the conditioning and gate-keeping principles of canonization in America: traditionally, in order for American literature to be both literature (as opposed to just writing) and American (as opposed to just literature, or just British literature), it must bear the marks of this ideology. It need not unconditionally accept the most optimistic claims of exceptionalism, but it must be clearly locable in relation to this ideology's themes – and generally, if not always, to the white, middle-class, male who is the dominant subject of this ideology, as well.[13]

It must be emphasized that this is the *traditional* way of looking at American literature, rather than the inevitable way, because this way is now being contested, perhaps more vigorously than ever before – as is the entire discourse of exceptionalism. While I am not eager or even willing, as some Americanists are, either to give up the canonical works or to discard the notion of aesthetic judgement as one criterion for deciding what to read and teach, I think this contestation is extremely healthy, both from a literary and a cultural point of view. In terms of literature it offers us more to be interested in, more texts to learn and to learn to love. In terms of culture it should offer us a deeper understanding of the historical and contemporary multiplicity of American life, and should help us to meet a future in which that multiplicity can no longer be papered over, no matter what those with a nostalgia for a homogeneous and homogenized, white and English-only America – a nostalgia for neverland – might prefer.

One example of such contestation with a broadly historical focus is Appleby's 'Recovering America's Historic Diversity: Beyond Exceptionalism'; for two examples of a more specifically literary contestation, consider Baym's now famous article and Annette Kolodny's essay, 'Letting Go Our Grand Obsessions: Notes Toward a New Literary History of the American Frontiers.'[14] The latter was recently published as the lead essay in

Michael Moon and Cathy Davidson's *Subjects and Citizens: Nation, Race, and Gender from Oroonoko to Anita Hill,* a collection whose opening sentence claims that it 'takes on one of the most vexed issues in American literary studies: American exceptionalism.'[15] Kolodny's essay offers a new way of defining the 'frontier' and its literature: a way new not only in its conception of what a frontier is, but also in its implications both for what texts it would include as canonical 'frontier literature' and for how it would read what it includes. Kolodny specifically rejects the conditioning assumptions of exceptionalism, assumptions that have valued certain texts for their place in a teleological account of America as the realization of European liberal ideals, while erasing others that suggest an other account (by which I mean not only a different account but an account offered by an other – by one who is not the subject of exceptionalist ideology).[16] Kolodny's essay is an excellent example of the way in which many scholars are trying to re-invent both American literature and American Studies.

Until recently I had accepted the widespread notion that our mystical exceptionalism was in large part a consequence of what has been called 'the Puritan origins of the American self.' It can be traced back to passages such as the following from what is perhaps the most famous exceptionalist text in colonial American literature: John Winthrop's 'A Model of Christian Charity':

Thus stands the cause between God and us. We are entered into Covenant with Him for this work ... Now if the Lord shall please to hear us, and bring us in peace to the place we desire, then hath He ratified this Covenant and sealed our Commission, [and] will expect a strict performance of the Articles contained in it[. ...]

[...] For this end, we must be knit together in this work as one man ... We must delight in each other, make other's conditions our own, rejoice together, mourn together, labor and suffer together, always having before our eyes our commission and community in the work, our community as members of the same body. So shall we keep the unity of the spirit in the bond of peace. The Lord will be our God, and delight to dwell among us as His own people, and will command a blessing upon us in all our ways, so that we shall see much more of His wisdom, power, goodness and truth, than formerly we have been acquainted with. We shall find that the God of Israel is among us, when ten of us shall be able to resist a thousand of our enemies; when He shall make us a praise and glory that men shall say of succeeding plantations, 'the Lord make it like that of NEW ENGLAND.' For we must consider that we shall be as a city upon a hill. The eyes of all people are upon us, so that if we shall deal falsely with our God in this work we have undertaken, and so cause Him to withdraw His present help from us, we shall be made a story and a by-word through the world. We shall open the mouths of enemies to speak evil of the ways of God, and all professors for God's sake. We shall shame the faces of many of God's worthy servants, and cause their prayers to be turned into curses upon us till we be consumed out of the good land whither we are agoing.

[...] Beloved, there is now set before us life and good, death and evil, in that we are commanded this day to love the Lord our God, and to love one another, to walk in His ways and to keep His commandments and His ordinance and His laws, and the articles of our covenant with Him, that we may live and be multiplied, and that the Lord our God may bless us in the land whither we go to possess it. But if our hearts shall turn away, so that we will not obey, but shall be seduced, and worship other gods, our pleasures and profits, and serve them, it is propounded unto us this day, we shall surely perish out of the good land whither we pass over this vast sea to possess it.[17]

It is no doubt the case, as Sacvan Bercovitch has argued, that Winthrop's description of the Puritans' covenant and of America as a city upon a hill – or, more broadly, that the genre his sermon exemplifies – is in fact one of the generative sources of exceptionalism as quasi-religious vision.[18] But the time has come lo ask what it is that makes this text, or this genre, canonical *as literature?* I do not believe that the answer lies in any inherently aesthetic or formal qualities. Winthrop is eloquent enough, but why this Puritan sermon and not others? Why, indeed, Puritan sermons at all, and especially why sermons of this sort? Bercovitch agrees with Perry Miller in calling 'the New England jeremiad America's first distinctive literary genre.'[19] But something becomes a distinctive genre only if its perceivers have an interest in distinguishing it as such. It may well be that there are many other patterns of similarity in texts of the colonial period that we could raise to generic standing if we had some reason to perceive those

patterns as significant. In fact, to some extent that is what Kolodny has done in her redefinition of frontier literature.

What, then, is it that makes the 'distinctive' elements of the
jeremiad distinguishable against, say, the general background of
biblical analogy in Puritan writing? Or against the general
background of the European encounter with the New World?
What makes the particular tropes and topoi of the jeremiad
significant enough to delineate a genre? The answer, I would
suggest, is that the literary canon itself was constituted, retro-
spectively, out of and in promotion of an exceptionalist ideology.[20] It may be that Winthrop and his genre – rather than, for
instance, Puritan biographies of 'great men,' or Amerindian texts
that witness the encounter with the Europeans (both of which
might be candidates for canonization as genres) – have stood at
the beginning of our tradition basically in a kind of cultural
*nachträglicheit*. I would suggest in fact that canon formation in
general operates at least in part in this fashion. If this is so, then
we see that exceptionalism as a theme has become constitutive of
what American literature is. At the very least, it seems safe to say
that if the tradition had not itself been constituted by men who
saw themselves as heirs to the Puritans and other exceptionalists
– if, for instance, the first anthologies used in American literature
courses had been edited by powerful critics who were also the
children or grandchildren of slaves – the canon might have
looked a good deal different.

One notable aspect of the claim that exceptionalism has been
constitutive for our literature is that it suggests that the canon has
been determined thematically and ideologically, rather than
formally or aesthetically.[21] This really comes as no surprise with
regard to the American scene. While formal and aesthetic traits or
judgements are never free of thematic or ideological determina-
tions, the disposition in America has been to see the former (the
aesthetic) as fundamentally trivial, and as worth attending to only
when redeemed by some higher seriousness; the 'merely' literary
or 'merely' aesthetic or 'merely' pleasurable isn't enough of a
value to define literature. Ben Franklin, a great lover of reading,
nonetheless says in his *Autobiography* that he 'approv'd the

amusing oneself with Poetry now and then, so far as to improve one's Language, but no farther.'[22] He found it of value only to the degree that it served a utilitarian end, such as increasing one's vocabulary. It may be in defense against this view of literature – or half in agreement with it – that Whitman insists in 'A Backward Glance O'er Travel'd Roads' that 'it is not on "Leaves of Grass" distinctively as *literature,* or a specimen thereof, that I feel to dwell, or advance claims. No one will get at my verses who insists upon viewing them as a literary performance, or as aiming toward art and aestheticism.'[23] Thus American literature must be exceptional not only by being American, but also by being more than mere 'literature': the latter is one of those rather effete European values that the new nation seeks to leave behind.

Moreover, as Nina Baym puts it, 'from its historical beginnings, American literary criticism has assumed that literature produced in this nation would have to be ground-breaking, equal to the challenge of the new nation, and completely original.'[24] In other words, it had to be as exceptional as the place. This meant that no established standards were relevant to it, so that, to quote Baym again, 'the early critic looked for a standard of Americanness rather than a standard of excellence. Inevitably, perhaps, it came to seem that the quality of "Americanness," whatever it might be, *constituted* literary excellence for American authors.'[25] We need not rehearse all of Baym's argument here, but she offers an incisive analysis of how the category of Americanness (which is also the category of exceptionalism – what makes something *uniquely* American) came to exclude women authors.

Of course, the specific exclusion of writing by American women from the canon of 'American literature' mirrored the more general exclusion that the ears of 1997 hear (as the ears of 1776 generally could not) in the assertion that all *men* are created equal, and endowed by their creator with certain unalienable rights. This formulation from the *Declaration of Independence,* which was in the revolutionary and federalist periods just the sort of thing that was offered as evidence for the exceptional nature of America, glossed over two other major structures of inequality as well. The first is the racism that excluded people of color from the category of men not because they were a different gender but because they were a different 'species' (or, in a wonderfully self-contradictory ideological formulation, a different 'species of men').[26] Looking ahead, we may note that the lesson Huck Finn has to learn on the raft is, precisely, that Jim is of the same species – that White and Black people share a common humanity. The second structure is that of class; the notion that all are created equal is that the individual is, in essence, free of circumstances – implicitly that those born poor are equal to those born rich.

This latter is a fine idea particularly in a judicial context: if one assumes that divisions between rich and poor are inevitable, it is a good thing – though of course never really the case – if they are nonetheless equal before the law. However, while the Enlightenment notion of individualism that this idea carries with it may have had a politically progressive inflection in its day (particularly in championing the bourgeoisie against the *droits de seigneur)*, over time it has (as often happens to ideas) been repositioned as a conservative defense of the vested interests of the dominant class – now, of course, the same bourgeoisie whom the idea helped to liberate. As Jehlen summarizes it,

The modern revision of identity in the seventeenth and eighteenth centuries had begun by projecting a new division. Countering the inequalities of social origin, it deeded each man with a natal estate in nature and pictured him then entering into political relations voluntarily and freely. This ontological separation and abstraction liberated the individual from a net of social and political interdependencies and, by rendering him inherently whole and self-sufficient, empowered him to act upon the world on his own (and his own behalf). No longer defined primarily by family or class, a man molded himself, then the world in his image.[27]

Despite its great usefulness in opposition to a European system of inherited rank, this idea has proved problematic in its application. For, as Appleby puts it, this way of thinking 'promotes more than a rejection of the past; it perpetuates the fantasy that we can uncouple ourselves from ... our society's cultural coding.'[28] In particular it assumes that class boundaries are completely fluid;

indeed the false consciousness that the USA is a classless meritocracy has persisted against all the evidence to the contrary. In suggesting that the individual exists apart from circumstances, middle-class Americans have all too often inferred that no matter what may be the accidents of one's birth, in America no one has a head start: hence the poor kid who remains poor does so not because she started the race on an unequal footing, but because she is slow – and probably willfully slow. This is part of the logic of opposition to affirmative action in America; the belief is that once legal and judicial restraints on equal opportunity were eliminated, the 'natural' equality of all citizens was re-insured. Any governmental help to any particular category of citizens is then seen as unfair, no matter what historical patterns of discrimination might still be in force.

I bring up the problems of race, class, and gender not only because they are now the common coin of cultural studies, or because they are among the major problems that are repressed in the simplistic, 'false consciousness' versions of an exceptionalism that sees America as the home of equality and possibility, and the model for the world's future. They are also worth raising because these three repressions are themselves highly productive of canonical American literature, a literature that becomes one significant site of the return of the exceptionalist repressed. This aspect of our literature picks up on the opposite side of the coin of being a chosen people: the promise of a special providence if we keep the faith is also the threat of one if we break the covenant, as Winthrop makes abundantly clear. In a more secular version, this way of thinking suggests that inequality in America constitutes a failure to live up to who we really, essentially are as a nation. Many of our canonical writers have been there to remind us of the tragic or ironic distance between America as dream and ideal – the dream of equality and well-being, liberty and justice for all – and the historical reality of America as place. In *The Last of the Mohicans* and *The Pioneers*, James Fenimore Cooper may do his best to affirm an ideology of white manifest destiny, but what makes him still worth reading is always what is left over, the pall that is cast (and the textual tension that is created) by the consciousness of and conscience about the genocidal effects on which this destiny depends. In 'Benito Cereno,' Melville gives us a savagely ironic portrait of Amasa Delano as the prototypical white American, the naive man of good will whose racism simply will not let him see – and who, when he does see, reacts as the mirror image of the 'savagery' he fears and loathes. Even more brilliantly, Melville positions the reader with Delano, enticing us to an identification with him by which we become implicated in his incapacities of moral vision. In *Huckleberry Finn*, Twain again shows racism to be the darkest blot on the American conscience and continent, the blot that puts all but the outcasts at odds with the positive potentialities of the natural scene. *The Scarlet Letter* examines the difficulties posed for the City on a Hill and its mission by the demands for freedom and self-realization, and the sexuality, of a strong woman – and the difficulties posed for her by the exceptionalist polity. In 'The Birthmark' Hawthorne shows how the dream of world-making and mastery over nature destroys the other and the possibility of love. 'Daisy Miller' shows how class snobbery and allegiance to European hierarchic values can make the American man not only a poor perceiver, but a killer, and a violator of that which is 'naturally' American. *Absalom, Absalom!* tells the story of the American intent on overcoming the classism he experienced as a child by carving his own world out of the wilderness, and of how he is brought down by his own failure to get beyond the strictures of racism, classism, and sexism. All of these texts – and they are among the greatest texts of our traditionally canonical fiction writers – gain a good deal of their force from the ground of American exceptionalism, from the notion that what is at stake in them is not just individual stories, not just a class or gender or race analysis and critique, but a failure of America: a failure to live up to our exceptionalist destiny. All of them, in varying degrees, invoke this destiny. At the least they are likely to do so by having a particular character who represents either 'the American' or 'America.' In other cases, they rather explicitly refer to exceptionalist discourse.

One of the most vivid examples of all is F. Scott Fitzgerald's *The Great Gatsby*, which is also one of the strongest novels ever

written by an American about money and class. Richard Chase
suggested some time ago that the force of this text is its staging of
a confrontation between the hero of American romance – the
questing individualist – and the traditional social world of the
novel: the world of manners, morals, money, and marriage that is
antithetical to the form and the hero of what Baym calls the
'melodrama of beset manhood.'[29] It is because Gatsby is the
exceptionalist hero – because he is the conscious amalgam of
Franklinian and Emersonian models of self-creation and transcendence of circumstances; because he 'sprang from his Platonic
conception of himself' – that he intrigues Americans, and that
Nick Carraway, Fitzgerald's moralistic narrator, can declare
Gatsby (despite his obvious corruptions), to be 'worth the whole
damn bunch put together.'[30] And what gives Fitzgerald's novel its
claim not necessarily to be the greatest novel ever written by an
American, but to be the 'great American novel,' is its analysis of
American society in light of the exceptionalist dream. At the very
least, this is what makes its ending one of the most resonant
passages in American writing:

[G]radually I became aware of the old island here that flowered once for
Dutch sailors' eyes – a fresh, green breast of the new world. Its vanished
trees [...] had once pandered in whispers to the last and greatest of all
human dreams; for a transitory enchanted moment man must have held
his breath in the presence of this continent [...] face to face for the last
time in history with something commensurate to his capacity for
wonder.

And as I sat there brooding on the old, unknown world, I thought of
Gatsby He had come a long way to this blue lawn, and his dream must
have seemed so close that he could hardly fail to grasp it. He did not
know that it was already behind him, somewhere back in that vast
obscurity beyond the city, where the dark fields of the republic rolled on
under the night [...]

So we beat on, boats against the current, borne back ceaselessly into
the past.[31]

For a more recent ending, by a writer who speaks from a very
different subject-position but who nonetheless invokes the same
tradition, consider the last lines of Toni Morrison's *The Bluest Eye*,

with their assertion that the destruction of Pecola Breedlove, a young Black girl, is a failure of the land, and their clear indication that the failure of the land is the failure of its people:

I talk about how [...] it was the fault of the earth, the land, of our town. I think even now that the land of the entire country was hostile to marigolds that year. This soil is bad for certain kinds of flowers. Certain seeds it will not nurture, certain fruit it will not bear and when the land kills of its own volition, we acquiesce and say the victim had no right to live. We are wrong, of course, but it doesn't matter. It's too late. At least on the edge of my town, among the garbage and the sunflowers of my town, it's much, much, much too late.[32]

Like James's Daisy Miller, Pecola Breedlove is an innocent flower cut off by the failure of America.

These two endings point strongly toward a key difference between the traditionally canonical sort of American novels on the one hand, and European – as well as many non-canonical or marginalized American – novels on the other. The difference, I would emphasize, is that the individual and social failures or tragedies in canonized American novels are rather consistently framed, by authors or readers or both, as failures or tragedies *of the nation* – rather than, on the one hand, of a particular class or gender or social system or, on the other, of humanity in general. Emma Bovary's death may be a function of the social system in which she lives, or of her nation at a particular moment, but it is not so specifically a failure of France as an ideological ideal (at least, I don't think it is). Dickens's innocents may suffer at the hands of a class system or a legal system or a failure of common humanity and charity, but they are not the victims of England's failure *to be England*. Among American novels, Edith Wharton's *The House of Mirth* is as vivid a narrative as *The Great Gatsby*, and as powerful an indictment of class prejudice. It also grippingly exposes and criticizes the kind of sexism that Fitzgerald's novel only reinforces. Yet in the past Wharton's novel has not had as much resonance for American audiences as has Fitzgerald's. The factors that Baym analyzes as contributing to the exclusion of women authors have everything to do with this. But I think one of the most important factors is that the novel is not framed by the exceptionalist myth: in particular, we are not invited to experience Lily Bart's death as a failure of the nation. Part of the reason for this is that she is not made to stand for America – that is, for the land – as women in general, and women victims in particular, have been made to stand in the traditional, male-authored American novel (as Baym and Kolodny, among others, have pointed out). One of the benefits of getting away from the nationalist/exceptionalist requirement for American literature is that we will longer require this problematic metaphor in order to feel the tragedy of such a death. Another benefit, already suggested above, is that we are thus given works of American literature to love that we were not invited to love before because they were not 'American' enough.

Exceptionalist ideology also depends upon at least one other key repression besides those of race, class, and gender – one other whose repressed returns in our canonically critical literature. That is the repression of the materiality and resistance, the otherness, of nature itself. Historically the guarantor of all the boons that make America exceptional is free land, and the landscape is regarded as hospitable to human activity – as, in the ideology's most radical versions, eager to be used (and used up) by and in human designs. Thus in 'Song of the Redwood-Tree,' one of his most troubling poems, Whitman has the tree, which is about to be cut, speak as follows:

> *Nor yield we mournfully majestic brothers,*
> *We who have grandly fill'd our time;*
> *With nature's calm content, with tacit huge delight,*
> *We welcome what we wrought for through the past,*
> *And leave the field for them.*
>
> *For them predicted long,*
> *For a superber race, they too to grandly fill their time,*
> *For them we abdicate, m them ourselves ye forest kings!*
> *To be in them absorb'd, assimilated.*[33]

A number of canonical texts could be cited against this one, as could a good deal of notable contemporary poetry. Consider, for instance, the pigeon-hunting scene in *The Pioneers,* where Natty Bumppo speaks passionately for nature against its victimization by the westward sweep of Euro-American designs. Or again recall 'The Birthmark' with its critique of the overweening scientific pride that would 'perfect' nature. Among contemporaries, the openly ecological writing of Gary Snyder and W. S. Merwin, among others, comes to mind. But perhaps the key text in this regard is *Moby-Dick,* in which nature persistently remains other to human readings of and designs for (or, more accurately, against) it. Surely the bitterness of the wounded transcendentalist, Ahab, results from the 'failure' of nature to live up to the exceptionalist promise. Surely Melville's portrait of overweening pride in relation to nature resonates against Whitman's appropriation of the voice of the tree to celebrate its demise in favor of manifest destiny – as, more generally, Melville's cautionary tale sounds against the entire transcendentalist and exceptionalist command, as Emerson puts it in 'Nature,' to 'Know then, that the world exists *for you.'*[34]

Thus in many ways our canonical literature has served as part of the conscience of exceptionalism, and of the nation. This critique from within the ideology helps explain why our literature may look highly political and subversive – as many critics, among the most recent of them Frank Lentricchia, have claimed – and why it may yet at the same time seem to be no more than what Nina Baym calls a 'consensus criticism of the consensus.'[35] Writing from the subject-position of an otherness (the feminine) that has been systematically excluded, indeed anathematized as an impediment to the exceptionalist encounter with the wilderness, Baym finds the political critique from within the tradition anything but radical: its problem is precisely that it does not change things radically in the etymological sense of 'at the root.' While it criticizes the material reality of America, it does not challenge the ideological paradigm. Interested parties can consult Sacvan Bercovitch's *The American Jeremiad* for another powerful analysis of the ways in which the energies of this traditional critique have 'served to sustain the culture, because the same ideal that released those energies transformed radicalism itself into a mode of cultural cohesion and continuity.'[36]

I want to align myself with those who urge that we attend to voices that pose a more radical threat – voices of others who have not been heard before, and who do not subscribe, even rhetorically, to the exceptionalist ideology. It is part of the business of contemporary American Studies to help us hear them. Yet it's interesting how, even in the case of voices from the position of the other, those who seem to have the most powerful impact are figures such as, in the African-American tradition, Frederick Douglass and Harriet Jacobs, Ralph Ellison, Martin Luther King, and Toni Morrison, who do invoke exceptionalism.

But we must not, in opening ourselves to others, cease to heed the voices whose critique come from within exceptionalism. There are two sides to what Bercovitch says: on the one hand, it is hard for any really radical critique to take place in America, because critique is so easily absorbed into cultural continuity, and thereby often neutralized. But the other side of this coin is that we have had a continuity of critique – an ongoing testing of our realities against our alleged values – and the effects of this have been in certain ways positive. The history of what has been, on social issues, a surprisingly conservative nation has been made more just (or at least less unjust) by certain critical uses of exceptionalism to hold our ideological feet to the fire. The critique that comes from within exceptionalism (like that which comes from the Enlightenment liberalism with which exceptionalism is so thoroughly imbricated) is not now nor has it ever been politically or culturally or ethically sufficient – but at times it has been effective, where a more radical critique simply fell on deaf ears.

What is the future of exceptionalist ideology in an age of the economic globalization that characterizes late capitalism, and the 'incredulity toward metanarratives' that, according to Jean-François Lyotard, constitutes the postmodern condition?[37] Both of these forces, it would seem, should tend to make exceptionalism less a dominant ideology and more a residual one, in Raymond Williams's terms.[38] And indeed, such a forecast has much in common with the vision of the future projected in the cyberpunk fictions of William Gibson (such as *Neuromancer, Count Zero, Mona Lisa Overdrive,* 'Burning Chrome,' 'Johnny Mnemonic') – fictions that Fredric Jameson sees as nothing less than a 'distorted figuration of ... the whole world system of a present-day multi-national capitalism.'[39] In Gibson's world, as in our own as the latter is described by many theorists of the postmodern, in the economically most highly developed countries national and nationalist categories seem to diminish in significance in light of the transnational flows of information and capital. In Gibson, the individualist small entrepreneurs who stand on the margins of the law, such as the computer 'cowboys' who steal data and money in *Neuromancer* and 'Burning Chrome,' have little or no sense of national identity, and no discernible relation to any national project.

On the other hand, both theoretical accounts of the present and recent fictions of America's future also provide an alternative vision, one in which exceptionalism could figure much more prominently. In contrast to those who see the role of the nation as diminishing, Michel Foucault points out that 'in contemporary societies ... power relations have come more and more under state control.'[40] If this is so, it is certainly possible for an exceptionalist discourse to have a significant ideological role to play, both in support of *and* in opposition to this concentration of power as the latter occurs in the United States. On the one hand, it can be one of the ideological frames by which this concentration is justified: 'America must be strong to fulfill her destiny.' On the other, it might be enlisted in the service of those who, invoking the Boston Tea Party and other icons of the American Revolution, claim the right of the people to throw off the 'yoke of tyranny.'

On a more specific plane, it seems clear that the forces of ideological reaction have grown radically in the last two decades: the presidency of Ronald Reagan, the growth of right-wing evangelical Christianity as a political force, the rise of Newt Gingrich and other young New Right ideologues, and the emergence of the militia movement are among the most visible examples. All of these developments are thoroughly imbricated with, and consciously trade on, various brands of exceptionalist ideology. A fiction that projects these trends (rather than the globalization of capital) as dominating daily life in the American future is Margaret Atwood's terrifying *The Handmaiden's Tale*. It is less difficult than it ought to be to imagine a future in the grip of a fundamentalist New Right totalitarianism; in such a future, one suspects, the most egregiously destructive versions of American exceptionalism (the belief in a programmatically white America with a Manifest Destiny allegedly ordained by an evangelical Christian God) might play quite a prominent role.

Nonetheless, despite this rather grim reminder of how destructive exceptionalism can be (and has been), I want to end by returning to a recognition of a more ameliorative and productive aspect, at least for literature, of a positive faith in it. In one way it is pleasing formally to end on a note of affirmation. But my doing so is in large part a consequence of the organization (or disorganization) of this essay as it has developed in composition, rather than an expression of any final faith in or desire to recuperate the exceptionalist ideology. Still, having disavowed the meaning of such a pleasurable closure, perhaps we can at least enjoy the fiction of it. The greatest pleasures and values of a positive exceptionalism in our literature, I believe, are to be found in the Whitman tradition, and particularly in the best poetry of Walt Whitman himself. Part of the reason for that is that Whitman took the ideology more seriously and viscerally – and literally – than any of our other significant writers. And by an act of sheer will and unbridled, erotic energy, he worked it into a vision that asserts the transcendence of difference and absence and even death. When Myra Jehlen discusses how America became the literalization, the 'incarnation of the spirit of liberal idealism,' and how 'the crux of the matter is the identification of certain abstract ideals with the physical American landscape'; when she discusses how 'Americans assume their national identity as the fulfillment of selfhood', when she tells how 'it is as an American that ... [the abstract individual] becomes not only singular but representative,' so that 'community ... comes from within' and 'it is by being autonomous that each man thus connects to others' – in all of

these instances she does no more, really, than to gloss Whitman.[41]
Here, then, is a passage that exemplifies Whitman's declaration of
the democratic vision to which exceptionalism led him. Would
that it had led our politicians and cultural gatekeepers to something similar:

These States are the amplest poem.
Here is not merely a nation but a teeming Nation of nations,
Here the doings of men correspond with the broadcast doings of the day
    and night,
Here is what moves in magnificent masses careless of particulars,
Here are the roughs, beards, friendliness, combativeness, the soul loves,
Here the flowing trains, here the crowds, equality, diversity, the soul
    loves.[42]

This scene of 'equality, diversity' is perhaps the nation to which
Allen Ginsberg referred as 'the lost America of love' when, in his
'In a Supermarket in California,' he paid tribute to Whitman as
'dear father, graybeard, lonely old courage-teacher.'[43] At its most
positively productive, American exceptionalism allows us to
dream that that America of love is not lost – and allows us to go
to *Leaves of Grass* to find it again, at least as hope and ideal. What
we need as a nation, beyond the exceptionalism that the rhetoric
of my ending is unable really to go beyond, is to learn that
courage, to find that love of equality and diversity, to give it an
American incarnation.

## Notes

1.  Joyce Appleby, 'Recovering America's Historic Diversity: Beyond
    Exceptionalism,' *Journal of American History,* 79 (1992): 419.
2.  Walt Whitman, *Complete Poetry and Selected Prose,* ed. James E. Miller, Jr.
    (Cambridge, MA: Riverside-Houghton, 1959), 154.
3.  Seymour Martin Lipset, *American Exceptionalism: A Double-Edged Sword*
    (New York: Norton, 1996), 17.
4.  Appleby, 419.
5.  Bill Ashcroft, Gareth Griffins and Helen Tiffen, *The Empire Writes Back* (New
    York: Routledge, 1989), 17.

6. Lipset, 18.
7. Raymond Williams, *Keywords: A Vocabulary of Culture and Society* (New York: Oxford University Press, 1976), 127.
8. Myra Jehlen, *American Incarnation: The Individual, the Nation, and the Continent* (Cambridge, MA: Harvard University Press, 1986), 4 (emphasis added).
9. Jehlen, 19 (emphases in original).
10. Louis Althusser, 'Ideology and Ideological State Apparatuses (Notes Towards an Investigation),' in *Lenin and Philosophy and Other Essays*, trans. Ben Brewster (New York: Monthly Review Press, 1971), 162.
11. Althusser, 171, 173.
12. See Ralph Waldo Emerson, 'Nature' (1836), *The Norton Anthology of American Literature*, 4th ed., ed. Nina Baym, et al., vol. 1 (New York: Norton, 1994) 1020.
13. Nina Baym, 'Melodramas of Beset Manhood: How Theories of American Fiction Exclude Women Authors,' *American Quarterly*, 33 (1981): 123–39.
14. Annette Kolodny, 'Letting Go Our Grand Obsessions: Notes Toward a New Literary History of the American Frontiers,' *Subjects and Citizens: Nation, Race, and Gender from Oroonoko to Anita Hill*, ed. Michael Moon and Cathy N. Davidson (Durham, NC: Duke University Press, 1995), 9–26.
15. 'Introduction', Moon and Davidson, 1.
16. Kolodny, 20.
17. John Winthrop, 'A Model of Christian Charity' (1630), *Norton Anthology*, ed. Baym, et al., 179–80.
18. Sacvan Bercovitch, *The American Jeremiad* (Madison: University of Wisconsin Press, 1978), 3–11.
19. Bercovitch, 6.
20. See Baym, 'Melodramas,' 125–27 and Kolodny, 20.
21. See Baym, 'Melodramas,' 125–29 and *passim*.
22. Benjamin Franklin, *The Autobiography*, *Norton Anthology*, ed. Baym, et al., 511.
23. Whitman, 454.
24. Baym, 'Melodramas,' 125.
25. Baym, 'Melodramas,' 125–6.
26. See Henry Louis Gates, 'Editor's Introduction: Writing "Race" and the Difference It Makes,' *'Race,' Writing, and Difference*, ed. Henry Louis Gates (Chicago: University of Chicago Press, 1986), 8.
27. Jehlen, 3–4.
28. Appleby, 427.
29. Richard Chase, *The American Novel and Its Tradition* (Garden City, NY: Anchor-Doubleday, 1957), 162–67.
30. F. Scott Fitzgerald, *The Great Gatsby* (1925; New York: Scribners, 1953), 99, 154.
31. Fitzgerald, 182.

32. Toni Morrison, *The Bluest Eye* (1970; New York: Washington Square-Simon, 1972), 160 (emphasis in original).

33. Whitman, 152 (italics in original).

34. Emerson, 1020 (emphasis added).

35. Frank Lentricchia, 'The American Writer as Bad Citizen - Introducing Don DeLillo,' *South Atlantic Quarterly*, 89 (1990): 241–43 (special issue on *The Fiction of Don DeLillo.*, ed. Frank Lentricchia); Baym, 'Melodramas,' 129.

36. Bercovitch, 205.

37. Jean-François Lyotard, *The Postmodern Condition: A Report on Knowledge*, trans. Geoff Bennington and Brain Massumi, Theory and History of Literature, 10 (Minneapolis: University of Minnesota Press, 1984), xxiv.

38. Raymond Williams, *Marxism and Literature* (Oxford: Oxford University Press, 1977), 121–27.

39. Fredric Jameson, *Postmodernism, or, The Cultural Logic of Late Capitalism*, (Durham, NC: Duke University Press, 1991), 37.

40. Michel Foucault, 'Afterword: The Subject and Power,' in Hubert L. Dreyfus and Paul Rabinow, *Michel Foucault: Beyond Structuralism and Hermeneutics*, 2nd ed. (Chicago: University of Chicago Press, 1983), 224.

41. Jehlen, 9, 12–13, 14–15.

42. Whitman, 243.

43. Allen Ginsberg, *Howl and Other Poems*, Pocket Poets Series, 4 (San Francisco: City Lights, 1956), 24.

# Writing, Criticism and the Imagination of Nation: American Exceptionalism and the Evolution of American Studies

*James Mendelsohn*

For years we studied American exceptionalism as if it were simply an examination of the character of the United States found in writing from the country and its colonial ancestors; today we more readily recognize that study itself to have contained an implied wish for national identity. I want to suggest the ways in which the imagination of the United States as a country has been complicated by the identification of that imagination within the discipline of American Studies – an identification which is, to be sure, its own imagining of the nation What I shall emphasize, therefore, is not only early writing in the United States that suggests the nation is an exceptional entity, but also the history of our writing and scholarship about such descriptions. I do not mean to suggest, however, that it is illegitimate to study or to generalize about the United States as a nation; in fact the study of national identity is a vital and unavoidable area of study. But this essay nonetheless implies that we need not frame our investigations of culture or history to further our emphasis upon nations even while studying them, and the point of the essay is we have often done just that: the state of American Studies today bears witness to the increasingly popular desire to find some other means of evaluating such things as territories, groups of peoples, and the shaping of identities within the series of continents America designates. For the ends I identify above, this essay briefly surveys writing from the United States about its character and then considers twentieth-century writing about such writings

*Marks of Distinction: American Exceptionalism Revisited*, ed. Dale Carter, *The Dolphin* 32, pp. 69–90. © 2001 by Aarhus University Press, Denmark. ISBN 87 7288 383 9; ISSN 0106 4487.

which are important to the formation of American Studies in the
United States.

I

I begin with a brief and general consideration of my premises. I
take it as a given that to be exceptional, like most ideas of identity,
requires the recognition of something by means of its difference
from others, and that it suggests some special recognition –
conscious or otherwise – of that exceptional status. Whether one
invokes, for example, Hegel's *Phenomenology of the Spirit* or one of
a number of more contemporary texts, from Emmanuel Levinas
to Homi Bhabha, we understand what we are in relation to what
we are not; and this *necessary* difference is sometimes explicit and
intentional and sometimes not. The me and not me of Hegel, the
other with a capital O – in each case the question of what we
identify results from establishing a difference from something
else, and the effects of doing so depends on how different that
otherness is, how remote we find ourselves to be, as a result of
that difference, from our own capacities to imagine the interests
of that other.

For the exceptionalism of a nation, we might further ask what
in the interest of defining a nation such remoteness creates in our
relations with those who are not part of it. A concern with the
cultural distinctiveness of a nation is of course one means by
which nations narrate their histories to themselves. It is one way
nations tell themselves this is what they are, this is what distinguishes them. The very question 'What makes the United States
exceptional?' is therefore full of the wish to imagine the world in
terms of nations, to shape how we think of the world in terms of
national entities. It is a question that carries with it the shadow of
nationalism. But for national identity to exist in cultural form,
those defined as outside of it play a vital role. This dynamic
occurs in our earliest records of Europeans on the western side of
the Atlantic. According to Bartholomew de las Casas, Christopher
Columbus honors Spain in his journal by naming an island 'San
Salvador,' and he describes the people he sees on his first voyage

as Indians. In so doing, his actions are complicated acts of imagination, in which what he sees before him results in part from the imperial task at hand. Before him are people he finds on what we now identify as San Salvador, Cuba, the Bahamas and Hispaniola. At the moment Columbus recognizes and names them 'Indians,' they become for him a kind of common people, thereby rendering invisible their different understandings of how they see themselves and their landscape. As an essential part of Columbus's identification, the New World is imagined as something which made another kind of past the land had for its inhabitants monolithic as well as invisible, because that other past had been neither written, to a large extent, nor nationally conceived. The pasts the inhabitants had before Columbus were largely the result of oral cultures and were thus literally written over by the domination of books (Western societies, after all, depend upon writing to function, documents are the means by which they perpetuate our history.)[1]

Therefore, in the earliest uses of the words 'New World' and 'America,' one finds something both exceptional and troubling: an imagination by Europeans of a land extending over multiple continents whose meaning, the result of the aspirations of Western nations – in particular Spain, Britain, and France – eclipses the histories of its oldest inhabitants. The New World is exceptional for the explorers, full of their longing to establish trade routes and thereby to see the land as part of this distinctive goal. The exceptional status of this New World thereby depends, albeit not implicitly, upon erasing a different, less usable past that belonged to the other peoples these explorers encountered there. For that other past, the explorers substituted a history that defines the New World as new, a part of the grand history of European empires; its previous inhabitants become the exemplary figures of that other world which these explorers imagined in order to identify themselves and their respective countries

As a result, the very language by which one now identifies what has preceded the invention of America becomes inadequate. How, for example, does one refer to its previous inhabitants – as first peoples or native Americans? – without effecting a similar, monolithic imagination of them that depends upon the acts of these explorers for its originating identification? Nonetheless, this earliest idea of America and eventually the United States nearly always comes up in discussions of its exceptional status: an imagination of landscape, land and country that furthers an imperial goal by imagining itself as someplace new, fresh, unpeopled, and exceptional; and which becomes something exceptional as a result. Paradoxically, this idea of the New World imagines the explorers themselves as first peoples in a profound, nearly unshakable way, and it exemplifies how these explorers identify themselves by identifying who they find in the New World as those other people they so desperately needed to imagine.

As Thomas Byers suggests in the previous essay, the religious imagination of the land by Puritans in what is now the United States performs a similar act in which the land itself is invested with a quality of promise, rebirth, and near salvation, and its previous inhabitants rendered nearly invisible, as if dissolved into the landscape and the religious allegory through which New England colonial settlers understood their experiences. In his lay sermon aboard the ship *Arbella* in 1630, en route to what was soon to become the Massachusetts Bay Colony, John Winthrop imagines the land he anticipates in a manner inseparable from his religious vision. In this speech, he defines America as special because it is the material manifestation of that religious vision. America is the place where a new Israel might be founded, where for the instruction of the rest of the world these Puritan colonists can live the life of the Lord. Significantly, Winthrop declares that they are not like other Englishmen: 'That which most in their Churches maintain as a truth in profession only, we must bring into familiar and constant practice.'[2] The role of other is performed here by the English. Winthrop anticipates a social compact which is fundamentally religious and depends upon the colonists' exceptional ability to follow the ways of God better than their fellow countrymen back in England. He declares the presence of a covenant, which implies his group of colonists is potentially a very special if not elect group, like the tribe of Israel:

'Thus stands the cause between God and us, we are entered into Covenant with him for this work, we have taken out a Commission, the Lord hath given us leave to draw our own Articles [...].'[3]

This covenant invests the future actions of the people with special import. According to Winthrop, the colonists are doing God's work in building this colony; all they do in their lives will be so governed. With this in mind, having preached these last words, Winthrop declares those often repeated words: The people and their community will be 'as a city upon a hill,' exceptional and constantly demonstrative of its exceptional status for the rest of the world.[4] Land itself is taken here as a sign of wonder. Using the metaphor of a city, which is both landscape and human settlement, Winthrop materializes America's exceptional condition, giving it not only social and religious but geographic meaning.

I am only alluding to the necessary texts in these examples; much else can and should be said about the early formation of America and the United States. My point, however, is to suggest not so much the importance of the land to an idea of American exceptionalism but the need for identifying a difference from something else to do so. This is the case not only before but after the colonies become a nation. In our idea of the revolutionary war today, the United States helps to imagine itself by a written declaration which defines the country according to its opposition to Britain and the declaration of an idea of life, liberty and the pursuit of happiness that would distinguish their lives from that under British rule. This imagination of the United States not only institutionalizes the soon-to-be former colonists' claims but, in one fell swoop, elides our own disturbing past and that of these colonists, who simultaneously called for freedom while maintaining slavery. In identifying themselves as independent, the colonists both acknowledge a sense of their difference from English colonists by their stated ideals, and yet suppress the wholesale exploitation of Africans that was so vital to the imagination of early economic life and post-colonial identity in the United States. The conditions of national identity appear a fragile balance of remembering and forgetting figures of 'otherness' that, whether visible or invisible, are nonetheless vital to its establishment.

That vital relation helps to explain why, during the Revolutionary War, we find enthusiastic reception of Crèvecœur's *Letters to an American Farmer:* because to be a nation requires a continual imagination of what it is and what it is not. Crèvecœur's 'What is an American?' letter effectively identifies Americans by its difference from Europe. The United States is distinct by virtue of the absence of monarchy, nobility, or Church domination and the pursuit, on more egalitarian terms, of an agrarian-based life. Hence Crèvecœur implies that the United States is exceptional because it is not like Europe and of course, paradoxically, physiocrats.[5]

Similarly, in his *Notes on Virginia,* Jefferson identifies the United States as exceptional through a defense of its natural resources and agrarian life against the claims of the Comte de Buffon and the Abbé Reynal that its animals (including people) were smaller and more degenerate. The vision of the United States that Jefferson's *Notes* proposes is once again a paean to the land as its unique feature – and also to the agrarian – but in the context of its difference from Europe, that necessary standard against which the United States measures its identity.[6] An agrarian myth, moreover, both distinguishes the United States and, as Henry Nash Smith and Leo Marx analyze, resolves the contradictory impulses toward civilized life and flight from it.[7] This idea of the agrarian implies that the frontier lands of the late eighteenth century are vital to the dynamic of flight and civilization through which the nation defines itself; and the interests of the earlier inhabitants of that frontier – the tribes of North Carolina, Virginia, and New York, for example – are rendered remote by the urgent need for imagining the nation.[8] We see this implication borne out in Jefferson's *Notes.* Following the French physiocrats, Jefferson argues that the magnificence of the natural landscape corresponds with the potential genius of its people. Jefferson thereby uses this book to suggest the exceptional nature of the American people. But his example of American potential is, of all things, the rhetorical brilliance in a speech by Logan, a

Mingo Indian Chief whose family has been murdered by whites and who has subsequently taken his revenge and been captured by the Virginia militia. There is a deep irony here that reflects on what exceptionalism does and what national identity perhaps requires. In this instance, the very act of taking over the land and making the nation results in the murder of earlier inhabitants, so that the creation of this exceptional country which Jefferson wants to show is represented by the speech of one victimized by that country. America is exceptional not for having committed this act, however, but for the potential of what the land can produce – 'genius' is the word Jefferson uses to describe Logan's speech.[9] So exceptionalism makes the plight of those inhabitants who define themselves in ways other than by the term 'United States' nearly invisible, a kind of instrument for proving American exceptionalism rather than an example of what might cast shadows over its value and understanding.

I am speeding toward the twentieth century in this survey of the United States as exceptional and imagined, so much so that I will all but overlook the Jacksonian period. With Emerson and later Whitman, however, the idea of Genius, present in all of us, is a virtual call for the equation of individual discovery with national discovery. Within this myth, America is, to paraphrase Sacvan Bercovitch, a great dream that is always on the horizon, always under formation, a dream that does cultural work.[10] This secular myth calls for identifying the United States by a rejection of the traditions of Europe and relying upon a form of revelation which is to be found by the individual within the country. To no surprise, such a myth is enormously suitable for the United States as it is transformed into an entrepreneurial and eventually urban, industrialized nation. In late ante-bellum and post-bellum America, American exceptionalism is most evident in the idea of manifest destiny, through which the United States justified wholesale attacks upon Indian tribes, the breaking of treaties with Indians, and the symbolic representation of the West as both the material resources for and the property of the United States and its citizens.[11] The special status of the country justifies its expansion, for which an imagination of the 'aggrandizing Mexican' and the 'savage Indian' played an integral role.

Of course, as Henry James writes in his famous list in his study of Hawthorne, the United States is, arguably, also exceptional for what it lacks.[12] The anxiety present in James's remarks reflects on his own ambivalent sense of belonging, at a distance, to the United States; but it also describes the United States as exceptional for what it would become but had not arrived at. While the country is defined by potential, that potential is in turn defined by how it is not like European countries in its cultural development though it promises to be so. Hence the exceptional status continues its special relationship with Europe by virtue of its continual and declared identification of itself by its difference. James's definition of the United States is part of what leads James in *The American Scene* to urge the creation through means such as writing of the rituals around which national symbols could be made and a national culture born.[13]


## II

One could cite many other texts now invoked as important documents or canonical writing or literature in the nineteenth century in the United States – the Seneca Falls Convention, Mark Twain, W. E. B. Du Bois, George Santayana. Each suggests the means by which writing served the formation of a national symbolic, an imagined identity of what the United States is by virtue of what it is not, which in a certain moment of its history, through its claim to be special, marks how the country shapes itself. In so doing one widens these few examples to include the ways in which those who were not powerful or privileged – African Americans and women, for example – invoked the exceptional character of the United States to argue for their inclusion in its national community.

But to go on in this way would not perhaps explain how I came to choose these texts to exemplify American exceptionalism, how this supposed history is not exclusively a reflection on the past but a sense of how American Studies narrates what the

United States is today. In this regard, there is a second story to be told, that in which twentieth-century intellectuals, critics and scholars identify the United States. It too bears relation to nationalism. When we examine the work of many writers and scholars whose goal is to identify an American tradition and, consciously and unconsciously, to describe American identity, we find it not simply identifying but contributing to the ideological development of nationalism via cultural tradition.

During the second decade of the twentieth century, for example, one sees emerging in the United States a call for identifying the country through literature, a call generated by those in opposition to the increasingly commercialized, industrial order of the country who seek explicitly a replacement in culture for what was in the past a political identity for the United States. Van Wyck Brooks, Waldo Frank, and more generally the members of the Seven Arts group sought in their lionizing of Walt Whitman, among others, a pre-industrial sense of the country and its workers, such that they would no longer be alienated by their place in the capitalist order. In the development of American Studies, Brooks's concept of 'the usable past' is a virtual call for pursuing a national identity via a literary legacy. Writing in *America's Coming of Age* (1915), Brooks declares that American culture must avoid what he calls its twin traditions of 'piety' and 'advertisement.' Piety is exemplified in the Puritans, Jonathan Edwards, Transcendentalists and professors, who create a kind of unreality, a 'priggish, paralyzing idealism'; advertisement is in contrast the product of crass commercialism, a 'catchpenny opportunism' found also in the Puritans, in Franklin, among American humorists, and of course in business life.[14] The usable past is primarily represented by the 'personal' approach of 'our poets' – especially Walt Whitman – so that writing, and especially literature, is exceptional to and distinguishing of the United States; a cultural identification of the nation can stand apart from capitalism and socially dominant forces in distinguishing the country.[15]

The United States is therefore exceptional to Brooks by virtue of its literature and literary tradition, or at least the tradition it has

begun but has yet to nurture adequately. With Whitman, moreover, Brooks signals his interest in a figure that celebrates an
evolving sense of potential citizenship that aspires to be deeply
democratic and populist. In both the traditions he wishes to avoid
and the poets he lionizes, however, the idea of the American past
and of the nation is problematic for a population that in the
second decade of the century was radically different in geographic origins than in the usable past he claims. As Claire
Sprague points out, Brooks calls for retaking the American past
from upstarts like H. L. Mencken, 'with a German-American
mind,' and he asserts that the writer and artist depends upon 'the
accretion of countless generations of ancestors, trained to one
deep, local, indigenous attitude toward life.'[16] Brooks's idea of
American exceptionalism either depends upon or encourages a
kind of cultural nativism that in turn potentially identifies non-
natives as ethnic, cultural, and indeed political outsiders and
wannabes. Such attitudes were not confined to Brooks nor should
Brooks's more laudatory contributions be ignored; but they do
suggest the ways in which the study and identification of American exceptionalism also served the national goals of some of the
population and further insinuated an idea of nation by virtue of
who did not belong. Studying American exceptionalism in this
way carries a nationalist implication and defines the country by
virtue of identifying who among its inhabitants do not uphold its
exceptional impulses; hence the figure of the other becomes more
explicitly located among the citizens or aspiring citizens of the
country. It identifies the nation through analyzing the character of
its literature and judging who best fits such an identification.
(This development finds its way into that bastion of piety, the
academy, at the same time. For example, the first publication of
the *Cambridge History of American Literature* was in 1917.[17] More
generally, as English departments shifted from the study of
philology to the development of literary studies, literary histories
of the nation played a vital part, so that the discipline of English
began to reflect not only a shift in methods of analysis but a
reflection upon national identity shaped in literature.)

Brooks, moreover, was but one of several liberal to left-leaning cultural critics of American exceptionalism who, early in the twentieth century, encouraged a particular form of nationalism while analyzing the nation. In *Main Currents in American Thought* (1927) – a book often associated with the beginning of American Studies – Vernon Parrington expands the scope of examination beyond American letters to something that prefigures cultural studies today but describes the United States as a country produced out of its differences and debts to European thought and culture. Rather than focus upon literature, Parrington devoted himself to identifying the values and concepts that have determined the 'form and scope of our characteristic ideals and institutions ... with their ramifications into theology and politics and economics'; literature is then valued as an expression of 'certain germinal ideas that have come to be reckoned traditionally American.' We must, he adds, 'follow the broad path of our political, economic and social development, rather than the narrower belletristic.'[18] Rich in its description of the complex and contradictory elements of national history, Parrington's study offers a new methodology for his era. He identifies America through ways we might recognize as prefiguring contemporary American studies, where American culture is construed more widely and where there are relationships found between the shape of institutions, politics, economics, and writing.

While Parrington is less of a proselytizer than Brooks, he nonetheless describes America in terms of a European legacy, exceptional for its ability to amalgamate European traditions to create the forms of its culture and thought. Parrington describes the exceptional character of the United States as the result of a 'grafting' of French, German, and English thoughts and institutions: 'bequests' of English independence, French romantic theory (by which he means Rousseau and the Enlightenment), the industrial revolution, laissez faire capitalism, nineteenth-century science, and 'Continental theories of collectivism.'[19] He identifies each of these elements in relation to specific formative moments in the United States, including Puritan settlement culture, Jeffersonian agrarianism, the rise of capitalism and industrialism, and in a final volume, what he calls the 'beginnings of dissatisfactions with the regnant middle class,' which is manifested in realism and naturalism. Here one sees the thesis that the earliest roots of the United States lie in twin traditions. On the one hand, there is independence from England and theories of natural rights and property deriving from the texts of John Locke and Rousseau; on the other hand there is the religious absolutism of what he calls a 'reactionary theology' that thought human nature to be evil and believed divine sovereignty to be absolute and arbitrary – so much so that it 'projected caste divisions into eternity.' The nation creates later roots by importing still more of the doctrine of natural rights and democratic theory, which substitute a more promising idea of human nature for the Puritan Idea of the corrupt soul. This later development, Parrington argues, is largely the result of the Physiocratic school, the consequent honor bestowed upon the farmer as an ideal citizen, and then the co-option of such beliefs by an emergent laissez-faire capitalism in the early nineteenth century, which believed 'human nature neither good nor bad, but ... acquisitive.'[20] On the one hand, Parrington analyzes with sophistication American exceptional-ism, which he describes as complex because of its different roots and potential forms within American culture and thought (a critical observation that is important for our sense of the union of form and content that F. O. Matthiessen later capitalized upon). On the other hand, he describes the United States as exceptional for its capacity to amalgamate Western traditions, so that the place and substance of Indian, African, Caribbean, and Latin traditions upon the continent and nation are understated in the name of identifying the country or the land as a product of a European past. Parrington's study exemplifies how the study of American exceptionalism develops an imagination of the nation as being born out of its recognized difference from Europe.

This effort continued with even greater urgency in the 1930s. In *The Great Tradition* (1933), Granville Hicks searches the post-civil war period to identify a literature that is able to interpret and oppose the times. Hicks champions belletristic writing against what he calls a dominant industrial culture, but his analysis is both a call for a new order, with explicit nationalist overtones, as well as a critique of the recent past in favor of a nativist tradition. For Hicks, the writer and artist himself is exceptional, needing and able to mirror the times especially when they are chaotic; but the writer is currently threatened by the industrial order which displaces the importance of literature:

In a society that regarded chaos as natural, that made greed a virtue, that placed financial achievement before personal integrity, culture was not likely to flourish. When things are in the saddle, the artist, if he deserves the name, is almost certain to trampled underfoot. Especially hazardous is the position of any artist who might venture to do what artists so commonly try to do, to mirror his own times.[21]

Nostalgic for the era before the Civil War, Hicks finds the artist to be the great synthesizer, the order he creates the enemy of capitalism. Hence the post-Civil War period, during which industrialism develops, means for him the potential end of such cultural possibilities. What is most American for Hicks is the possibility of a literature that can produce a contemporary vision of American culture and which, he goes on to write, can incorporate the wide variety of American types into active myths of the United States. Surveying Longfellow, Whittier, and Holmes among others, he finds no equivalent to Emerson, Thoreau, Hawthorne or Melville. James Russell Lowell provides a momentary possibility but Hicks criticizes him for abandoning socialism – which Hicks describes as the opposition to the pull of economic life in favor of a kind of enlightened humanism, collectivism and a valuing of the common woman and man. Lowell, moreover, ignores the changing demographics of the nation. Hicks's complaint recalls George Santayana, especially when he declares that more recent writers 'cast a fog of gentility over our literature.' His dissatisfaction with many post-Civil War writers implies much about what he believes made the nation exceptional in the past: 'kindly men, well-informed, well-intentioned [...] but they were nevertheless parasites – parasites upon the past, upon foreign culture, upon an industrial order that they did not try to understand, did not think of reforming, and did not venture to defend and advance.'[22]

Although Hicks disparages Lowell for nativism, he calls for an advancing army of writers who cast off foreign influence and who develop a modern, urban idea of national culture. Like his predecessors Waldo Frank and Van Wyck Brooks, Hicks finds the proper tradition not in contemporary writers of different origins but in Whitman. Whitman's belief in individualism is generous enough for the factory worker and the farmer, among other things, and therefore able to generate a kind of myth that is constitutive of the conflicts and complexities of American life in the industrial age.

In the texts of Brooks and Hicks, one can see the momentum for forming a national literary tradition which, while analyzing the character of the country, urges a particular past upon it. Matthiessen's *The American Renaissance: Art and Expression in the Age of Emerson and Whitman* (1941) canonized a group of writers still further and encouraged a sense of American exceptionalism, dating the now familiar 1850–1855 period as the time in which American culture emerges, its social significance manifested in the very literary form and content of these works, which consti-tute a complicated, exhilarating national legacy:[23]

It may not seem precisely accurate to refer to our mid-nineteenth century as a *re-birth;* but that was how the writers themselves judged it. Nor as a re-birth of values that had existed previously in America, but as America's way of producing a renaissance, by coming to its first maturity and affirming its rightful heritage in the whole expanse of art and culture.[24]

Matthiessen's goal, therefore, is to show how in form and content the art and culture of this period claims an identity – a first identity – for the United States, that he will in turn claim in the series of essays that make up American Renaissance. His goal is explicitly to avoid the 'descriptive' narrative of literary history that Brooks sought and the evaluation of how these writers interpreted their time, of which Hicks is for Matthiessen exemplary.[25] Without ignoring the relation of these writers to the development of the republic, Matthiessen wishes to examine belletristic writers for their capacity to write about writing and to practice what their theories of writing assert, which together describe a common literary legacy that identifies the country and indeed 'illuminates' even more than 'reflects' the age: This is literature, to adapt Emerson, as the pole star of an era and a country.[26] As a work exemplary of methodology, of what can and should be made of the relation of writing and art to one another, Matthiessen's book can hardly be overrated. But its contribution to forming a sense of the nation via the identification of a complex literary heritage is what I wish to emphasize here.

A similar contribution results from Perry Miller's monumental intellectual history of Puritan culture *The New England Mind*, which led him eventually to declare Puritanism 'the fundamental theme,' the 'origin of origins' that describes the 'uniqueness of the American experience.'[27] This theological errand into the wilderness is anything but material in Miller's assessment, history having been relegated to a minor place in relation to the spiritual and mythifying status of Puritanism and eventually to transcendentalism. Here, too, one finds a precursor for the identification of myths by American studies, which Miller identifies specifically with the early religious settlers of the northeastern United States rather than, for example, southwestern settlements, or the Virginians, or previous inhabitants of the continent.[28] Even more so than their predecessors, Matthiessen and Miller are exemplary figures in the founding of American Studies as an academic discipline. As colleagues at Harvard, their attempts to do just that are hardly surprising, and indeed Matthiessen cites Miller's *The New England Mind* in his introduction as a work that, once finished, will contribute greatly to the development of American Studies (only its first volume had been published as of 1941).[29] But in each of their cases, the identification of the nation urges a certain form of nationalism.

That tendency begins to change in the late forties. Henry Nash Smith's *Virgin Land* begins what came to be known, pejoratively and perhaps unfairly, as the myth and symbol school.[30] In *Virgin*

*Land* and later Leo Marx's *The Machine in the Garden* (to name just two examples), one sees an explicit consideration of myth, a cultural symbology whose activity it was to study how myths fuse conflicting and diverse strains in the United States' imagination of itself. Smith's book investigates how, in the continuing treatment of the frontier and the garden, cultural formation leads to and from ideological formation. Similarly, Marx's book argues that pastoralism arises from the capacity of a literary form to be adapted for the construction of a national, social myth. Smith has been criticized and has strongly criticized himself for the lack of attention to Indians in his characterization of how a myth of virgin land contributed to westward expansion and national formation, and both he and Marx have been critiqued for not emphasizing ideology enough, so that in describing cultural symbolism, they produce a hegemonic vision of the nation. Arguably, Smith notes how such myths had devastating effects upon the tribes that westward expansion all but destroyed.[31] In both *Virgin Land* and *The Machine in the Garden,* moreover, the emphasis is upon how the nation forms itself, and they are therefore more self-consciously descriptive of the country's evolving sense of its national identity than their predecessors. Rather than urging a national legacy, they provide a means for studying the evolution of national identity that later scholars of American studies capitalize upon.

Such discussion of myths and symbols is part of what underlies Sacvan Bercovitch's work since the 1970s, when he turned to Puritan texts as well as the writings Matthiessen promoted and found within them the rhetorical formation of an American ideology, fantastic for its capacity to represent the United States as an ongoing project that is always being reborn.[32] Bercovitch noted the exceptional status of this ideology. It makes dissent implicit in the status quo, a consensus born out of it. Such ideology is especially present, moreover, in the invocation of ordinary and everyday life within these writings, so that what makes the United States exceptional is that it locates its history, culture, even philosophy according to Stanley Cavell, in the ordinary. For Bercovitch, this ideology is both pervasive and limiting of the capacity for change in the United States, so that the underlying tone of his analysis is hardly celebratory and the identification of the nation, while monolithic in implication, does not inspire unreflective nationalism.

Even more so today, the focus upon ideology has led many in American Studies to cast a colder eye upon exceptionalism and to re-examine yet again the role of American studies in the twentieth century – to consider how culture is a distinct but often reinforcing entity of nationalism. It has led many to pursue ways in which we might characterize the place of culture in the definition of the nation rather than assume it exists independent of nationalism. A few typical, perhaps obvious questions underlie much of this work: How do the myths of the country use a sense of difference or otherness to define what the nation is? How does it, for example, use ethnicity, race, gender, sexual preference, and class to produce national identity? How is the experience of the nation distinct according to differences produced by the social formations of gender and race? From such questions, the canon of American literature and the characterization of its past has been reassessed, nearly continuously, to both widen the range of texts used to describe the country and to argue against our capacity to describe the country succinctly or monolithically, given the vast differences in experience.[33] Foregrounding the need to create an other to define national identity, these re-evaluations describe not only a dominant culture but its subalterns.

Still other areas of inquiry lead us to consider what kinds of deceptions exceptionalism may promote. For example, it may create the illusion the United States has not been an imperialist power. This effect may arise from the myth of the isolation of the country and its *sui generis* nature. William Appleman Williams has argued and Amy Kaplan has more recently urged us to consider, in an illuminating critique of Perry Miller and others, that the United States is exceptional for its ability to avoid the status of empire.[34]

Such recent developments have led us to look at the idea of America in the designation American Studies. What it has most often meant in the last century, many point out, has been not

America as it was generally conceived by most of the early European explorers but the United States. In response to this usurpation of the term, a growing body of scholars and educators (at least) have widened their analysis to include Canada, Mexico, and the countries of Latin America, South America and the Caribbean Basin. It has also led many to pursue an analysis of writing and culture that is not beholden to nations and that wishes to avoid tacit promotion of them. For example, these studies consider what we can understand about the constellation of forces that make nations and make identities when we examine those on their margins who do not identify themselves so readily by nationality. How does the need for national identity affect the constituents of the United States, those identified as outside its domain, or those who think of themselves as both within and without the nation? What can such questions tell us about national formation and extra-national ideas of subjectivity? Hence there has recently been interest in analysis that is influenced by the work on boundaries and borders begun by anthropologists such as Victor Turner and Frederick Barth and then revised by Renato Rosaldo and James Clifford as well as theorists such as Homi Bhabha.[35] There have also been studies such as Eric Sundquist's *To Wake the Nations* that assert American literature should not be defined as exclusively national because it is inextricably composed of at least African and Anglo-European legacies.[36] Other studies assess *Comparative American Identities,* to use the title of one collection of essays, or they focus upon exile, gender, race, class and sexual identities to note the mechanisms by which the nation is formed as well as to describe worlds that are dependent upon but not of national formation.[37] And it has led us to evaluate the implication of our own studies and of the role of academic institution – as I have been attempting in modest ways in this essay.

But it may be more accurate to assert that we have simply refashioned an idea of the United States in a manner less deliberate and more anxious about national identity and about our own identification with our studies than scholars and writers about American exceptionalism in the past. Gone, then, is the celebratory connotation of the term, but in its place remains the interest in nationalism which past scholars have exhibited. The form of that nationalism may be as idiosyncratic, its presentation every bit as blind to history, as its predecessors. The use of multiple descriptions of American culture and of America; the identification of differences according to gender, 'race,' class, and sexual identity; and the suspicion of nationalism – all of these are forms of inquiry in the present, which Larzer Ziff – reviewing the most recent *Cambridge History of American Literature* – describes as a 'new exceptionalism,' in which 'only in America' no longer designates a single culture but conflicting 'cultures.'[38] This comment may be a gloss, however polemical, upon the idea that we write out of a present which we cannot help but assume advances an understanding over the past and in which our own superior ability to study America is proved by our critique of past scholars and writers. But one does not avoid imagining the country any more than in the past. What emerges, then, in the multiple stories of America in American Studies is more than an analysis of the ruling class and its subordinates and more than an account of American exceptionalism, furthered by our own self-awareness – although it certainly is all of these; what emerges as well is an implicit identification of the scholar and citizen of the moment, whose necessary 'other' includes elements of the present, his or her predecessors in the field, and the past he or she studies. The movement between self-identification and analysis of the past is neither surprising nor to be avoided. As if it could be.[39] But it does suggest that at present the study of America develops out of both a sense of identifying oneself in what one studies and of attempting to study something we imagine as a distant but usable past. Whether or not American exceptionalism should be avoided might well be answered best by a question directed toward the former impulse – what does such an idea mean for us? – whose answer delivers an account of the present we might well include in our accounts of the past, as we have been doing, knowingly or unconsciously, all along.

## Notes

1. For further discussion of the relation of writing to the development of nations, see Benedict Anderson, *Imagined Communities: Reflections on the Origin and Spread of Nationalism* (London: Verso, 1983); Homi Bhabha, *Nation and Narration* (London: Routledge, 1990); and *The Location of Culture*, ed. Homi Bhabha (New York: Routledge, 1994).
2. Perry Miller and Thomas H. Johnson, *The Puritans*, vol. 1 (1938; New York: Harper and Row, 1963), 198.
3. Miller and Johnson, 198.
4. Miller and Johnson, 198.
5. J. Hector St. John de Crèvecoeur, *Letters from an American Farmer* (London: Dent, 1926), 'Letter III: What Is an American?'
6. Thomas Jefferson, *The Complete Jefferson*, ed. Saul K. Padover (New York: Tudor, 1943).
7. Henry Nash Smith, *Virgin Land: The American West as Symbol and Myth* (Cambridge, MA: Harvard University Press, 1950); Leo Marx, *The Machine in the Garden: Technology and the Pastoral Ideal in America* (New York: Oxford University Press, 1964).
8. For further discussion of the relation of land to the identification of the United States in early national texts, see Myra Jehlen, *American Incarnation: The Individual, the Nation, and the Continent* (Cambridge, MA: Harvard University Press, 1986).
9. Jefferson, 608–09.
10. See Sacvan Bercovitch, *The Rites of Assent: Transformation in the Symbolic Construction of America* (New York: Routledge, 1993).
11. For further discussion of manifest destiny, national identity and the expansion of the United States westward, see Richard Slotkin, *The Fatal Environment: The Myth of the Frontier in the Age of Industrialization, 1800–1890* (New York: Atheneum, 1985); and Alan Trachtenberg, *The Incorporation of America: Culture and Society in the Gilded Age* (New York: Hill and Wang, 1982).
12. Henry James, *Hawthorne* (Ithaca, NY: Cornell University Press, 1966).
13. Henry James, *The American Scene Together with Three Essays from Portraits of Places*, ed. W. H. Auden (New York: Scribner, 1946). See, for example, his comments on New York opera goers and Laurence Holland's comments upon these passages in Laurence B. Holland, *The Expense of Vision: Essays in the Craft of Henry James* (Princeton: Princeton University Press, 1964).
14. Van Wyck Brooks, *The Early Years: A Selection from His Works, 1908–1921*, ed. Claire Sprague (New York: Harper and Row, 1968), 84.
15. Brooks, 95–98.
16. Brooks, 80, xvi.
17. For a discussion of how American literary history 'assisted the gradual displacement of philology by literary studies,' see William Spengemann, *A*

*New World of Words, Redefining Early American Literature* (New Haven: Yale University Press, 1994), 12.

18. Vernon Louis Parrington, *Main Currents in American Thought: An Interpretation of American Literature from the Beginnings to 1920*, 3 vols (New York: Harcourt, Brace and Company, 1927), iii.

19. Parrington, iii.

20. Parrington, v.

21. Granville Hicks, *The Great Tradition: An Interpretation of American Literature Since the Civil War* (New York: Macmillan, 1933), 3.

22. Hicks, 19–20.

23. Of course, Matthiessen adds Hawthorne to the group of writers Hicks identifies. For Hicks, Hawthorne is too 'remote from his period' and isolated from the 'occupations and preoccupations of his fellowmen.' Consequently, the characters of his book are 'remote and insubstantial.' Hicks, 5–6.

24. F. O. Matthiessen, *The American Renaissance: Art and Expression in the Age of Emerson and Whitman* (1941; New York: Oxford University Press, 1968), vii.

25. Matthiessen, viii.

26. Matthiessen, x.

27. Perry Miller, *Errand into the Wilderness* (Cambridge, MA: Harvard University Press, 1946).

28. See Introduction to *Cultures of United States Imperialism*, ed. Amy Kaplan and Donald Pease (Durham, NC: Duke University Press, 1993).

29. Perry Miller, *The New England Mind: From Colony to Province,* 3 vols (Cambridge, MA: Harvard University Press, 1953).

30. For the identification and critique of the myth and symbol school, see Bruce Kuklick, 'Myth and Symbol in American Studies,' *American Quarterly*, 24 (1972): 435–50.

31. See Henry Nash Smith, 'Symbol and Idea in *Virgin Land,' Ideology and Classic American Literature*, ed. Sacvan Bercovitch and Myra Jehlen (Cambridge, MA: Harvard University Press 1986), 21–35.

32. Sacvan Bercovitch, *The American Jeremiad* (Madison: University of Wisconsin Press, 1978); Sacvan Bercovitch, *The Puritan Origins of the American Self* (New Haven: Yale University Press, 1976).

33. For a volume that exemplifies such work, see *The American Renaissance Reconsidered*, ed. Walter Benn Michaels and Donald E. Pease, Selected Papers From the English Institute, 9 (Baltimore: Johns Hopkins University Press, 1985).

34. William Appleman Williams, 'The Frontier Thesis and American Foreign Policy,' *Pacific Historical Review*, 24 (1955): 379–95; Kaplan and Pease, eds, *Cultures*.

35. Victor W. Turner, ed., *The Anthropology of Experience* (Champaign, IL: University of Illinois Press, 1986); Victor W. Turner, *Process, Performance and Pilgrimage: A Study in Comparative Symbology* (New Delhi: Concept, 1979); Victor W. Turner, *The Ritual Process: Structure and Anti-Structure* (London:

Routledge, 1969); Frederick Barth, *Cosmologies in the Making: A Generative Approach to Cultural Variation in New Guinea* (Cambridge: Cambridge University Press, 1989); Frederick Barth, *Ethnic Groups and Boundaries: The Social Organization of Cultural Difference* (Bergen: Scandinavian University Books, 1969); Renato Rosaldo, *Culture and Truth: The Remaking of Social Analysis* (London: Routledge, 1993); James Clifford, *The Predicament of Culture: Twentieth-Century Ethnography, Literature and Art* (Cambridge, MA: Harvard University Press, 1988; James Clifford and George E. Marcus, eds, *Writing Culture. The Poetics and Politics of Ethnography* (Berkeley: University of California Press, 1986); Bhabha, *The Location of Culture*; Bhabha, *Nation and Narration*.

36. Eric Sundquist, *To Wake the Nations* (Cambridge, MA: Harvard University Press, 1993).

37. Hortense J. Spillers, ed., *Comparative American Identities: Race, Sex, and Nationality in the Modern Text* (London: Routledge, 1991).

38. For Ziff this is no cause for celebration. Rather than describe a democratization of study, in which differing communities are represented, this new exceptionalism conforms to a present that Ziff names as 'the time of the mall.' Ziff asserts that the description of conflicting cultures describes a refusal to study differences in languages and nations with depth or to make willful, intellectual judgements about what 'American' might mean. Larzer Ziff, 'The New Exceptionalism,' *Modern Language Quarterly*, 56 (1995): 191.

39. For an elegant description of this tendency in literary history, see Mitchell Breitweiser, 'The Vagaries of Historical Reading,' *Modern Language Quarterly*, 56 (1995): 197–206.

# Technologies

# Technology and Cultural Difference

*David E. Nye*

The United States is generally understood to be a capitalist, industrial offshoot of Europe, whose culture has been transformed by contact with Native-American, African, and Asian cultures. It is currently unfashionable to assert the existence of a common American cultural experience. I want to confront head-on the question of national character and its relationship to technology. Americans long believed that both their machines and the way they used them made them unique, and it is emphatically not my aim to revive these claims. However, in rejecting the idea of an American exceptionalism based on a uniquely democratic technology, one need not dispense with the idea of divergent national patterns that are expressed in both behavior and material culture.[1]

The United States, as a newly emerging nation in the nineteenth century, sought to shape a separate identity for itself. This story is best known in a literary form, as the struggle of antebellum American writers to free themselves from English dominance and create a distinctive national literature. Less remembered is the effort to industrialize without repeating the errors of European nations, which had created polluted industrial areas and a miserable proletariat that shocked early American travelers, particularly in England. While many nations have taken pride in particular technical achievements, Americans saw themselves as an ingenious people, a nation of tinkerers and inventors who would industrialize without creating either a proletariat or unhealthy industrial cities. This self-perception has largely disappeared today, as part of a general renunciation of the idea of American exceptionalism, the once popular idea that the history

*Marks of Distinction: American Exceptionalism Revisited*, ed. Dale Carter, *The Dolphin* 32, pp. 93–111. © 2001 by Aarhus University Press, Denmark. ISBN 87 7288 383 9; ISSN 0106 4487.

and development of the United States is fundamentally different from that of Europe.

To see how matters now stand, consider a lead essay of the fall 1992 issue of the *Journal of American History* written by the then President of the Organization of American Historians, Joyce Appleby. Her title, 'Recovering America's Historic Diversity: Beyond Exceptionalism,' underlines how for many Americanists the idea of 'exceptionalism' now posits an unacceptably radical difference between the United States and the rest of the world.[2] Appleby deftly traces some of the ideological underpinnings to 'exceptionalism,' showing how a good deal of eighteenth-century American history had to be suppressed from view in order to make the nation seem fundamentally different from Europe. Technology, which was once a central part of the exceptionalist argument, is not mentioned at any point in her argument.

This is a remarkable omission.[3] During most of the nineteenth century and a good deal of the twentieth, the national character was thought to be exemplified by a pantheon of inventors, including Eli Whitney, Robert Fulton, Alexander Graham Bell, Thomas Edison, Henry Ford, and the Wright Brothers, to name but a few. The argument has recently been relaunched by Newt Gingrich in *To Renew America*, which celebrates individualism, 'the spirit of free enterprise' and 'the spirit of invention and discovery.' Gingrich declares 'We have no caste system, no class requirements, no regulated professions, no barriers to entry.' He rejects the idea that 'America is no different than Europe.'[4] This is a nineteenth-century argument, which in its classic form claimed that Americans were ingenious Yankees who focused on practical results. They were less interested in science than engineering, less concerned with aristocratic theory than with the democratic dispersal of useful improvements. Compared to Europeans, Americans were unfettered by guilds, state monopolies, and other artificial restraints on trade.[5] The nation industrialized rapidly after c. 1825, and if in the beginning it necessarily imitated European machinery, there were soon claims for an American style in machine building, in manufacturing, and in business organization. I will take up these three topics in turn, moving from individual machines to their organization in factories and then to how these factories were managed. After this focus on production, I will then briefly turn to the American popular reception of technology. In all four areas some differences between Americans and Europeans can be documented. Do these differences collectively merit the 'exceptionalist' label?

Are American machines different from those made in some or all of the European countries? John Kouwenhoven argued in his once influential *Made in America* that there was a distinctive American machine design, exemplified in such artefacts as the American ax, the clipper ship, the loosely jointed American locomotive, and the Model T. Ford. All were characterized by simplicity, plainness, efficiency, and a functional aesthetic.[6] Furthermore, Americans early began to build machines designed to last only a short time. This practice, often criticized by Europeans, emphasized immediate practical results, and assumed that machines would be replaced frequently. Where the English built locomotives to last indefinitely, Americans expected better ones to be invented before long. Likewise, where Europeans early demanded efficiency from stationary steam engines, Americans at first preferred cheapness and simplicity in operation, and willingly used more fuel. Oliver Evans invented just such a device, a new kind of steam engine which ran at high pressure and quickly became standard on American steamboats. 'It was smaller, cheaper, and less complex,' but it had one serious drawback: it was exploded easily.[7] In short, one might make a case for American machines as being distinctively pragmatic, temporary, and functional.

Yet a powerful counter-argument has been in the ascendancy in recent years. Studies in the history of technology have emphasized the exchange of technical information through international networks. For example, the American iron industry was started by English and German immigrants in the colonial period. Major nineteenth-century advances such as Bessemer steel and later the open-hearth process were developed in Europe and transferred to the United States.[8] Likewise, canal construction, almost unknown in the new United States of the 1790s, was attempted at first without much success, until aided by William Weston, an immigrant engineer who had worked under the great English canal-builder, James Brindley. From Weston, men in Massachusetts, New York, and Pennsylvania learned surveying, a canal's proper dimensions, the superiority of stone to brick (and of brick to wood) in constructing walls, the design of locks, and the necessity of puddling, or laminating the walls of the canal repeatedly with a clay paste, to make them water-tight.[9] Similarly, the indispensable ingredient in creating an American textile industry was the largely non-verbal knowledge of design brought across the Atlantic by immigrant textile machine builders.[10] Likewise, French immigrant, Eleuthère Irénée du Pont transferred superior techniques of gunpowder manufacturing to the United States, establishing an extensive works on the Brandywine.[11] Americans already manufactured gunpowder, but of uneven quality. Du Pont had superior techniques, learned in years of training in the French government's industry. Using his contacts he imported a complete set of equipment 'essential to every phase of black powder manufacture' and kept abreast of French developments in the trade after he built his American factory.[12] Even Fulton's famous steamboat used a steam-engine made in England, and he engaged 'at least one mechanic who had worked for Boulton and Watt to cross the Atlantic and set up the engine.'[13]

The carriers of information were often immigrants, but there were also more formal channels. Technical publications and magazines, world's fairs, congresses, and official visits all sped the flow of innovations, so that even a small factory along the Appalachian fall line, such as the one that Anthony Wallace studied in *Rockdale*, kept abreast of the latest innovations. He found that in the textile industry 'nearly all of the several hundred master mechanicians of the English-speaking world knew each other by name and reputation,' and 'each man probably had met with and talked with most of his peers on one occasion or another or had corresponded in writing.'[14] In short, the weight of evidence about American machine-making seems to go against the 'exceptionalist' hypothesis, although there are cases that point the other way. Clearly Americans were alert to the newest

European ideas and innovations, which they combined with their own.

Yet if their machines must be seen as part of a trans-Atlantic dialogue, did Americans nevertheless manufacture in a distinctive fashion?

At the Crystal Palace exhibition of 1851, European observers found some American machines on view unlike their own. Yet they did not speak at once of an 'American system of manufacturing.' This idea was invented in the early twentieth century and until recently remained unquestioned. Kouwenhoven argued that 'the technology of mass production is as indigenous to the United States as the husking bee,' and saw automation, interchangeable parts, and the assembly line as national characteristics.[15] Many historians heralded mass production as a defining national hallmark. Two characteristic heroes in this account were Eli Whitney and Henry Ford.[16] From the moment that Whitney displayed ten muskets with interchangeable parts to President-elect Thomas Jefferson in 1801, he was credited with creating a uniquely American approach to production. Machines would make identical parts for other machines. Historians have found, however, that Whitney did not mass-produce interchangeable components for muskets in 1801; they remained an idea more than a reality for many years.[17] Furthermore, the idea of interchangeability itself was first dreamed in France, during the eighteenth century, by General Jean-Baptiste de Gribeauval. Whitney's workmen made reasonably standardized parts, to be sure, but they did so by hand-filing what came out of the moulds. An astute self-publicist, Whitney emphasized the possible results of his system and made it the ideal toward which many manufacturers strove. Yet the 'American system' was not as well-defined or as self-conscious in 1851 as historians once claimed, and a British Parliamentary committee found that even in 1854 Samuel Colt had not yet managed the precision necessary to make identical parts. Rather, they were 'very nearly alike.'[18]

Even if the term 'American system' was not used and interchangeability itself was more a goal than an achievement, many first-hand witnesses found American production methods distinctive. An English workingman who came to the United States during the Civil War found that 'there are few trades which have not been materially changed' after they crossed the Atlantic. He emphasized that 'division of labour is carried out in all the various branches of skilled labour to the fullest possible extent; this system not only facilitates production, but it conduces to perfection in the workmen; machinery, too, is used for every purpose to which it can be applied.'[19] This was a difference less in technology than in its organization, turning the focus to management, which pursued interchangeability most vigorously in the United States. Half a century later, the end result of this process was the assembly line perfected by Henry Ford at his Highland Park Plant in 1912. Because of standardization, Whitney's factory required fewer skilled workmen than any previous armory, but Ford went much further. He not only used interchangeable parts, but also sub-divided work more thoroughly than anyone before, and because his semi-skilled workmen could learn their tasks in a matter of days they became largely interchangeable as well.

Mass production has many forms, however, and while Ford led the world automotive sector for at least a decade, transforming the nature of capital-intensive industry in the process, Americans did not lead in all areas. If one looks closely at a mature industry such as textile manufacturing in the early twentieth century, at precisely the time that Ford was in the ascendancy, American facilities lagged behind much of continental Europe. A comparative study of the textile industry by a German expert, Wilhelm Stiel, revealed that in the 1920s considerable differences existed among the textile-producing countries. England lagged the farthest behind, as they 'rested on old tradition ... supported by the fact that a successful spinning industry has grown up on the basis of substantially built mills with well-designed and smoothly running line shafting.' Exhaustive efficiency tests showed that, compared to this overhead shafting, group drive [one electric motor to a small number of machines] was better and individual drive [one motor to one machine] was best. Nevertheless, the English retained the line-shaft mill driven by a few large electric motors. In contrast,

Germany, Holland, Switzerland, and Sweden converted most of their textile factories to individual electric drive, and as a result had higher productivity, because their machines ran at faster and more constant speeds. American manufacturers were in an intermediate stage of development. They early adopted group drive, most typically with one motor mounted on the ceiling to drive four machines by belt. Stiel commented that their practices were 'founded on the American principle, viz. utmost economy of man-power (production per head and not per machine!) to which a bit of spindle speed is willingly sacrificed, so that American working speeds cannot bear comparison with those in use in Europe.'[20] This analysis of one industry is highly suggestive for others. Stiel had noted an American propensity to keep wages as low as possible, which was possible in a largely non-union country. Lower wages made it unnecessary to maximize capital investment in machinery. In other words, Stiel found America distinctive for reasons that were not technological, but social.

The conclusion that United States' industries varied considerably also emerges if one examines the way that workers were paid. Work by piece-rate in the twentieth century enjoyed a revival in labor-intensive industries, such as the shops of General Electric and Westinghouse. In contrast, the heavily-capitalized assembly line encouraged manufacturers to adopt fixed hourly wages, because workers had no choice but to keep up the pace. More highly skilled work increasingly was done on the basis of daily quotas, with incentives for overproduction.[21] In short, there was not a single 'American system' of manufacturing in the early twentieth century, by which time the production system certainly had matured. Rather, there were at least three systems in place. Older industries, such as textiles, kept wages low and modernized equipment with that factor in mind. Newer mass-production industries, epitomized by Ford, developed a high wage policy, for which they demanded fast-paced routine work on assembly lines. Highly-skilled work developed in yet a third direction, as companies adopted piece-rates and individual incentives. In short, there was no monolithic 'Fordist' system of production, contrary to what many humanists all too casually assume. Rather, the characteristic American factor was the weakness of organized labor, so that the workforce had to respond to the quite different strategies of large corporations, depending upon whether they were capital or labor intensive, skilled or unskilled. The labor market, more than technology, made America distinctive when compared to Europe, where unions were strong and corporations few. Note that while these comparisons are all between highly developed industrial economies they are further confirmed by looking at labor in developing economies. In the early twentieth century newly industrializing countries such as China and India, even when they purchased up-to-date machinery, were unable to produce as efficiently as England or America because their labor force was not yet sufficiently skilled.[22] Culture is often a more important factor than technology in fostering or limiting economic growth.

While exceptionalism based on American machine design or a distinctive system of manufacturing is implausible, Alfred D. Chandler has advanced a theory of business organization based in part on American uniqueness. He argues that in the United States the private corporation developed a distinctive form in response to the sheer size of the continental market served by railroads and canals. Unlike the fragmented, small, and protected European markets of the nineteenth century, which encouraged small-scale production, American businessmen faced a market that was unified, large, and highly competitive. These conditions encouraged both economies of production and large organizations. In response, Americans early began to move away from partnerships and family firms toward corporations. In the process they developed new forms of accounting, production, and marketing. Most important of all, they invented a new form of the corporation, which no longer was created by a special act of the legislature, but rather could be formed by any group of people who wished to limit their personal liability to the amount they invested in a new firm.

In contrast, when partnerships and family firms went bankrupt, the investors could lose all their capital. Such companies, which need to be more cautious in management and which have more difficulty raising large sums, were still the norm in most of Europe until World War II. They grew to a large scale less frequently, first because they operated in small markets, and second because they depended on a family or small group to be talented, united, and well-capitalized over extended periods. Thus it was the United States, not Europe which emerged at the end of the nineteenth century as the premier site of the corporation. Nor did this result from blind economic forces at work. Chandler attacks the traditional *laissez-faire* notion of the 'invisible hand of the market,' arguing instead that it was the *visible hand* of management that shaped American corporations, which he regards as the dominant institution in the life of the United States.[23]

Yet while Chandler may at first appear to be an exponent of American exceptionalism, his subsequent work reveals an interest in how corporations developed outside the United States. German development was directed more by banks than in the United States. British firms resisted incorporation and tended to remain family-run or partnerships down to World War II. Japanese trading companies developed into manufacturing firms in close cooperation with the government.[24] In short, Chandler's work can in fairness only be used to make an argument for American exceptionalism if one is also prepared to argue for a degree of 'exceptionalism' in other nations as well. Chandler's work ultimately only makes a case for a certain soft determinism. In his scenario large, private, diversified, corporations catering to a mass market have a decisive competitive advantage over businesses that are small, that are public, that produce only one thing or a small number of things, and that cater to smaller markets. In other words, if the original idea of an 'exception' is that there is a 'rule' followed elsewhere, then Chandler grants American business exceptional status only in that its managers grasped the key factors of corporate development sooner than others and in that Americans have chosen to institutionalize these factors somewhat differently than Germany, England or Japan. Such a theory does not really grant America an exceptional status, but rather argues for certain ground rules of capitalist development that permit a range of cultural variation.

Economic geographers Michael Storper and Richard Walker corroborate this general approach, while developing their own typology. They identify four distinctive patterns of capitalist development. That in the United States has been characterized by high wage levels, high worker consumption, moderate profits, and moderate investment. An Asian model, exemplified by Japan, sets more modest levels for wages and consumption, with higher rates of profit and investment. The Brazilian economy represents yet another path, with low wages, permitting high investment levels and many exports but weak domestic consumption and erratic overall performance. Finally, the British system is characterized by modest wages, moderate mass consumption, low profits, and weak investment.[25] As these comparisons suggest, capitalism is not one system, but rather a variety of culturally inflected developments. Energy use is an important part of each of these forms of capitalism, and not surprisingly, the United States, with its emphasis on high rates of consumption, uses more energy per capita than any other nation.

If one looks at the first three sections of this chapter together, rather than separately, Chandler's theory does not contradict either the notion that American machines were built for maximum short-term efficiency or the idea that Americans pioneered mass production within an international context of technology and information exchange. Indeed, Chandler allows us to replace the rather woolly and undefined idea of 'national character' as the driving force at work, with the far more specific idea that managers selected machines and organized factories in a distinctive American way because they catered to and competed in the world's first mass market. In other words, it was not that Americans *lacked* the traditional monopolies and government restrictions of Europe, a negative argument that focuses on an *absent* obstacle that did not stand in the way of vaguely-defined actors. Rather, American managers faced the demands of a large market which offered competitive advantages to those who could produce and sell on a large scale. This is a positive argument that

focuses on incentives to clearly-defined historical actors. However, such an argument leaves most Americans out of the discussion, as it focuses on the management elite. What of the 'mass' in
the 'mass market?'

The French traveller Michael Chevalier noted in the 1830s
that, 'There is a perfect mania in this country on the subject of
railroads.'[26] This enthusiasm could be seen among virtually all
citizens. For example, in Baltimore the entire city turned out to
celebrate the construction of the nation's first railway line. That
they held this celebration on Independence Day in 1828 suggests
how technology early intertwined with American nationalism.
The event went off without a dissenting voice, with a huge parade
in which most of the artisans of the city participated. In contrast,
two years later when the Liverpool and Manchester Railway
opened, it drew a much larger crowd estimated at 400,000, which
lined the tracks for most of the distance. If Baltimore's citizens
had eagerly gathered to celebrate technological advance, many in
the English crowd protested the new railway. Some spattered
mud on the clothes of the ladies and gentlemen who were the first
passengers. On a prominent spot above the crowd, a poorly
dressed hand-loom weaver sat as a silent protest, understood by
Fanny Kemble to be 'a representative man, to protest against this
triumph of machinery, and the gain and glory which the wealthy
Liverpool and Manchester men were likely to derive from it.'[27]
The English, more than the Americans, viewed industrialization
in terms of class exploitation, satanic mills and Frankensteinian
monsters.

Americans have long embraced new technologies with far less
criticism than Europeans. A particularly striking example was the
American enthusiasm for spectacular electrical displays, first at
expositions in the 1880s and 1890s and later in the commercial
zones of American cities. Where English and French communities
successfully legislated against enormous electrical signs, only a
minority of Americans opposed them, almost entirely without
success. Times Square and the Great White Way became the
models that other American cities imitated when they strove to be
glamorous and modern.[28] Nor was extensive lighting merely a

ploy on the part of businessmen. They spent millions of dollars on electrical displays because the public demanded it, and patronized the areas of the city that were most brilliantly (Europeans would say garishly) illuminated. Spectacular lighting displays still remain popular in the United States today, as, for example, in the extensive use of laser beams in the ceremony rededicating the Statue of Liberty in 1986.[29] Perhaps the clearest example of the difference between American and European views of technology is the popular response to the two space programs. Where hundreds of thousands, and on some occasions millions, of Americans turn out to see a launching, Europeans display little enthusiasm for their space program. Launchings have never inspired a great deal of European newspaper or television coverage, and almost no one would consider using vacation time and money to travel to French Guinea to see a rocket go up. Americans have long enjoyed technological display more than Europeans, and these displays have often been understood in terms of a nationalism that borders on the claims of exceptionalism. As one women at a Cape Kennedy launch put it succinctly, 'There isn't another country in the world that's going to do this – you've got to say America's first.'[30]

Just as Appleby made no reference to technology, so too today's technological historians seldom refer to 'exceptionalism.' The once acceptable ideas that American machines and manufacturing methods were fundamentally distinctive have given way to discussion of international networks of information exchange, flowing through immigration, trade journals, world's fairs, joint work on engineering projects, and other kinds of technological transfer. While American mills and factories had distinctive features, they were clearly related to European facilities, sometimes ahead of them, at times not. In short, when emphasizing technology alone, *exceptionalism* proves to be a lame horse, if not a dead one. But if one looks instead at business organization and the popular reception of technology, the United States appears distinct from Europe. The social construction of technology in America, whether examined in terms of institutional arrangements or in terms of the formation of popular consciousness, suggests a national pattern.

Why does Appleby prefer to omit American technological history from her account, if recent research in the field does not lend support to the exceptionalist thesis? She notes that 'Remembering and forgetting determine the history we tell.' Appleby also attacks the penchant Americans have had for erasing much of the past, in order to create the clean slate of an exceptionalist nation, 'born free' on 'virgin land.'[31] But in her brief for multicultural history, she has erased areas of the past as well. In her account, rather significant areas are simply wiped out, including business, technology, invention, and science. Furthermore, theories of multiculturalism, such as Appleby's, seem to require the suppression of observed commonalities in the United States. Indeed, the multicultural approach has the very faults that are usually attributed to 'exceptionalism' itself. Each ethnic, racial, and gender minority claims to be radically different from every other. In this 'essentialism,' each group claims to have a cultural essence that is in danger of being polluted or destroyed by the larger society. The history of technology thus has not only been associated with the exceptionalist thesis, it is widely understood as a central part of the hegemonic culture that multiculturalism opposes. It is the unspoken absence at the heart of many multicultural texts. There is considerable irony in the situation. Many have cast aside 'American exceptionalism' only to embrace instead a 'multi- exceptionalism' in which America is rewritten as a nation of heterogeneous groups, each of which can only be interpreted by cultural insiders.

Such an approach focuses on details and overlooks the larger structures of American culture. For example, Americans may crave a variety of ethnic cuisines, but increasingly these are processed foods cooked in a microwave or bought at a fast food restaurant. The specific food is distinctive, but the packaging, advertising, preparation, and the consumption time are commonalities. This may be seen, for example, at the immigration museum on Ellis Island, where a variety of ethnic fast foods are available, each being sold and consumed in the same way. Is this multi-ethnicity?

Many other similarities exist among Americans, but those embracing multiculturalism spend little time looking for shared characteristics or shared technical systems.[32] There is a common core to American culture which makes it distinctive and identifiable, although not exceptional, and the social construction of technology reveals part of that common core. There are many characteristic American patterns, including wasteful consumption habits, the world's highest energy use, heavy reliance on processed foods, longer work hours and less vacation time than in European countries, the sprawling layout of cities and suburbs, the general rejection of mass transit, and so forth. Those living in the United States seem blind to such commonalities, but they immediately strike any outside observer.

For more than a decade Americans have been over-emphasizing their differences, and there is not a little irony in this development. At the very moment when interchangeability, mass production, television, and the computer have fully penetrated not only production but also the spheres of consumption and cultural reproduction, at the very moment when virtually all Americans are enmeshed in advanced technological systems that bind them together, they have chosen to ignore their material connectedness and to insist on the primacy of inherited or newly rediscovered cultural values. The very elimination of technology from Appleby's text and from most discussions of multiculturalism signifies a reluctance to confront the structures that have penetrated thoroughly into every aspect of daily life. Meanwhile, Newt Gingrich and the Republican Party win elections by championing individualism, free enterprise and exceptionalism, in combination with a nineteenth-century vision of liberating technology.

In contrast, historians of technology question both the idea that American machines and manufacturing systems are hallmarks of national identity and the Whig idea of history as the story of amelioration. Questioning the idea of a national character and the idea of progress leads one to focus on the cultural meaning of technological systems themselves. Do different ethnic and racial groups work on assembly lines in fundamentally distinctive ways? Do they drive automobiles on different kinds of roads and follow different traffic rules? Do they plug their electrical appliances into different grids? Do they use different credit cards or use them in fundamentally different ways? Do some of them reject items made with interchangeable parts in favor of hand-made items? By such tests, only a few groups really merit the name 'multi- cultural,' including the Amish, many Native-Americans, some of the rural poor, and some of those living in communes. Most Americans are inextricably bound up with their technological systems, which they use to shape their lives as producers and consumers within the world's most energy-intensive culture. Indeed, this quantitative difference in energy use is so large that it translates into important qualitative distinctions between the United States and other nations. The American organization of production and consumption displays a discernible pattern, whose lineaments can be traced through history, and whose existence undercuts the more extreme claims for multiculturalism.

Americans of different ethnic and racial backgrounds usually resemble each other more than they do people from their nations of origin. Their similarities emerge in habits of energy use, which include the electrified home, automobile, and air-conditioner, and which touch virtually all aspects of life, including even those that seem most distinctive. For example, production and consumption of food is a central part of maintaining a cultural tradition. In the United States, food requires 17% of all the energy used, with 6% for production, another 6% for processing, and 5% for transport, refrigeration, cooking, and washing dishes. Ethnic differentiation in cuisine thus exists within an energy-intensive framework. By the 1980s a typical large supermarket stocked an average of 30,000 items. The price of achieving this variety was a decline in the total number of markets in the 1980s, while the average floor space of the remaining stores doubled. The ethnic variety on the shelves is based on capitalist rationalization, packaging, and distribution. At the supermarket multiculturalism and advanced capitalism prove compatible, just as they do in merchandizing by mail, in narrow-casting in the broadcast media, and in other forms of market segmentation.

Furthermore, whatever the preferred cuisine, Americans of all ethnic and racial backgrounds tend toward high sugar and high fat diets that lead to the 'diseases of affluence.' Finally, much of the variety of ethnic cuisine is maintained as a business: '55 percent of America's consumer food budget is spent on restaurant meals and ready-to-eat convenience foods.'[33] This is a far higher percentage than in most other cultures, and further indicates how market forces maintain a veneer of ethnic diversity. The businesses of transportation, food preservation, marketing, and advertising prove central to the creation of a surface appearance of variety, in stark contrast to the small grocer of c. 1920 who bought from local farmers and regional suppliers.

Virtually every foreign observer from Tocqueville to Weber to our own time has noted the centrality of business in American culture, a fact perhaps so obvious that those living inside the United States tend to overlook it. As the Dutch historian Johan Huizinga noted a lifetime ago in *Life and Thought in America,* 'The progress of technology compels the economic process to move toward concentration and general uniformity at an ever faster tempo. The more human inventiveness and exact science become locked into the organization of business, the more the active man, as the embodiment of an enterprise and its master, seems to disappear.' By extension the distinctiveness of whole groups of immigrants and minorities was eroded both by immersion in corporate work cultures and by the all pervasive character of American consumption. Note that, as in Chandler's argument, this is not a brief for technological determinism. Rather, Huizinga argued, like Tocqueville before him, that 'The American *wants* to be like his neighbour,' and he went one step further, expressing the power and importance of the idea of interchangeability, noting that the American 'only feels spiritually safe in what has been standardized.'[34] If one doubts this statement consider the popularity of national merchandizing chains that guarantee a consumer the same products and services coast to coast. The uniformity in American life has become so great that a European, flying a thousand miles to a new city inside the United States, can frequently be disappointed, because the new place seems so much like all the other places.

Multiculturalism is perhaps best understood as a reaction against the uniformities noted by Tocqueville, Weber, and Huizinga. It is an attempt, focused primarily within the realm of consumption, to counter the pressures toward standardization, efficiency, and business-directed routines in both the work place and private life. If advocates of multiculturalism such as Appleby ignore technology, it is not because they reject the almost forgotten exceptionalist history of American technology, but because they mistakenly (and implicitly) conceive of technology as a deterministic system.

## Notes

1. For comments on this paper I am indebted to members of the Danish American Studies Consortium who participated in a two day Ph.D. seminar in February 1996.
2. Joyce Appleby, 'Recovering America's Historic Diversity: Beyond Exceptionalism,' *Journal of American History*, 79 (1992): 419–32.
3. Appleby is not idiosyncratic in omitting the history of technology. In a debate over historical method that pitted the 'old history' versus the 'new' Gertrude Himmelfarb also ignored the history of technology. Himmelfarb, 'Some Reflections on the New History,' *American Historical Review*, 94 (1989): 661–70.
4. Newt Gingrich, *To Renew America* (New York: HarperCollins, 1994), 41–43. Gingrich goes on to name, on the same page, Bill Gates, Steve Jobs, Edison and Ford. He later mentions the older pantheon of Fulton, Whitney, Morse, and the Wright Brothers (44).
5. Of course there was also a counter-tradition, emphasizing the natural landscape (and/or the frontier) as the seedbed of national identity. Thomas Jefferson and Alexander Hamilton argued over how much the nation should industrialize, and had Jefferson's policies prevailed the nation might have been more agrarian, importing many of the finished goods it needed from Europe. Jefferson was not as rabidly anti-technological as many once thought, however. See John Kasson, *Civilizing the Machine* (New York: Penguin, 1977), 36–38.
6. John Kouwenhoven, *Made in America: The Arts in Modern Civilization* (New York: Doubleday, 1962), 26–33, *passim.*

7. Brooke Hindle, *Emulation and Invention*. (Washington, DC: Smithsonian Institution, 1981), 55.

8. An American named William Kelly had independently hit upon something like the Bessemer process, and he was granted a patent. But his discovery was not fully translated into a method and set of equipment, and American steel makers had to buy licenses from both Kelly and Bessemer. For an excellent account of the introduction of the Bessemer process into the United States, see Elting E. Morison, *Men, Machines, and Modern Times* (Cambridge, MA: MIT Press, 1966), 123–205. For a brief account of the iron industry, see W. David Lewis, *Iron and Steel in America* (Greenville, DE: The Hagley Museum, 1976).

9. Elting Morison, *From Know-How to Nowhere: The Development of American Technology* (New York: Basic Books, 1974), 22–30.

10. David J. Jeremy, 'Innovation in American Textile Technology During the Early 19th Century,' *Technology and Culture*, 14 (1973): 41–45.

11. Darwin Stapleton, *The Transfer of Early Technologies to America* (Philadelphia: American Philosophical Society, 1987), 72–121.

12. Stapleton, 88, 114, *passim.*

13. Hindle, 53.

14. Anthony F. C. Wallace, *Rockdale* (New York: Norton, 1978), 219.

15. Kouwenhoven, 40.

16. Other figures who usually appeared in these narratives were Elias Howe (sewing machine). Oliver Evans (automated flour mill), Robert Fulton (steamboat), Samuel Morse (telegraph), Alexander Graham Bell (telephone), the Wright Brothers (the airplane), and Thomas A. Edison (phonograph, electric lighting system), plus many more. For a deconstructivist account of how the mythology of the inventor was inscribed on the documents of Thomas Edison, see David E. Nye, *The Invented Self: An Anti-Biography of Thomas A. Edison* (Odense, Den.: Odense University Press, 1983).

17. Merritt Roe Smith, 'Eli Whitney and the American System of Manufacturing,' *Technology in America*, ed. Caroll W. Pursell, Jr. (Cambridge, MA: MIT Press, 1981), 45–61.

18. David A. Hounshell, *From the American System to Mass Production, 1800–1932* (Baltimore: Johns Hopkins University Press, 1984), 25–29.

19. J. D. Burn, *The Years Among the Working-Classes of the United States During the War* (London, 1865), 178.

20. Wilhelm Stiel, *Textile Electrification* (London: Routledge, 1933), 150–51. Note that these comparisons are all between highly developed industrial economies.

21. Ronald Schatz, *The Electrical Workers: A History of Labor at General Electric and Westinghouse, 1923–1960* (Urbana: University of Illinois Press, 1983), 138.

22. See Gregory Clark, 'Why Isn't the Whole World Developed? Lessons for the Cotton Mills,' *Journal of Economic History*, 47 (1987): 141–73.

23. Alfred D. Chandler, *The Visible Hand* (Cambridge, MA: Harvard University Press, 1977).

24. Alfred D. Chandler, 'The Beginnings of "Big Business" in American Industry,' *Managing Big Business*, ed. Richard Tedlow and Richard John (Boston: Harvard Business School Press, 1986).

25. Michael Storper and Richard Walker, *The Capitalist Imperative: Territory, Technology, and Industrial Growth* (Oxford: Blackwell, 1989).

26. Michael Chevalier, *Society, Manners, and Politics in the United States* (1839; New York: Doubleday, 1961), 71, 73–74. For more on the tendency of Americans to see their railroads in nationalistic terms, see James A. Ward, *Railroads and the Character of America, 1820–1887* (Knoxville: University of Tennessee Press, 1986).

27. Cited in Francis Klingender, *Art and the Industrial Revolution,* ed. Arthur Elton (New York: Augustus Kelley, 1968), 147.

28. See David E. Nye, *Electrifying America: Social Meanings of a New Technology* (Cambridge, MA: MIT Press, 1990), chapter two: 'The Great White Way.'

29. I devote a chapter to this event in my *American Technological Sublime* (Cambridge, MA: MIT Press, 1994).

30. *New York Times,* 13 April 1981.

31. Appleby, 427, 430.

32. The crowd at a mass sporting event or at the launching of a space shuttle comes from all segments of the population. See chapter nine in Nye, *American Technological Sublime.*

33. Alan Durning, *How Much is Enough? The Consumer Society and the Future of the Earth* (New York: Norton, 1992), 69, 74, 68, 45.

34. Johan Huizinga, *Life and Thought in America: A Dutch Historian's Vision, From Afar and Near* (New York: Harper Torchbooks, 1972), 234, 237.

# No Special Relation: British Perceptions of Ante-Bellum America's Growing Pains

*Inger Hunnerup Dalsgaard*

> The youth of America is their oldest tradition.
> It has been going on now for three hundred years.
>
> Oscar Wilde, *A Woman of No Importance* (1893)

## 'America is the Country of Young Men'

Soon after the execution of the Oklahoma bomber, Timothy McVeigh, at the US Federal Penitentiary in Terre Haute, Indiana, in June 2001, Keith Graves, a Sky News reporter covering the execution, was challenged by London studio anchorman Martin Stanford as to whether this was 'the right and proper way for a grown-up country to behave?'[1] At a time when less astute European observers were dismissively describing yet another US president as immature in some peculiarly American way (this time on the basis of his 'irresponsible' stance on international security and environmental issues rather than his unchecked libido), the slip of Martin Stanford's tongue also suggested that a deeper existential belief survives in the Old World: that the United States itself can somehow be seen as an autonomous, 'teenaged' being, still having troubles growing up and meeting British standards of 'adult' or civilized behaviour. Stanford was scarcely alone. Over the past two hundred years, in fact, Americans and Europeans as diverse as Ralph Waldo Emerson and Count Hermann Keyserling have agreed that the United States as a nation is somehow best described as being in a distinctive state of near-perpetual adolescence. On the European side of the Atlantic, in particular, the United States appears forever fixed in the public imagination – and constantly reinvoked in advertising,

*Marks of Distinction: American Exceptionalism Revisited*, ed. Dale Carter, *The Dolphin* 32, pp. 112–36. © 2001 by Aarhus University Press, Denmark. ISBN 87 7288 383 9; ISSN 0106 4487.

films and popular classics – in the guise of a gum-chewing teen rebel or a fishing rod-carrying Huck Finn.

As with other tropes used to gloss American exceptionalism, it seems that 'symbols teach more than facts': the unity of a singular identification – here dubbed 'centrism' – displacing the minutiae and diversity of plural facts.[2] Casting national identity under Hamiltonian and Jacksonian influences increasingly in terms of a young, entrepreneurial spirit may have helped render what one might call 'Americentrism' exceptional in terms of content: the range of symbols, including contradictions, being particular to this national self-perception (albeit at the expense of those who did not fit the model). At the same time and according to Joyce Appleby, however, the resulting figure also retained its Eurocentric ancestry. Though the United States strove to see itself as self-created almost *ex nihilo*, in other words, it remained subtly subject to its heritage. As what follows argues, half a century after independence it was more specifically subject to continued British influence, as the nation's own re-configuration of its exceptional nature was confronted by those alternative definitions and values ascribed to the predominant character in 'the country of young men' by still-influential British draftsmen.[3]

Insofar as it constituted (to reconfigure Appleby's notion of foreclosure) a kind of blindness, 'centrism' may have been an inherited and long unchallenged disability; many exceptional values were certainly identified in colonial times or (by enthusiastic French authors) soon after the revolution. Some of the unchallenged 'original' contents of American exceptionalism therefore clearly had European roots. However, when the British and Americans were ready to meet each other again some decades after their last military confrontation in 1815, the renewed sense of untimely interference and unwanted criticism made American tempers flare. As a result, contrasts more than similarities were emphasized in popular literature. While certain kinds of literature may have stressed parallels and 'equality' between the two nations, the shrillest voices left the impression that British and American definitions and evaluations of American exceptionalism had diverged: not in relation to the nation's genesis or original nature so much as to its industrialized 'com-ing-of-age,' involving as the latter did the establishment of a successful economy and infrastructure, and an increasingly independent literary opinion-forming community. Thus champions of American exceptionalism in both the arts and industries themselves appealed to a rhetoric of adolescence, as did their British detractors. Within this rhetorical field, however, 'newness' could signify promise as well as ignorance, while 'youth' might imply vigour or immaturity, depending on the inclinations of the interpreter. Between the Jacksonian Era and the Civil War, such preferred images and associated expectations were reflected back and forth: resisted, co-opted, incorporated and internalized through a transatlantic discourse fraught with pain and defiance. Arranged around the metaphor of growing up, what follows looks at the changing nature of this 'special relationship' as the New World grew, in British writing (and American responses), from the aberrant child of the Old World into a distant, exotic or ridiculed cousin.

If this period is aptly described as the United States' 'puberty,' a troubled process resulting in its final, significant break with authority, it is in part because of the impression some hyper-sensitive American writers gave that 'parental' approval was still being sought in the comments of Old World observers.[4] When sought, such approval was not always found. Early on, for example, *The Edinburgh Review* (amongst other publications) had declared America 'to be the land of the future, "emphatically the New World".'[5] British people duly crossed the Atlantic to see whether the new nation lived up to its revolutionary promises, whether it was an improvement on the old, or whether its new-found freedom had caused the developing democratic republic to descend into complete uncultured backwardness. Yet many of these British visitors arrived with perhaps overly-inflated expectations about the radical political potential and democratic institutions of the young nation, and were disappointed. Others, meanwhile, discovered that their patronizing cultural observations of taste and manners sold well both at home and abroad. Touring the New World and publishing their findings in the

United Kingdom, they often found that disparaging remarks about the behaviour and ideas of the young independent nation, down to the way in which some individuals handled their cutlery or abused their 'common' language, sold more books – on both sides of the ocean.[6]

The kinds of writings dealt with here include a number of different guidebooks and travelogues with varying degrees of serious, comic and sensational intent. Thanks to the revolution in steam transportation ('such an easy method of spanning the broad gulf between the Old and New World,' according to one hopeful writer), both the writers and readers of such literature were able to travel more easily to and within the United States: visiting relatives or being tourists, as emigrants or sojourners, depending on their class and background.[7] Overrun by writers of varying ability and often dubious intent, Americans grew to feel that the English had turned their country into 'a sort of continental sideshow to be exploited by any literary hack who could afford the fare.'[8] More precisely, the draftsmen of this 'sideshow,' a literary market generated and underwritten by successful industrialization, were sketching (to extrapolate from Appleby) 'the lineaments of [an] exceptional, new' *and industrializing* nation in which the special relationship metaphor informed an articulation of its position within a Euro- and an Americentric worldview.[9] Ultimately, in the debates that raged in response to British condescension towards 'the young American,' symbolic 'youth' became a popular but ambivalent term within a broader parent/child discourse applied to relationships between nations. Writers used the same metaphors to explain how the United States had grown into an exceptionally good or exceptionally bad 'teenager.' Such language signified the broadening gulf between British 'parental' expectations and optative American self-perceptions – whether in contemporary writings about the new republic or in 21st century news commentary – which neither steam trains nor steamboats would bridge.

## Industry and Identity

If adolescence is defined as the stage at which a child first en-
deavours to break with parental authority and styles, and to
assert its own distinctive identity, then the beginnings of the
United States' prolonged adolescence, in its own and British eyes,
came half a century and more after its birth as a nation. In his
1844 lecture 'The Young American,' for example, Ralph Waldo
Emerson highlighted the way in which the United States by that
point was able to cut the last, cultural, umbilical cord, adding that
in material terms railroad construction had made the country self-
sufficient and financially independent while reducing the mother
country 'to a third of its size.'[10] If so, then this period also com-
mends itself as worthy of closer scrutiny from the perspective of
American exceptionalism, since (as Joyce Appleby, James Mendelsohn and others argue elsewhere in this volume) exceptionalism may have to do less with the real complexities of a nation
than with just such a desire for an autonomous, homogenous
identity.

Immediately, however, the conditions under which such a
national identity might be adopted, constructed or imposed
become clear. For by emphasizing the uniformly progress-
oriented nature of America's 'young men,' the opinions or literary
productions of Others – those not so oriented – within the *United*
States found themselves divided off and banished to an unreachable wilderness. The results included a covert remoteness in
internal relations, the maintenance of a mental back-woods area
in a forward-looking nation, where, in Emerson's words, 'the
locomotive and steamboat, like enormous shuttles, shoot every
day across the thousand various threads of national descent and
employment and bind them fast in one web, an hourly assimilation goes forward, and there is no danger that local peculiarities
and hostilities should be preserved.'[11] Emerson's relentlessly
mechanized image of a 'fabricated' America evinces a 'textual
materialism' in which metaphors and mechanical means merge.
In the lecture as a whole, and in the metaphoric syncretism
common to the rhetoric of American exceptionalism, the desire

for a unified American literature, a canon of the new world, blends with the need – underwritten by the nation's devotion to the ethos of mechanized progress – to weave regional (and other) differences industrially together. Those not streamlined in the weft and woof are banished to margins or interstices unreachable even by steam-transport. As one English observer, saddened that the prairie had been 'disturbed by the snorting locomotive,' poetically put it: 'and the Indian at the burial-place murmured – ... fast they follow, as we go / Towards the setting day, – / Till they shall fill the land, and we / Are driven into the western sea.'[12]

In discussing the earliest roots of exceptionalism within the United States, therefore, Appleby explains how the determination to perceive the new nation as a political prodigy meant that, just as Europeans had 'learned to make the other invisible,' so citizens of the United States worked to disable their own multiple vision.[13] British observers who subsequently pointed out more or less trivial differences between themselves and their hosts (slavery and poverty at one end, lack of civility at the other) threatened simultaneously to expose the ways in which American self-presentations effaced multiplicity within. American retorts in turn re-homogenized exceptionalism by projecting domestic differences outwards onto the imagined gulf between the United States and Britain, thereby rendering differences exogenous to a re-asserted exceptionalism. One American critic insisted in 1843 that if Dickens chose to remark on the nation's poor and uncultured people, this was only because (being British and therefore class-ridden) he allegedly thought they were not kept in their 'proper place,' as in Britain, but were allowed to mingle and receive 'education from society.' Such education was in fact intended to enable them, the American went on, to rise from 'the habits of the labourer' and, if successful, to earn enough to send their 'children to college or to travel in Europe.' So phrased, the issue was quickly reformulated around 'youths and maidens' and their attraction to 'antiquated' countries. In order to defuse analogous situations, other writers would seek out a very different exceptionalist chestnut, the future in a country short on history, because the latter was already rhetorically contained and less problematic. After all, as Emerson quipped, it was 'one thing to visit the Pyramids, and another to wish to live there.'[14]

The story the United States *wanted* to tell itself and its visitors was one of young men and exemplary young women in model factories, not one of poorhouses, asylums, sculleries or slave quarters. The latter did come to the attention of some British writers, notably Dickens and W. E. Baxter. But in the United States, even the silent misfits were subordinated to the mantras of industry and streamlining. Thus Dickens's sentimentality attracts him to write the 'instructive history' of Laura Bridgman and Oliver Caswell, both 'deaf, and dumb, and blind' but taught to work and study in pursuit of 'Noble Usefulness.' After their institution he next visits an asylum so enlightened that the patient, fettered only by 'moral restraint,' is trusted with the 'tools of his trade as if he were a sane man' in the 'labour department.' This is less occupational therapy than a lesson in being American. Next on Dickens's list of American institutions is the ironically-named House of Industry – home, in fact, to elderly paupers. Orphans and juvenile delinquents are also taught agriculture through song and 'sober industry' through 'basket-making and the manufacture of palm-leaf hats' respectively. All such institutions, Dickens writes, contribute to a system for 'the inculcation and encouragement, even among such unhappy persons, of a decent self-respect.'[15] If self-respect was believed to be found in agriculture, learning and industry, it is no surprise that Dickens later recognized the Lowell Mills, the industrial institution which brought them together, as the most exceptional American sight, from a British perspective.

At this point, in the early to mid-nineteenth century, American technology and industrialization were being championed at many levels as capable of delivering a progress at once exemplary and exceptionally different from that of the Old World. This was not just because such progress would eradicate internal differences and present a united front, as Emerson's textual image suggested. It was also because a unique blend of egalitarian ideology and industrial nationalism would reinforce the brand of exceptionalism with which American writers were starting to defend themselves as British writers grew ever more critical of the democratic United States. American writers and opinion-formers thus sought to direct public attention to new realms – notably mechanization and the entrepreneurial spirit – through which the nation's unique and superior qualities might be articulated. Far from all visitors were convinced, however, and many clung to the horrific fatality statistics associated with frequent steamboat explosions 'sending a score or two of parboiled passengers to an inconvenient altitude in the atmosphere.' However, even the spiteful Mrs. Trollope herself had to admit that, in the case of steamboats, the United States was superior, in some indefinable way, to Europe.[16]

## Training an Exceptional Generation

The early nineteenth century, when railroads started to expand explosively (sometimes literally), was the period which really put Americans on the map as technology-mad in all senses of the word. Their technological enthusiasm and initiative were advertised as exceptional (a rebuttal of the other criticisms levelled against them) and linked to the argument that technological progress was the best, or only, way for the newly independent nation to prosper in the world – and a way the United States had to follow at any cost. This version of the metanarrative of progress was powerfully Americentric and particularly useful for instilling in a nation looking to industrialize rapidly a sense that industriousness (applied to labour and education) and ingenuity (supported by natural inquisitiveness and a pioneering spirit) were large parts of a shared ethos.[17]

One element of the identity Americans seemed happy to embrace, and to which droves of British writers almost ritually referred, saw the United States as the 'go-ahead!' nation. This term was well-nigh obligatory in travelogues of the period and appeared to emphasize the deplorable irresponsibility of a country which could not progress fast enough; whether in the construction or actual running of sea and land transportation, it was one of those ambiguous terms which even British travel writers seemed to realize Americans would find positive, notwithstanding its use by hostile critics. In a country where assertions were regularly made about the need to conquer the land technologically, to invent labour-saving machinery in order to compensate for lack of skilled labour, and to gain international competitiveness through manufacturing, there was no time to lose looking backwards. American writers did not, therefore, quibble with British correspondents who labelled them part of a 'go-ahead!' nation. On the contrary, the stronger the belief that these were indeed areas in which the United States excelled and was advancing, the more pride they took in the term, and the more backwards it made British writers seem for having thought it a *critical* bon mot. The overall effect of this reinforced ethos was to make Americans more willing to welcome mechanization as a positive force. Without the resultant territorial and financial gains, it might seem the United States would have remained a geographically and psychologically limited 'New England' instead of an (imaginative) expanse of 'empty' space rapidly filling up with entrepreneurs (including the literary ones of the American Renaissance). Few English observers were as enamoured of this strategy's promise as Americans themselves had reason to be. In light of comparisons between the reception and running of factories and railroads in either country, it seemed that Americans really felt their industrial progress benefited the majority.[18]

British criticisms of American domestic manners, rather than of the American system of domestic manufacture, started to appear insignificant as industrialization accelerated and beliefs in progress spread. Indeed, even British observers came to accept and helped cement the 'fact' that Americans were exceptionally ingenious since, according to Alfred Bunn in *Old England and New England* (1853), in 'every place in the Union ... they have each peculiar [notions] of their own, whether it be in singular ideas on passing events, or in serious or simple inventions, from a steam engine to an apple-parer.' In this realm, exceptional America appears unique in the world and its citizens equal amongst themselves, betraying an independence of mind, down to the individual level, even in foreign eyes. However, having admired a few of the material 'trifles' for mechanical fruit peeling 'on which the intellect of such a creative set of people is for ever employed,' Bunn quickly returns to the associated youth metaphor to suggest that such inventiveness is a prerogative of 'younger minds,' and that wisdom and the older generation are pushed aside in the process. Ostensibly describing a typical American family, Bunn paints an almost allegorical picture of the emerging shift in the balance of (world) power towards the Old World's adolescent offspring, his tone reflecting the growing self-confidence which had entered the 'special relationship' after American exhibitors had returned triumphant from the Great Exhibition in London two years earlier, in 1851:

The son, at a very early age, is of the opinion that his father knows nothing about it, whatever 'it' might be – that his time is gone by, long ago – ... In all business matters ... he very soon substitutes *I* for *we*, and, in short, takes the lead in everything. The daughter is not a whit behind her brother; she arranges parties ... and gives such general directions, that your first impression is, the mother is dead.[19]

Many reluctant observers of the rapid increase in American self-sufficiency during the early nineteenth century used elaborate familial metaphors to rehearse their assumptions of a special relationship between the 'overgrown baby America' and its mother country to whom, they felt, it should still owe its living, or at least show due respect. As C. Vann Woodward notes, the built-in youth metaphor applied to the United States had long allowed 'nations of the older generation, those of the Old World,' to assume 'parental roles of responsibility, discipline, and admonition' at the expense of a respectful tone between equals.[20] An anonymous 1843 reply to some misplaced paternal criticism, perceived in Dickens's *American Notes*, put it this way:

Nearly all these travelled writers [from England] profess a wish to cultivate and improve good understanding which should prevail between a child and parent countries, and they then, with some honorable exceptions, proceed to shew – strange means to such an end – how rude and perverse is the overgrown baby America, disregardful of parental admonitions, and perseverant with ridiculous obstinacy in thinking, speaking, and acting for herself.[21]

Placing the United States in that sort of relationship marked out a set of rules for the 'special relationship' which the Old World expected or hoped the New would obey. Between these two descriptions from 1843 and 1853, however, the nation had grown in self-confidence and self-sufficiency to the point where thinking of or addressing it as a mere 'child' no longer seemed appropriate.

Even as youth- and family-related metaphors became ingrained in descriptions and understandings of the nature of the United States and its relationship with both Great Britain and technology, therefore, the growing coolness and distance in the relationship prompted the growth of two metaphoric variants. Firstly, referring increasingly to Americans as 'cousins,' family ties were upgraded from hypotactic to paratactic, reflecting perceived changes in the relationship by acknowledging a kind of parity. This idea was explored in particular by some of the nation's more serious chroniclers, who tentatively suggested that the United States and Britain were no more different, in terms of manners and unintelligible dialects, than London and Lincolnshire. More soberly than the best-sellers, such writers drew similar parallels between populations, arguing that a certain heterogeneity existed not only *between* the two peoples and nations but also *within* the American public, in spite of the universal equality both travel writers and many Americans trumpeted.[22]

Entertained in some of the more scholarly works, such parallelisms eventually gained prominence in the metaphoric guise of the 'special cousin' relationship, one boosted on both sides of the Atlantic by the fame and popularity of Tom Taylor's three act play, *Our American Cousin*. Later titles would include *Our American Cousins at Home* (1873), *Our American Cousins and Their Political Life: By One of Themselves* (1887) and *Our English*

*Cousins* (1894). In contrast to the idea that contemporary Britons were somehow ancestors of the American population, as if time had stood still on the British Isles while only their progeny had 'gone-ahead,' cousinhood at a metaphorical level implied equal standing: common roots from which different branches had grown simultaneously. The implication of the nations being cousins-german was, however, tellingly undermined in Taylor's play, where the eponymous American Cousin, Asa Trenchard, is both culturally and genealogically far removed, representing a forgotten branch of a clearly British family. It was not only in Taylor's drama, moreover, that their quaint language, clothing or dining habits made distant but rich cousins (or uncles) from America (like Asa) the butt of humour at one moment even as they are appealed to for financial support the next. Though beliefs might not have changed at heart, the symbolic mode of address was at least considered more respectful, and *Our American Cousin* was in fact found amusing by Americans themselves, so much so that President Abraham Lincoln took his wife to see the play on 14th April, 1865.

The second variant on ingrained youth- and family-related metaphors was used less explicitly to identify alleged 'childish' characteristics defining Americans in relation to the British. As the United States grew larger (physically at least) than its parents, so it became more difficult to address a whole nation as if it were a child. Instead, British authors turned to describing not the 'overgrown baby America' but the babies *of* America – American children themselves – as symbolic of what was exceptional about their native land. If, as we have seen, both young men and extending railway lines were to Emerson simultaneously symbolic of and instrumental to growth, so for British writers this symbolic complex of trains and youths also signified. In their case, however, such images were juxtaposed to express an essential *difference* about the first 'real' Americans: the new generation who felt not displaced but disinterested when the machine rushed through their garden idyll:

On [the train] whirls headlong, [it] dives through the woods again, emerges in the light, ... suddenly awakens all the slumbering echoes in the main street of a large town, and dashes on haphazard, pell-mell, neck-or-nothing, down the middle of the road. There – with mechanics working at their trades, and people leaning from their doors and windows, and boys flying kites and playing marbles, and men smoking, and women talking, and children crawling ... close to the very rails – there – on, on, on – tears the mad dragon of an engine with its train of cars.[23]

Because even they embraced the machine, children (and women) were often used to demonstrate what was conceived of as exceptionally *American* behaviour. The creation of a special American child metaphor served, here and elsewhere, to exemplify a basic truth about the peculiarly fearless or uncritical American relationship with advancing technology, the presence of which had become so accepted, its manifestations so thoroughly absorbed, that humans were not only undisturbed by, but indifferent to, the snorting monster. If Emerson's train crisscrossing the width and breadth of the continent had been blind to the original native population, this new 'freeborn progeny' growing up in the early- to mid-nineteenth century were themselves as blind to the train as if they had been born in the 'revolutionary prize of an empty continent' previously found only in the minds of eighteenth-century European observers.[24] The United States thus proved an Americentric model for the rest of humanity not because the land was devoid of Indians or engines but because both could be largely ignored, the former through 'othering,' the latter via absorption. Indeed, the way in which the train was incorporated into the image of cosy, small communities may well be one of the first demonstrations of the insidious effects of successful industrialization on the ability to see beyond the ideological framework accompanying such 'progress.'

The independent American children, to whom British authors now turned to describe what might be called 'Industrial exceptionalism,' were reared as if the mechanized society were still an Edenic resource. Indeed, Nature and Industry might well have appeared to mesh together seamlessly in fledgling American minds, were we to believe these texts in which machines only intrude violently on the perceptions and writings of British visitors, 'unaccustomed horses' and trespassing cows, the latter 'cut into atoms' by the locomotive 'spearhead of progress.' There *were* Americans who resisted and protested, unsuccessfully, against the coming of the railroads, but these have subsequently been largely forgotten and ignored.[25]

No doubt Captain Marryat and Charles Dickens alike believed that the United States was both young and reckless, a 'go-ahead' nation pursuing 'the almighty dollar.' Clichéd statements about time being money and speed desirable at any cost to 'these Americans' served to explain why tourists witnessed trains speeding through small communities without fencing around the tracks to protect valuable livestock and offspring. Marryat interpreted such phenomena as a 'development of the English character under a new aspect, arising from a new state of things.' By this he may have had in mind not only material equality in a 'country where factory-girls carry parasols, and pig-drivers wear spectacles,' for he also cited (as 'rather a singular feature') 'a recklessness – an indifference to life – shown through all America.'[26] American children, meanwhile, appeared to have imbibed the spirit of technology, playing undisturbed next to the tracks even as the mad dragon of an engine tore past, hissing and screeching. Fearless young Americans, he anticipated, would inherit the mixed blessings of self-evident technological progress, blind to the dangers of mechanization and industrialization.

An English émigrée living in Philadelphia, claiming to be engaged in a revision of Dickens's *American Notes* twenty-five years down the line, gives a sketch which is very similar but also of its own time, in terms not only of its respectful tone of address but also of the gentle and non-insulting humour with which it renders what it perceives as the still-noteworthy American attitude to trains (and life threatening speed):

In spite of [their advantages in the technological field] our cousins **do** enjoy a singular pre-eminence in railway accidents it must be admitted: and it does look odd to see a great long train go Pell-Mell through a village, now dashing past a potato stall, now making a detour round a confectioner's window close enough to enable one to pocket a piece of candy, now dodging some perambulator containing young Americans out for an airing, and all as unconcerned, passenger, perambulators, villagers, as if it were a water-cart drawn by a blind donkey. Far from any concern being evinced, some of the servant maids in charge of these perambulators seemed to me to regard the train with an air of mingled defiance and contempt, as who should say 'If you will make less fuss and abate your hurry, I'll get this out the way and let you pass'; while the little things, in their <u>gigantic</u> conveyances, appeared to me to wink to the engine-driver, and only wanted tongue to say, 'go-ahead; don't be alarmed; the <u>Locomotive</u> is quite safe.'[27]

By the 1850s, in other words, the cousins 'across the pond' were being thought of as being raised to be fearless in the face of the inevitable onrush of industrial progress. As such, this new generation – born with technology as second nature, as though this (symbolic) locomotive had also always been integral to American Nature – fostered the erasure of a past in which different ideologies had co-existed. The attitude of blind, irreverent confidence found in America's new generations, these overawed British writers concluded, effaced niggling criticisms of domestic manners and instead put flesh on the bones of the metaphor then tying children, technology and America together: the promise of the future. The Americans of tomorrow not only appeared defiantly confident in their 'gigantic conveyances'; they already perceived the railroad of their youth as an old, slow cart, drawn by a blind donkey.

## Exceptionalism: Who Needs It?

Texts such as these might have been read as a portent of things to come. A new industrial and technological mind-set in place, the United States was threatening to become more powerful, if not more well-mannered, than the old countries: daring enough to achieve dominance through manufacture; a financial and later a political force to be reckoned with; perhaps ultimately an agenda-setter in the world community. While the condescending version of the youth metaphor lingered, it could not hide the growing sense that this was a powerful child over which the Old World yielded diminishing influence – except, perhaps, to the extent that European criticism continued to pain Uncle Sam. Yet because ante-bellum Americans (also) took notable pride in the achievements of their country, the British were constantly surprised to discover that the braggadocio nation was unusually thin-skinned when confronted with criticism and unfavourable descriptions. Dickens had thought Americans were a people who could 'bear the truth, when told good humouredly and in a kind spirit' precisely *because* they loved their country so much.[28] It was as if the rest of the Western World was, for a while, more convinced by the frequent assertions of 'American Superiority' (for which read 'exceptionalism') put forward by the proudly-progressing nation than Americans were themselves, judging at least by their strong reactions to their portrayals at the hands of foreigners they believed had not empathized sufficiently with the American ethos. 'It is true, the public wants self-respect,' Emerson agreed: 'We are full of vanity, of which the most signal proof is our sensitivity to foreign and especially English censure.'[29]

The apparent lack of confidence or self-critical faculties may have been a sign that Americans had established a perfectionist self-image; that an insistence on exceptionalism had them living more within such a constructed, optative, vision than their own immediate reality (one is reminded, too, of Richard Hofstadter's dictum – made, ironically, in reference to Crèvecœur – that 'the United States was the only country in the world that began with perfection and aspired to progress').[30] If so, the habit proved problematic when the image reflected in the writings of foreign visitors conflicted with their own. Refusing to accept that the British might reject the superior American model of industrialization, and thus belittle their source of pride, achievement and self-definition, many American writers preferred to explain such criticisms to themselves as 'English jealousy.' That they should alight on 'jealousy' as a legitimating explanation may suggest that the correspondents were convincing themselves that, deep down, the Old Country surely wished it could reinvent itself and become a reflection of the New.

The fact that British travel books sold so well in the United States, even as they encouraged so many enraged retorts, implies that the American public at this time were painfully curious about their own reflection in the Old World. Trying hard not to see themselves *in* the countries and cultures of the past, they nevertheless relied on evidence of their own identity extracted from whatever perceptions Britons might have of them, even though directed towards a British readership. It is thus intriguing to wonder by whom and for what purpose American exceptionalism was conceived or elaborated on during these years, when views were passed back and forth, and across the Atlantic, in written form. A number of books were clearly written with political motives or to enhance domestic understandings of Great Britain itself, rather than the United States; to assure British readers, that is, of the stability of their own social and political systems should readers ever be tempted to embrace the American brand of equality. Significantly, perhaps, at precisely the time the travelogue and guidebook genre was fixing the United States in its sights, the Reform Bill of 1832 'signalled England's tentative movement toward a broadening of democracy' – another reason, essentially domestic, why American society and its institutions remained under close scrutiny for decades.[31] Then as now, many books written about the United States were ultimately written as commentaries on what Britain ought, or ought not, to become: part crystal ball, part 'mirror, mirror on the wall.'[32] Whatever insights Americans might hope to obtain from observing their reflections in the eyes of Britons, therefore, might have them looking not so much at a second hand reflection of themselves as at a thoroughly distorted third hand view of Britain. Insofar as Americans attempted to make sense of the fragmented image of the United States by reading British reflections on their nation, they – much like the characters in the celebrated shoot-out at the end of *The Lady From Shanghai* (Orson Welles, 1948) – were trying to find and position themselves in a hall of mirrors.

If being watched was unsettling then stability might be found at home, where Republican *amour propre* and political reality confirmed the usefulness of adhering to a metanarrative of progress for which industrial capitalism was the guarantor. One might speculate, however, whether American industrial exceptionalism was not also a necessity for *Europeans*, insofar as it enabled other industrializing nations to encounter fears and worries at a safe distance by acquiescing in the role the United States was forging for itself as humanity's industrial laboratory, having already served as a comfortably distant testing ground for democracy during the first fifty years of its existence. The new nation might eventually also serve as a scapegoat for industrialization's subsequent faults, having endorsed, and in some regards pioneered, this latest experiment as an integral part of its egalitarian democracy. Whether informed of such thinking or not, British writers (in addition to making money on this lucrative genre) were certainly able to develop their own agendas by adding another volume to their already copious outpourings. Disregarding the poorest hack writing on the table manners of Americans, a survey of the literature of the 1830s to 1850s suggests that those arguments which accept the premise of 'American superiority' and then defend or attack it, rest on technological, political and socio-cultural comparisons (fuelled by ideology and rhetoric). By contrast, those arguments which challenge the existence of any such essential distinctions and hierarchies are made in works which either (a) are more scholarly and sensitive to relative historical, demographic and geographical differences, or (b) downplay exceptionalist rhetoric for other reasons, such as thinly-disguised nostalgia for the colonial days, when America was just another rural province, like Lincolnshire, and differences were of degree, not substance.

Of course, a critique or defence of exceptionalism may have offered a more attractive angle for sensationalist writers (and more of a reason to write a book for other prospective tourists) than the identification of similarities. Some British observers certainly *wanted* America to be the Other, and since these were also best-selling books they became influential in promoting many of the prejudices or simplifications which some of them exploited knowingly and for supposedly comic effect. American readers may have suspected that the British were trying to make a fast buck by savaging an easy target; as one bitter American put it: 'considerable railwaying, horror at tobacco, awe at Niagara, and Lo! an English work upon the United States of America.'[33] Many stories American readers found so outrageous that they were unable to identify with events or the behaviour of fellow citizens in other places and occupations. To do so would undermine any sense of common national identity, so that the colourful regional characters and behaviour depicted by visiting 'reporters' were often ascribed to pure invention or the common practice of repeating or embellishing uncritically the claims and anecdotes of preceding travel writers. As they made yet another circuit amongst travellers, some such reports (about dramatic steamboat accidents in particular) were easily ten years old or approaching the status of urban legend; others, sadly, were both up-to-date and true. To citizens in many parts of the country, they did not necessarily have to be fanciful or antiquated in order to appear as so many descriptions of some un-assimilated society: a society which, if it ever existed, had long been outgrown, and one with which ordinary Americans found it impossible to identify.

Captain Frederick Marryat, on the other hand, thought that Americans were 'often themselves the cause of their being misrepresented' in outrageous tourist fictions, because the latter were often based on their own exaggerated tall-tales and deceptions. If Americans 'have the slightest suspicion that a foreigner is about to write a book, nothing gives them so much pleasure as to try to mislead him.'[34] His is a partly spurious comment, but it does raise important (and partly anthropological) questions about who was really describing the national 'lineaments' and on what basis collaborations between reporters and subjects took place. During this early period, exceptionalism was, on different levels, a co-production of Great Britain and the United States: the two jointly defined wherein the latter's differences lay, and why, while they simultaneously differed, so to speak, over what their *real* differences were. In the course of such discussions, British statements spurred the United States on towards a proud national identification with industrialization, one which further removed them from the 'Old World's dreams, fantasies, imaginings, hopes and yearnings' which had created an Edenic fiction about the Western Isles long before Columbus arrived.[35]

The early nineteenth century might therefore be termed a pivotal phase in the separation process, between ideals and expectations, on both sides. The familial metaphors identified above may appear to have been drawn on loosely yet they are telling: not only for the ways in which each side's reflections on the other changed, but also for the ways in which the distinctive nature of the *American* (taken either as a whole or as regional types) was perceived by British observers. The definition of the United States as *exceptional* rather than objectively *different* implies, in the terms of Joyce Appleby and others, that enviable qualities were projected on to its national identity from either within or without. More acutely, however, insofar as the United States is perceived as an adolescent nation or a 'special relation' in need of civilizing education, we might speak of 'exceptionalism' as a kind of 'expectationalism.' In their projection of (relationally defined) expectations onto the 'silver screen' or 'Mirage in the West,' writings about the United States (during this period by British and Americans alike) therefore tell us much about the formation of exceptionalist ideas. They do so particularly as the latter shift: fading French admiration for American democracy being supplanted by British mockery of personal habits and admonitions against inflated self-worth, and both of these intersecting with abiding American convictions concerning the nation's uniform difference, achieved through superior technology and progress, about both of which their old relatives were impotently jealous.[36] In light of these interactions, and from a European perspective, it is tempting to adapt once more the dictum of nineteenth-century Czech historian, nationalist and politician Frantisek Palacky: 'if the United States had not existed, we would have had to invent it.' In some ways, as the above shows, we did, as much as the United States invented itself.

## Conclusion: Go-ahead to the Future?

'In the beginning, there was *American* exceptionalism,' Byron Shafer writes in his introduction to *Is America Different?*[37] Though his definition of the concept may rest on the idea of uniqueness beyond mere 'difference,' Shafer's formulation also suggests that such uniqueness may lie as much in being exceptional *first* as in either the way both the United States and American exceptionalism continue to stimulate comparisons with other societies or the ways in which the nation appears to have been created, developed or understood as distinct from the rest of the world. And yet these other practices and perceptions show no sign of faltering. President George W. Bush's apparent disregard for the world's climate has been perceived, for example, as an exceptional blindness: not (just) to (ideological and bio-) diversity within the United States but also, given his prioritization of the needs of the domestic US economy over the objectives of the Kyoto Protocol on Global Warming, to multicultural and alternative perspectives and needs on a global scale. Not only does progress still appear to exclude from its narrative those whose ideas and interests differ; as a result, many observers beyond the United States are also having latently reconfirmed long held suspicions that the 'go-ahead!' nation remains devoted, more than anything else, to the quest for the 'almighty dollar,' the sign behind which all Americans become one in pursuit of personal gain, precisely as many of their ante-bellum detractors had claimed.

As President Bush travelled from Madrid via Brussels and Gothenburg to Warsaw and Moscow during the summer of 2001, showing the nation's official human face, many demonstrated: not only against him personally but also against that most abstract of post-industrial, late-capitalist entities, 'globalism,' burning the stars and stripes and parading dummies with cowboy hats. However justified or understandable, such behaviour is also informed by a kind of nostalgic retrospection insofar as the United States, in an age of globalism, may be no more exceptionally 'capitalist' than anywhere else, except perhaps in degree and consequence, given the sheer size of the US economy.

If that size is in part an indication of the material plenty that has long underwritten American industrial exceptionalism then, whatever else they may have been, the demonstrations were testimony to the fact that the imaginative or ideological appeal of such exceptionalism also remains powerful, in both the Old World and the New. Many remain wedded to an image created almost two centuries ago, in part because it saw the first, and most explicit, national identification with industrialism and capitalism which pretended to be blind to distinctions or divisions within society. As Charles Dickens's nineteenth-century visits to the asylums showed, even outcasts in the United States were united, albeit institutionally and forcibly, in the pursuit of profitable industry.

Do Americans today find themselves figuratively hostages of super-capitalist fortune and imaginatively harnessed to visions of unscrupulous entrepreneurs because of their nation's pursuit of exceptionalism or because of the way such pursuit was from the outset reflected on scornfully in Europe? Young people today can seem as ignorant of the diversity and complexity of the United States as British visitors were then, and as simplistically opinionated about and prejudiced towards the United States' lack of welfare provision and gun control, as much as their racism and eating habits (American ways of using knives at dinner remain a staple of condescending comment). Just as in the early nineteenth century, when British writers were accused of both incredulity and bad research when relating uncorroborated or outdated stories about outrageous steamboat accidents, so today, it seems, many assumptions remain based on unsubstantiated hear-say and 'urban legends,' on sensationalism, distortions and simplistic opinions amplified and disseminated by popular global media keen to tell us that a whole nation needs to grow up and 'behave.'

## Notes

1. Martin Stanford, *Sky News*, 9:06 PM (British Summer Time), 11 June 2001.
2. Joyce Appleby, 'Recovering America's Historic Diversity: Beyond Exceptionalism,' *Journal of American History*, 79 (1992): 430; Count Hermann

Keyserling, *America Set Free* (London: Cape, 1930), 161, 267. In Keyserling's view American adulation of the juvenile was an expression of deep-rooted primitivism.

3. Appleby, 420–23; Ralph Waldo Emerson, 'Old Age,' *Society and Solitude* (Boston: Houghton, Mifflin, 1904), 331.

4. Some of the better known ones being Frances Wright, *Views of Society and Manners in America* (1821), Capt. Basil Hall, *Travels in North America in the Years 1827 and 1828* (1829), Mrs Frances Trollope, *Domestic Manners of the Americans* (1832), Harriet Martineau, *Society in America* (1837), Capt. Frederick Marryat, *Diary in America, with Remarks on its Institutions* (1839), and Charles Dickens, *American Notes for General Circulation* (1842).

5. Constance Wright, *Fanny Kemble and the Lovely Land* (London: Hale, 1972), 15.

6. Frances Trollope provides endless examples of the 'social defects and absurdities which our near relatives had adopted in their domestic life.' Among their 'universal deficiency in good manners' were their 'strange uncouth phrases and pronunciation,' their 'loathsome spitting' and 'the frightful manner of feeding with their knives, till the whole blade seemed to enter the mouth; and the still more frightful manner of cleaning the teeth afterwards with a pocket knife.' Dickens also complained of fellow diners who sucked their knives. A general lack of understanding for the unwillingness of Americans to 'compromise their independence in any material degree' by paying homage to English norms of good behaviour pervades such anecdotes. Nonetheless, in 1840 *The Art of Good Behaviour* had become a best-seller by telling Americans that 'if possible, the knife should never be put in the mouth at all.' Malcolm Bradbury, *Dangerous Pilgrimages: Trans-Atlantic Mythologies and the Novel* (London: Secker and Warburg, 1995), 92; Charles Dickens, *American Notes for General Circulation* (1842; Harmondsworth: Penguin, 1972), 203; Captain Basil Hall, *Travels in North America in the Years 1827 and 1828*, vol. 2 (Edinburgh, 1829), 43–47.

7. Vera, *Our American Cousins at Home* (London: Sampson, et al., 1873), 1. A closer relationship was not just rebuilt by improved transportation but also by the fact that the 'troubled Anglo-American relations of twenty-five years earlier had largely disappeared into the past' and, allegedly, that British condescension 'to their American cousins ... was generally in a spirit of far greater sympathy.' See Bradbury, 115.

8. Captain Frederick Marryat, *Diary in America*, ed. Jules Sanger (1839; London: Vane, 1960), 12.

9. Appleby, 420.

10. Ralph Waldo Emerson, 'The Young American,' *Nature: Addresses and Lectures* (Boston: Houghton, Mifflin, 1903), 364.

11. Emerson, 'The Young American,' 363–64.

12. W. E. Baxter, *America and the Americans* (London, 1855), 46–47.

13. Appleby, 421.

14. 'An American Lady' [Thomas G. Cary], *A Letter to a Lady in France* (Boston, 1843), 26–27; Emerson, 'The American Scholar,' 392.

15. Dickens, 79–99. It is worth keeping in mind Tocqueville's idea that democracy was the reason why all Americans were called to leave agriculture in favour of industry: Alexis de Tocqueville, *Democracy in America* (1835, 1840; Ware-Wordsworth, 1998), 249–52.

16. Thomas Hamilton, *Men and Manners in America*, vol. 2 (Edinburgh, 1833), 181; Marvin Fisher, *Workshops in the Wilderness: The European Response to American Industrialization, 1830–1860* (New York: Oxford University Press, 1967), 172.

17. Bruce Mazlish, 'Progress: A Historical and Critical Perspective,' *Progress: Fact or Illusion*, ed. Leo Marx and Bruce Mazlish (Ann Arbor: University of Michigan Press, 1998), 35.

18. David E. Nye, *American Technological Sublime* (Cambridge, MA: MIT Press, 1994), 46–54.

19. Alfred Bunn, *Old England and New England: In a Series of Views taken on the Spot*, vol. 2 (London, 1853), 126–28.

20. C. Vann Woodward, *The Old World's New World* (Oxford: Oxford University Press, 1991), vii.

21. 'An American Lady,' *Change for the American Notes: In Letters from London to New York* (London, 1843), iii.

22. William Gore Ouseley, *Remarks on the Statistics and Political Institutions of the United States* (London, 1832), 45; John McGregor, *The Progress of America, from the Discovery by Columbus to the year 1846*, vol. 1 (London, 1847), 199–200.

23. Dickens, 113.

24. Appleby, 420.

25. Dickens, 113; Captain Frederick Marryat, *A Diary in America with Remarks on Its Institutions*, ed. Sydney Jackman (1839; New York: Knopf, 1962), 368; Nye, 54.

26. Dickens, 174; Marryat, ed. Sanger, 42–3, 265; Marryat, ed. Jackman, 371.

27. Anon., *Some Notes on America to Be Rewritten: Suggested, with Respect, to Charles Dickens, Esq.* (Philadelphia, 1868), 10–11.

28. Woodward, viii; Dickens's dedication was deleted from the book in 1859; Dickens, 45.

29. Emerson, 'The Young American,' 392.

30. Richard Hofstadter, *The Age of Reform: From Bryan to FDR* (New York: Vintage, 1955), 35–36. Interestingly, though, in a preceding passage, Hofstadter explicitly links technology to a perpetual American quest for improvement and a corresponding dissatisfaction with 'the evils of life.' He goes on: 'Americans ... are forever restlessly pitting themselves against them, demanding changes, improvements, remedies, but not often with sufficient sense of the limits that the human condition will in the end insistently impose upon us. This restlessness is most valuable and has its most successful consequence wherever dealing with *things* is involved, in

technology and invention, in productivity, in the ability to meet needs and provide comforts. In this sphere we have surpassed all other peoples' (16).

31. Richard L. Rapson, *Britons View America: Travel Commentary, 1860–1935* (Seattle: University of Washington Press, 1971), 4.
32. Two recent examples would be Jonathan Freedland, *Bring Home The Revolution: The Case For a British Republic*, new ed. (London: Fourth Estate, 1999); and Gavin Esler, *The United States of Anger*, new ed. (Harmondsworth: Penguin, 1998).
33. 'An American Lady,' *Change*, v.
34. Marryat, ed. Sanger, 38.
35. Woodward, 3.
36. Appleby, 419; Woodward, 18–21.
37. Byron Shafer, ed., *Is America Different? A New Look at American Exceptionalism* (Oxford: Clarendon, 1991), v.

# Newt's Clean Slate, or American Exceptionalism in the Information Age

*Eric Guthey*

If we can reform ourselves, there is every reason to believe our best days are still ahead. A renewed and reinvigorated America that educates all its children could compete with any country. An America that has replaced the culture of poverty and violence with a culture of opportunity would be the safest, most prosperous place on the globe. An entrepreneurial America that embraces science and innovation would progress at a fantastic pace, opening a vastly greater range of choices to its people than any civilization in history. Such a revitalized America could sustain its military and diplomatic responsibilities with ease and still find the world eager to be led toward greater prosperity, security, and freedom. Once again, America would be the last, best hope on earth.

Erstwhile history professor and Speaker of the House of Representatives Newt Gingrich opened his 1995 book, *To Renew America,* with a litany of such appeals to a vision of America as the 'last, best hope on earth,' fashioning himself as an ardent reformer and a card-carrying American exceptionalist of the first order. The book – for which Gingrich eventually had to turn down a $4.5 million advance from a publishing company owned by Rupert Murdoch amidst cries of influence peddling and conflict of interest – initially enjoyed twelve weeks on the *New York Times* best seller list, seven of those in the number one spot.

But the erratic speaker fell from his pinnacle of political and popular grace in the fall of 1995 after he publicly blamed the Democrats and the welfare state for the grisly murder of a Chicago mother, her two children, and her unborn baby, and after he admitted that he had precipitated a shut-down of the Federal government largely because he didn't like the seating arrangements on Air Force One during the 25 hour flight back and forth

*Marks of Distinction: American Exceptionalism Revisited*, ed. Dale Carter, *The Dolphin* 32, pp. 137–63. © 2001 by Aarhus University Press, Denmark. ISBN 87 7288 383 9; ISSN 0106 4487.

from the funeral of Israeli Prime Minister Yitzhak Rabin. Soon thereafter remaindered on the book shelves along with the presidential aspirations of its author (at least for the time being), *To Renew America* has been pilloried by critics, and with good reason. In an article in *The New York Review of Books,* Joan Didion used Gingrich's own clichéd and self-contradictory words to ridicule his thought patterns as relentlessly schematic, largely occult, and pointlessly specific, observing at one point, 'we have here a man who once calculated the odds on the survival of his second marriage at 53 to 47.'[1]

When Didion pounces on Gingrich's advocacy of honeymoons in space, his effusive praise of the uniquely American spirit of companies that have contributed hundreds of thousands of dollars to his campaign coffers, or his description of how America is a land of opportunity because it might soon be possible to learn over the internet how to make batik you can sell at the mall, her acerbic glee is infectious. But she herself points out that in his 'Renewing American Civilization' video lecture series, Gingrich declares that 'there is an American exceptionalism that can be understood through history.'[2] As intellectually and ethically challenged as *To Renew America* may be, then, it still deserves scrutiny as an example of what has become of American exceptionalism, still alive and kicking as the doctrine approaches another millennium.

In the book, Gingrich uses exceptionalist ideology to pillory the very notion of a multicultural approach to American identity as historically suspect, socially detrimental and downright anti-American. In fact, he goes out of his way to commit every heresy Joyce Appleby deplores in her 1992 *Journal of American History* article 'Recovering America's Historic Diversity: Beyond Exceptionalism.'[3] For this reason, Appleby's analysis can serve to delineate the contours of Gingrich's particular brand of American exceptionalism. A closer look at Gingrich's book serves to highlight certain blind spots in Appleby's own vision as well.

As David Nye points out in this volume, Appleby fails to discuss the crucial relationship between technology and exceptionalism. Gingrich's exceptionalism, however, pivots on the potentials he perceives behind new information and communication technologies. Mention of technology also points toward a weakness professors Gingrich and Appleby share. They both work from an understanding of American exceptionalism that seems to have sprung full-grown from the eighteenth century and ossified at the latest by the 1830s. Consequently, they both ignore historical pressures that have shaped or altered exceptionalist doctrines since that time.

Although he is clearly the less distinguished historian, Gingrich's static and anachronistic understanding of exceptionalism is the more striking, since his whole book hinges on the great historical/technological transformation he calls 'The Third Wave.' Gingrich's use of this term (borrowed from his futurist gurus Alvin and Heidi Toffler) is highly simplistic and wracked with technological determinism. But by another name we might call it the shift towards late capitalism, towards a regime of flexible accumulation, or towards a high-tech, postmodern service economy centered on new information and communications technologies. The central irony of Gingrich's book is that he preaches *both* American exceptionalism and the Third Wave at the same time, although the two work at cross purposes. That is, the globalizing and decentralizing tendencies at work within the shift towards this new kind of economic order threaten to dissolve the usefulness of the nation state and further confuse and fragment the already-problematic notion of an American national identity itself.

This contradiction arises in large part from the history of the interaction between exceptionalist ideology and the development of new technologies of communication in the American context. In the first part of this essay I will measure what Appleby would consider Gingrich's oppressively unifying ideology against the three insistent themes of American exceptionalism she outlines – 'the autonomy of the individual with its accompanying disparagement of dependency; the clean slate with its implicit rejection of the past; and the concept of a uniform human nature with its ascription of universality to particular social traits.'[4] Next I will review how these same themes appear as constants within the social construction of new technologies of communication, from the telegraph all the way up to the internet. American reformers have celebrated each of these in turn as a force that would wipe the slate clean of all unjust power relations and simultaneously unify the population, empower the individual citizen, and secure the nation's historical preeminence as an exemplar of democracy. But powerful corporate interests have always also been busy promoting their own vision of a communications revolution with exceptionalist rhetoric. These competing exceptionalisms became fused together during the broadcast reform era of the late 1960s and early 1970s, when corporate America succeeded in cementing into conventional wisdom the notion that progressive reform and individual empowerment can result only from deregulation and the machinations of an unfettered marketplace. As the heir to this tradition and the premiere contemporary spokesman for this point of view, Newt Gingrich needs to be understood in the context of these historical developments.

*To Renew America* opens in the manner of a jeremiad, describing in the starkest terms possible the moral crisis facing American society. 'Either we will pull ourselves together for the effort or we will continue to decay,' Gingrich predicts. 'There is virtually no middle ground.'[5] He opts for the former path, of course, and declares that the great challenge facing the nation today is the imperative to 'renew and reassert American civilization.' All such alarmist cries of decline presuppose some former state of grace, and indeed, Gingrich presupposes the existence of one continuous American civilization which he wastes no time in celebrating as 'the greatest the planet has ever known.' That greatness, Gingrich insists, rested on one 'clear sense of what it meant to be an American,' and on the strength of 'a set of commonly accepted legal and cultural principles.' Those principles had existed 'from the arrival of the English colonists in 1607 until 1965,' Gingrich states with a semblance of historical precision, and appear crystallized in such diverse sources as de Tocqueville's *Democracy in America* and Norman Rockwell's paintings of the 1940s and 1950s (25).

As Joan Didion has pointed out, Gingrich's thoughts most often arrange themselves according to the self-help, outline form favored by motivational and managerial therapists using overhead transparencies – he is constantly isolating two choices which give way to six challenges, which themselves stem from the five basic principles, all of which relate crucially to three historical 'waves' or epochs, and so on. His list of the five basic principles that form the heart of American civilization (in the lectures they appear as 'Five Pillars') reads as follows:

1. The common understanding we share about who we are and how we came to be.
2. The ethic of individual responsibility.
3. The spirit of entrepreneurial free enterprise.
4. The spirit of invention and discovery.
5. Pragmatism and the concern for craft and excellence, as expressed most recently in the teachings of Edwards Deming. (33)

Gingrich's list is tautological: the first basic principle that provides the basis for our common understanding we share about who we are is none other than 'the common understanding we share about who we are.' His list is also fundamentally confrontational, since the only precision his otherwise vague principles exhibit derives from their immediate opposition to some trumped up and demonized other that threatens the continued viability of American civilization. Thus, in his elaboration on the first principle, which he calls 'the spiritual dimension,' Gingrich pillories the rest of the world for not maintaining the correct relationship to the Creator. 'In nearly all countries, power belongs to the state and is occasionally loaned to individuals,' he says. 'In America, power comes from God to the individual and is loaned to the state.... It would be hard to imagine a greater difference in first principles' (34). In this manner Gingrich claims divine sanction for 'who we are,' and also legitimizes the second principle of American civilization, individual responsibility. 'Precisely because our rights are endowed by our Creator,' Gingrich explains, 'the individual burden of responsibility borne by each citizen is greater than in any country.' Here the counter-cultural left, contemporary liberals, and pregnant teenagers come under fire for blaming everything on 'society' and the modern welfare state receives special mention as a system that subsidizes idleness and violates the ethic that everyone should work hard to improve their own lot without government help. 'By blaming everything on "society," contemporary liberals are really trying to escape the personal responsibility that comes with being an American,' Gingrich admonishes. 'If you are not prepared to shoulder personal responsibility, then you are not prepared to participate in American civilization' (39).

'True Americans' are innately prepared to shoulder the individual responsibility that derives from their special relationship with God, Gingrich continues, because they share in the uniquely American spirit of free enterprise, his third principle. Gingrich credits American entrepreneurial genius, the desire to get up in the morning and 'invent a slightly better mousetrap for the world,' with the happy fact that at every level of American society, 'people can improve their own lot.' Again, the flaccid platitude sharpens its rhetorical teeth on its supposed opposite, as Gingrich insists that unlike Europe and other class-dominated cultures, 'we have no caste system, no class requirements, no regulated professions, no barriers to entry' to hold us back from entrepreneurial achievement. In France, Gingrich explains, only graduates of the École Nationale d'Administration can hold important government positions, but in the U.S. 'even a professor from a small college in Georgia can aspire to the highest levels of government' (41). He concludes:

Generosity, trust, optimism and hard work – these are the elements that drive the American entrepreneurial system, creating the most powerful and vibrant economy the world has ever known. Unfortunately, this isn't as easy as it used to be. Taxes, regulation, and litigation have all thrown a blanket over the entrepreneurial spirit. Elite criticisms of the can-do spirit have undermined that ethic. Credentialing of the professions has raised barriers to entrepreneurial inventiveness. The welfare system has sapped the spirit of the poor and made it harder to climb the first rungs of the economic ladder. (43)

Although Gingrich insists that a 'true American' confronted with a problem will never ask 'Who can I blame this on?,' a consistent pattern of blame undergirds his book. Every time he cites an American virtue, he immediately indicts an elite cabal of nefarious, left-leaning intellectuals and counter-cultural special interest groups for conspiring to undermine it. On the very first page of *To Renew America*, he states:

> While we as a people were winning our battles around the world, here at home our elites were deserting us. For the past thirty years, we have been influenced to abandon our culture and seem to have lost faith in the core values, traditions, and institutions of our civilization The intellectual nonsense propagated since 1965 – in the media, on university campuses, even among our religious and political leaders – now threatens to cripple our ability to teach the next generation to be Americans. (3, 4)

So the problem stems from the 1960s when the counterculture began to use 'situational ethics' and 'deconstructionism' to repudiate solid middle-class values and universal standards of right and wrong 'Multiculturalism switched the emphasis from proclaiming allegiance to the common culture to proclaiming the virtues (real or imagined) of a particular ethnicity, sect, or tribe,' Gingrich complains, while 'traditional history has been replaced by the notion that every group is entitled to its own version of the past' and 'moral standards have been replaced by "role-playing"' (30). In Gingrich's mind, these heretical kinds of thinking have led to the dissolution of the consensus about what American civilization should be. In the context of his jeremiad, this represents the breaking of the covenant, and the reason why American civilization has to be renewed at all.

Joyce Appleby traces how exceptionalism originated in Europe even before America became a nation, but only began to flourish as a unifying ideology on the other side of the Atlantic in the mid–1790s, when it became a potent weapon in a plebeian radical attack on the aristocratic pretensions of a federalist elite. Exactly two centuries later, Newt Gingrich carries on this legacy of exceptionalist attack politics, painting himself as a representative of the common people, and directing his animus against the straw figure of a 'liberal elite,' a cadre of counter culture intellectuals, multiculturalists, and Washington insiders who want to promote teenage pregnancy, raise taxes, increase the size of government and take as much power as possible away from the individual American. By his own design a modern-day version of Appleby's 'undistinguished citizen,' Gingrich has capitalized on such attack rhetoric to effect a change of personnel within Congress, to defeat venerable traditions of authority within the House of Representatives, and to paint himself as a hero for pulling the responsibility for the national political agenda down the social ladder.

Like Appleby's propagandists of American democracy, Gingrich has achieved this feat by taking full advantage of a 'dense new communications network' – in his instance, cable television, satellite delivery systems, and right-wing talk radio – in order to wrest away 'the control over information and opinions once exercised exclusively by an elite.'[6] Along the way he has offended even many conservatives with his crass self-assertion and bombastic new form of politics. He also has succeeded, to borrow Appleby's words, in elevating 'what might be construed elsewhere as uninterestingly plebeian' to the level of 'a new goal for mankind.'[7]

The three central themes Appleby perceives behind the nascent doctrine of American exceptionalism all resurface in Gingrich's rhetoric. The first of these – the autonomy of the individual with its accompanying disparagement of dependency – crystallizes into Gingrich's second pillar, and motivates his attacks on welfare. 'The classic American is an independent, self-reliant, hard working, honest person of no great wealth or social status,' Gingrich tells us, but 'nothing could be less traditionally American than the modern welfare system,' because it breeds a cycle of dependency and 'violates the American ethic that everyone should work hard' (39). The certainty with which Gingrich advances these opinions brings to the fore the second theme Appleby isolates. 'By construing their own liberty as liberation from historic institutions,' says Appleby of the early exceptionalists, 'the enthusiasts of democracy made the United States the pilot society for the world.' Gingrich likewise universalizes particular American social traits as normative and proscriptive ideals for all humankind, and then proceeds to use this same self-evident universality to turn dissent into deviation and thereby to exclude whole groups of Americans from his definition of American national character altogether. This is how he comes to the conclusion that welfare recipients and those who swear allegiance to a particular ethnicity, sect or tribe are not 'true Americans.' The real bad apples to be sorted out of the bunch, of course, are the liberal elite who have conspired to pollute and degrade American civilization with their deviant ideals.

The third and most important exceptionalist theme Joyce Appleby highlights is the notion of the clean slate, with its rejection of the past and of all European cultural baggage, and with its vision of a new frontier where all of the old institutions and problems would simply vanish. 'The clean slate suggests most powerfully a freedom of choice – the freedom to be the designer of one's own life unaided or impeded by others,' Appleby explains. 'It also denied the force of history, for it is past actions that clutter up the metaphorical slate.' Garry Wills has pointed out that in spite of Gingrich's animus towards intellectual elites, he insists upon his status as a history professor in order to legitimize his ideas ('How many of us have taken a history class,' asks Wills, 'in which the professor tells you in class, every class, sometimes several times in one session, that he is a professor?'[8]) As Wills also points out, Gingrich's approach to American history is 'celebratory, based on static symbols for enduring values.' Gingrich does away with those bothersome historical realities that do not affirm conservative values by means of his own particular brand of clean-slatism. For Gingrich, the slate is wiped clean by technology, and his peculiar posture towards technology bears special mention, as it is the source of his most 'occult' ideas.

'Imagine a morning in just a decade or so,' Gingrich encourages readers of *To Renew America*. 'You wake up to a wall-size, high-definition television showing surf off Maui (this is my favorite island – you can pick your own scene).' As the day progresses, Gingrich tells us, we never have to go outside, since we can 'do Stairmaster while catching up on the morning news,' and we can all telecommute to work from home via computer, thus avoiding rush hour traffic. When you are sick, you sit in your diagnostic chair and communicate with the local health clinic,' he predicts. 'Sensors take your blood pressure, analyze a blood sample, or do throat cultures.' Since medical information systems have become so advanced, we won't really need any doctors, and we can save money by deciding on our own treatment. Legal trouble? No problem, says Gingrich 'you can write your own will, file your own adoption papers, form your own partnership or corporation – all with software programs available in your home.' According to Gingrich, these technological developments will cause no great displacement of workers in the medical or legal professions. 'Fortunately, since most lawyers were reasonably smart and well-educated people, they have been able to find other lines of work' (55).

Gingrich is clearly in the thrall of a space age, even science-fiction conception of technology and technological change. His formulations are stridently technologically deterministic and naive, sometimes even childlike in the extreme. 'Absent an idea that can be sold at Disney World,' Joan Didion observes, 'he has tended to lose interest.'[9] At one point later in the book he suggests that it would not be all that impossible to construct a real Jurassic Park, and that such an endeavor would be 'one of the most spectacular accomplishments of human history' (190). Gingrich's romance with technology becomes most literal in his bizarre description of the possibility of honeymoons in space, an idea he recycles from his 1984 book, *Window of Opportunity:*

I believe that space tourism will be a common fact of life during the adulthood of children born this year, that honeymoons in space will be the vogue by 2020. Imagine weightlessness and its effects and you will understand some of its attractions. Imagine looking out at the Earth from your honeymoon suite and you will understand even more why it will be a big item. (192)

No commentator can fail to marvel at how ridiculous Gingrich appears willing to sound, but the Speaker's unself-conscious inanity tends to distract attention away from the significant development in the kind of exceptionalist thought he advances. As Tom Byers and James Mendelsohn stress elsewhere in this volume, land, wilderness, and the frontier have often served as the foundational justification for exceptionalism itself. Gingrich's exceptionalism eclipses the natural world altogether. He doesn't invoke the surf off the island of Maui, but rather a wall-sized television image thereof. He dreams of replicant dinosaurs. He is so distanced from the natural world that in his fantasies, even the fertility ritual of the honeymoon itself can only gaze on the earth from space – a great view, no doubt, but a view none the same, and a very distant one at that. There is no direct experience of nature in Gingrich's imaginary future, which leads Joan Didion to describe it as 'a kind of endless Delta hub.'[10] Without any intimate connection to the iconic American landscape, we have here an exceptionalism of a very different order.

The concept that replaces the land in Gingrich is the Third Wave Information Revolution, this radical transformation or discontinuity as he calls it, that allows him to summarize all of world history in a few short paragraphs and then to chuck it out of the window altogether, since it simply doesn't apply anymore. Citing his friends Heidi and Alvin Toffler, authors of *Future Shock, The Third Wave,* and a host of other pop-futurist analyses of technological change, Gingrich explains that 'the transformation we are experiencing is so large and historic that it can be compared with only two other great eras of human history – the Agricultural Revolution and the Industrial Revolution' (52). As he elaborates further in his foreword to the Toffler's 1994 book, *Creating a New Civilization: The Politics of The Third Wave:*

The Tofflers correctly understand that development and distribution of information has now become the central productivity and power activity of the human race. From world financial markets to the worldwide, twenty-four-hour-a-day distribution of news via CNN to the break-throughs of the biological revolution and their impact on health and agricultural production – on virtually every front we see the information revolution changing the fabric, pace and substance of our lives.[11]

The Third Wave functions as Gingrich's New Frontier, clean slate, and *deus ex machina*, automatically returning America to its important core values. According to Gingrich, for example, contemporary liberalism is an outdated, 'Second Wave' phenomenon, and the coming of the Third Wave will discredit liberal ideals once and for all. 'While the Industrial Revolution herded people into gigantic social institutions – big corporations, big unions, big government,' he explains, 'the Information Revolution is breaking up these giants and leading us back to something that is, strangely enough, much more like de Tocqueville's 1830s America.' In this 'Back to the Future' scenario, every new technological change promotes greater individual autonomy and personal choice, and Gingrich harbors no doubts about where the benefits of the Third Wave Information Age will accrue. Americans should not fear the rush of changes associated with the Third Wave, he insists, since those changes will restore the nation to its rightful preeminence as a world leader. 'The coming of the 3rd Wave brings potential for enormous improvement in the lifestyle choices of most Americans,' Gingrich predicts. 'If we can grasp the true significance of these changes, we can lead the world into the Information Age and leave our children a country unmatched in wealth, power and opportunity' (57, 7).

In classic exceptionalist fashion Gingrich attaches such weight to his concept of the Third Wave that his every observation becomes universalized and invested with certitude and inevitability. 'Aside from the Third Waves concept there is no effective system of analysis which makes sense of the frustration and confusion which characterizes politics and government virtually everywhere in the industrial world,' he asserts in his foreword to the Tofflers' book. 'There is no language to communicate the problems we face, no vision to outline the future towards which we should strive, and no program to help accelerate and make easier the transition.'[12]

At first glance, Gingrich's visions of the future may seem downright wacky, but in the context of the history of the reception of new technologies in America, they appear quite familiar. American culture always has made room for those with an almost unswerving faith in technological progress and in the notion that advances in technology translate directly into advances in the perceived democratic nature of American society and in the ultimate triumph of the 'American way of life.' Enthusiasts of this point of view, especially those within the media industry, have reserved their most exuberant praise for the various technologies of communication, promising that those technologies would unify the nation, promote the democratic exchange of ideas, and champion each individual citizen's right to free speech under the First Amendment. Newt Gingrich did not import an enthusiasm over new technologies of communication into American exceptionalist rhetoric himself. Rather, he stands in a long line of American exceptionalists hopeful that some new technological fix will wipe the slate clean of aberrant historical developments and return the nation to the kind of imagined Toquevillian idyll he holds so dear.

For example, as Daniel Czitrom points out in *Media and the American Mind*, the 'universal communication' made possible by the advent of the telegraph in the 1850s, was celebrated as a force that would bring the Republic closer together, help fulfill America's 'manifest destiny,' and, in the words of the editor of *American Telegraph Magazine*, allow for 'nearly all our vast and widespread populations [to be] bound together, not merely by political institutions but by a Telegraph and Lightning-like affinity of intelligence and sympathy, that renders us emphatically "ONE PEOPLE" everywhere.'[13] Another commentator in an 1858 issue of the *New Englander* declared that the telegraph 'gives the preponderance of power to the nations representing the highest elements in humanity.'[14] By 1866, however, Western Union had become the largest firm in American history to that point, and its monopolistic stranglehold on the glorious new technology of telegraphy allowed it to charge exorbitant rates for its use; by the

1880s Bell telephone had done almost the same for telephone communications.

In this climate, Susan Douglas points out in *Inventing American Broadcasting*, hopes for the realization of the democratic potential assumed to lie dormant in communications technology, or at least the rhetorical expression thereof, were transferred to the new technology of wireless telegraphy, which was introduced in 1899. Power-hungry trusts could easily control lines and wires, reasoned many critics of Western Union, but corporations would have a more difficult time monopolizing the airwaves, which were often described in the popular press as a sort of mysterious ether vested with magical powers. When wireless technology itself evolved into the institution of broadcast radio, and individual sets became available for the reception of sound transmissions in the home in the early 1920s, commentators again declared that communications technology would finally spread 'mutual understanding to all sections of the country, unifying our thoughts, ideals, and purposes, making us a strong and well-knit people.'[15] Douglas isolates the pattern according to which new technologies of communication would be introduced again and again:

Radio was portrayed as an autonomous force, capable of revolutionizing American culture. It was a machine that would make history. It was also portrayed as a technology without a history. Rarely, in those heady, breathless articles about the radio boom, was reference made to the twenty-five years of technical, economic, and cultural experimentation that had led to and produced radio broadcasting. Radio was thus presented as an invention not burdened by a past or shackled to the constraining conventions of the established social order, but as an invention free to reshape, on its own terms, the patterns of American life.[16]

Not surprisingly, the advent of the ability to transmit not only sound, but images as well, gave rise to a similar flourish of enthusiasm. In a speech in 1931, RCA executive David Sarnoff waxed grandiloquent about the virtues of the next major development in the communications and broadcasting industry:

When television has fulfilled its ultimate destiny, man's sense of physical limitation will be swept away and his boundaries of sight and hearing will be the limits of the earth itself. With this may come a new horizon, a new philosophy, a new sense of freedom, and greatest of all, perhaps, a finer and broader understanding between all the peoples of the world.[17]

Willard D. Rowland Jr. has stressed the intimate connections between this faith in communications technology as an agent capable of restoring an ideal democratic community and the core beliefs of American progressivism. Some forty years ago Richard Hofstadter isolated the general theme of the progressive movement as 'the effort to restore a type of economic individualism and political democracy that was widely believed to have existed earlier in America and to have been destroyed by the great corporation and the corrupt political machine, and with that restoration to bring back a kind of morality and civic purity that was also believed to have been lost.'[18] The rationalizing tendencies within the progressive movement, Rowland elaborates, led it to cling to the notion that modern man, possessed of an analytical mind and the latest advances in science, technology and education, could yoke the power of modernization and industrialization to the task of restoring the communitarian ideal. 'Underneath the progressive program was an explicit faith in a reconstituted human nature, and an implicit belief in the utility of modern communications,' explains Rowland. 'That faith in the ameliorative power of communications carried forward with redoubled strength into the coming age of radio and television.'[19]

This enthusiasm served as a significant shaping force behind Progressive Era communications legislation. The Radio Act of 1927 and the Communications Act of 1934 started from the notion that the electromagnetic spectrum constituted a limited natural resource owned in common by all the people of the United States. Lawmakers and regulators insisted that since the spectrum could support only a certain number of broadcast outlets operating on certain frequencies, those licensed to use it must act as trustees of that precious resource serving in the public interest. The doctrine of the public interest in broadcasting held up an ideal of a truly democratic broadcast system managed by private companies serving in the public interest according to the community-oriented principle of localism. That principle held that local broadcasters must fulfill their public trustee function by serving their individual communities with programs of local interest and concern and by providing for a broad range of local expression over the airwaves.

Jeffersonian ideals of local broadcasters serving an enlightened citizenry may have undergirded the framing of the earliest federal communications legislation, but as Robert Horwitz stresses in *The Irony of Regulatory Reform,* the power of the communications industry has always been such that federal regulation has done little more than graft these kinds of lofty egalitarian and communitarian principles onto a preexisting industrial structure characterized by intense concentrations of capital and private ownership.[20] After all, the communications industry had had more than three quarters of a century to grow into a monopolistic and profit-hungry monolith by the time federal regulation began to develop in earnest. In this situation mutually beneficial turf agreements hashed out between the communications giants were presented to federal regulators as done deals. Rather than challenge these collusive arrangements, the state wrote them into federal law in such a way that what had been merely profitable for the interested parties came to seem natural and inevitable.

For this reason, Susan Douglas maintains, the romantic rhetoric applied to technological advances 'helped legitimate the private, corporate control of machines as the only equitable and progressive method of management.'[21] Most of the money spent to explore and develop these new technologies (especially television) came from these same corporations, which further pushed the resulting advances in communication into the service of private profit. The federal government also encouraged the development of a private, commercial infrastructure for the communications industry by means of promotion, subsidy, and sanctioning of corporate control. One important example of this is the manner in which the US Navy handed all of its patents for long distance radio communication over to General Electric after World War I, leading to the creation of the Radio Corporation of America, which would dominate radio and television for years to come.[22]

Committed to a market-based system by the sheer power of the communications conglomerates such as RCA, yet blinded to market realities by the swirl of rhetoric surrounding communications technologies, federal communications regulation failed to address squarely the two most salient aspects of the broadcasting industry itself. The first of these was the fact that money would have to be made, and this would end up being achieved by advertising. The lofty hopes and ideals surrounding broadcasting initially created a situation in which all parties involved agreed that advertising would sully the new media with impure motives and crass moneymaking. None other than David Sarnoff, the president of RCA, originally called for the financing of radio programming by means of a national fund fueled by a percentage of the profits realized by radio manufacturers and dealers. As late as 1924, then-Secretary of Commerce Herbert Hoover stated that 'the quickest way to kill broadcasting would be to use it for direct advertising.'[23] But such attacks on the direct advertising of consumer goods had the effect of smoothing the way for the 'indirect selling' implicit in commercially sponsored programming, which quickly became the norm.

Manufacturers soon became enamored of the effectiveness with which attaching their names to popular broadcasts could help boost sales, and by 1925 nearly half of the 547 radio stations in operation in the United States sold air time to commercial sponsors.[24] By 1927, the resistance to direct advertising had been overcome, and admen like Edgar Felix could exclaim of the practice, 'What a glorious opportunity for the advertising man to spread his sales propaganda... American business men, because of radio, are provided with a latch key to nearly every home in the United States.'[25] Federal regulation 'in the public interest' clearly encouraged such a presumptuously invasive attitude. In his work on the broadcast sponsor, Erik Barnouw quotes a 1935 study in the *Harvard Business Review* which concluded that 'the Federal

Radio Commission has interpreted the concept of public interest so as to favor in actual practice one particular group ... the commercial broadcasters.'[26]

The second reality of the broadcasting marketplace was that *lots* of money had to be made, both because broadcasting (especially television) is very expensive and because companies always want to make more money. This was achieved by the creation of broadcast networks. Networking allowed broadcasters to take advantage of massive economies of scale, spreading the cost of production out amongst a number of distribution outlets and offering advertisers blanket coverage in a variety of markets at once during choice hours of the broadcast schedule. AT&T began experimenting with the connection of local radio stations by means of coaxial cables for special events as early as 1922. After 1926, when AT&T got out of the business of owning radio stations in exchange for the exclusive right to interconnect broadcast networks over its wires, RCA, Westinghouse, and General Electric formed the National Broadcasting Company (NBC), which would operate both a 'Red' and a 'Blue' radio network (the government would later force the latter to break off and become the American Broadcasting Network [ABC]). By the time the Columbia Broadcasting System formed in 1929, less than 20% of all radio stations had affiliated themselves with a network, but those same stations raked in a full 72% of the $27 million spent on radio advertising.[27]

The preeminence of chain broadcasting flew in the face of the regulatory principle of localism, because it took almost all of the decision-making power over programming away from individual, local broadcast licensees and handed it over to large national corporations. Networking ensured that the big money in broadcast advertising would come primarily from national coverage, and this gave national advertisers a strong say over programming content and left local television broadcasters with little incentive to serve the idiosyncratic needs of their own community in any real sense. By the 1960s, then, federal broadcasting regulation 'in the public interest' came to protect a centralized system of three advertising-supported, national television networks as the American, democratic system of television. The big three television networks held an oligopoly over what the public saw, and treated television viewers as a mass market. Moreover the Federal Communications Commission used the regulatory principle of localism to justify actions that protected the big three networks – who by their very existence effectively sabotaged any hope of realizing a truly community-based, democratic television system. As Horwitz concludes, the very ideals undergirding federal communications regulation led those who framed it to 'misconstrue the nature of a capitalist communications system,' while the image of the broadcaster 'in the mythic haze of the small-town Jeffersonian public sphere served only to veil the actual practices and consequences of a commercially organized, national system of network broadcasting.'[28]

It did not take much to recognize that something had gone awry, and the same ideals that undergirded the network system eventually ignited a movement to reform it. Amidst the general climate of citizen activism that characterized the late 1960s, a loose but broad-based and diverse coalition of minority groups and community organizations now labeled collectively as the broadcast reform movement sought to challenge the regulatory status quo on such matters as minority programming and hiring practices, television violence, the nature of children's programming, truth in advertising, and the responsiveness of the networks and their affiliates to community input. These groups pursued three strategies to achieve their goals. The first two were technical and legal attempts to hold the broadcast regulatory process accountable to its own first principles. Many community groups, armed with the rhetoric of the Communications Act, sought to block the renewal of individual broadcast licenses by filing 'petitions to deny' on the basis that the broadcasters had not lived up to their public interest obligations. Other groups argued that the FCC's Fairness Doctrine gave them the right of mandatory access to the airwaves to express their views. Neither of these strategies met with much direct success. The 342 petitions to deny filed between 1971 and 1973 did not result in the suspension of a single broadcast license, and the FCC has only taken away one such license in its entire history. Although attempts to gain citizen access to the airwaves eventually led to a complete ban on cigarette advertising on television, the Supreme Court ruled in 1973 that the public did not have anything like a mandatory right of access to the broadcast airwaves.[29]

The third front on which the members of the broadcast reform movement sought to advance their various interests ended up exerting the most impact on the industry – although certainly not in the way the reformers themselves may have envisioned – because it returned to the core of cultural beliefs concerning the transformative and beneficent power of technology that had undergirded the formation of federal communications regulation in the first place. The same dissatisfaction with the power of the networks that had inspired the wave of petitions to deny and the many attempts to gain access and equal time also gave rise to a movement to seek out viable alternatives to commercial network broadcasting altogether. This impulse clearly lay behind the Public Broadcasting Act of 1967, which united struggling educational stations from around the country into the Public Broadcasting Service. The search for alternatives caught fire when it united with the notion that new technologies of television signal delivery could circumvent the traditional broadcasting structure altogether, rendering the power of the commercial networks obsolete and ushering in a democratic communications revolution. Specifically, this 'new technologies' rhetoric attached itself to the expansion of cable systems and to the development of satellite communications .

Cable had been around since as early as 1948, but the new enthusiasm ignored its technical, economic, political and cultural entanglements in the television industry over the past twenty years and treated it as a technology without a history, very much in the manner radio had been celebrated in the 1920s. The new technologies rhetoric seized upon cable's ability to import multiple channels into the home as a means of finally insuring the kind of diversity that would serve the public interest, giving a voice to minorities, the elderly, handicapped persons, and other previously disenfranchised groups through electronic conferences and 'town meetings.' It also maintained that the technical capability of two-way communication over cable would allow individuals and groups to 'talk back' to their television sets, instantly ushering in a democratic communications revolution that would solve the problem of public access.

The grandiose heights to which the new technologies rhetoric could soar is well reflected in Don LeDuc's introduction to his otherwise sober study of cable regulation, published in 1973. Enthusiasm for cable had not arisen because it offered a closed-circuit means of distribution that would allow for selective price discrimination, LeDuc argued, but because of its ability to provide the public with an abundance of viewing alternatives from which to choose. He went on:

The competitive strength of cable, then, seems based upon the same fundamental human urge, an apparently insatiable desire for ever more extensive communications service, which has spurred the evolution of each successive mass medium since the advent of the industrial age in Western society. It may be that industrialization, in diluting the strength of the oral tradition, instilled in modern man a craving for the certitude that was once drawn from countless springs of communal and kinship custom – a thirst no narrow and mechanized message channel has the capacity to quench. In this context the cable medium could represent the first communications force capable of ending man's Tantalus-like quest; its vast array of channels offering the diverse, variant, and thus more human message bonds which mass-produced units of entertainment and news have supplanted but have failed to replace.[30]

Horwitz points out that this kind of rhetoric was not the exclusive province of idealistic liberals and grass-roots organizers. Free market economists waxed just as enthusiastic about cable in studies funded by such sources as the Rand Corporation, the Alfred Sloan Foundation, the Ford Foundation, and the John and Mary Markle Foundation.[31] And the Johnson, Nixon, and Ford administrations all formed task forces and commissions that strongly advocated the development of new technologies, especially cable, as the solution to the problems plaguing broad-casting in the US. These groups helped channel the debate over broadcast reform in the direction of neo-libertarian economic rhetoric, whereby a free and open marketplace would solve all of the problems of corporate perfidy and public disenfranchisement in broadcasting by effecting the efficient development of new technologies of delivery.

This kind of rhetoric gained a wide hearing because it comported well with the designs of the major players in the communications industry themselves, whose interests lay in quieting criticism of their power while simultaneously opening new markets to increase that power into the future. Other corporate players, chief among them defense contractors that had performed communications and aerospace research for the military, had a vested interest in challenging the regulatory protection of the broadcast networks so that they could move into commercial cable and satellite signal delivery themselves. 'The reform movement had done much to focus the attack on the regulatory process as too protectionist of established industrial hegemony and too little concerned about the public service component of the public interest standard,' points out Willard Rowland in his study of the broadcast reform movement. 'For a much longer period of time, though, the industry had been making assaults on the regulatory process as unnecessarily bureaucratic, economically inefficient and an infringement on its right as an extension of the press, operating under First Amendment freedoms.'[32]

The broadcast reform movement ended up realizing its most significant gains when it joined in this chorus of voices calling for the deregulation of cable and satellite technology as a means of achieving content diversity, public access, and free information flow through the good graces of a free and open marketplace. But this turned out to be a Faustian bargain. 'By the time deregulation began to take shape, the reasons for the reform concerns had been forgotten and the longstanding major industrial interests had reasserted themselves,' explains Rowland. 'Deregulation was to go forward, but public service considerations were ignored – or at best they were assumed to be realizable through marketplace forces.'[33] By the end of the 1970s, the FCC was actively promoting cable as an alternative to the network oligopoly. Under the Reagan administration it moved further to abolish ownership limits, restrictions on cross-ownership, the Fairness Doctrine, rules regarding children's programming and advertising, and almost anything else that stood in the way of unbridled competition and expansion in the media industry.

Of course, all of this deregulation did not really democratize the media. Because financial barriers to full participation in the media economy are so high, it merely opened up the industry to let a few more heavily capitalized players in – such as Ted Turner's Turner Broadcasting System and Rupert Murdoch's News Corp. Inc. – and allowed the telephone giants and the film industry to move into television and cable, and vice-versa. These corporations quickly divvied up the spoils of the newly liberalized market, then began looking overseas for even larger vistas. This process has led to the complete abandonment of the public interest obligations formerly imposed on media entities, and to previously unimaginable levels of globalization, concentration and conglomeration in the media industry, as witnessed most recently by the mergers of Disney and Capital Cities/ABC and of Time-Warner and the Turner Broadcasting System.

This media concentration has occurred in the name of empowering individual citizens and promoting greater freedom. Signing into law the Telecommunications Reform Act of 1995, which further dismantled barriers to media concentration and steered clear of imposing any positive public interest obligations altogether, President Bill Clinton declared that it would 'stimulate investment, promote competition, provide open access for all citizens to the Information Superhighway, strengthen and improve universal service and provide families with technologies to help them control what kind of programs come into their homes over television.' He concluded, 'As a result of this action today, consumers will receive the benefits of lower prices, better quality and greater choices in their telephone and cable services, and they will continue to benefit from a diversity of voices and viewpoints in radio, television and the print media.'

The American social construction of new technologies of communication appears permeated with exceptionalist ideology, and Newt Gingrich's flights of technological fancy appear quite mainstream in this context. All three of the insistent themes Joyce Appleby highlights in her analysis of the development of American exceptionalism resurface again and again in the rhetoric surrounding the development of telegraph, broadcasting, cable, and other forms of electronic signal delivery. American lawmakers, regulators, reformers, and industry leaders have greeted these technologies as instruments that would promote individual liberty and personal autonomy. In their enthusiasm, they have made sweeping claims about human nature, interpreting the inevitable culmination of technological and historical developments as the triumph of American democratic ideals. In order to make these claims in the face of often overwhelming evidence to the contrary, they have treated each successive new technology of communication as if it had no history, thereby participating in their own form of clean slatism. The histories wiped off the slate in the process have had little to do with idealized Jeffersonian communities of enlightened and empowered citizens and everything to do with what has been *truly* distinctive in America – which David Nye describes elsewhere in this volume as the centrality of business to American culture and that peculiarly American form of business organization, the private corporation.

As the preceding discussion has shown, for example, the predominance of commerce in American culture meant that almost from the beginning the broadcasting public was effectively synonymous with the competitive broadcasting market. For the vast majority of the population, broadcasting never represented a means of communication, but rather a means of consumption, and the freedom promised by the enthusiasts of the new technology of broadcasting was in reality the freedom to choose from a limited range of programming options. In the context of the progressive era rhetoric that informed the framing of federal communications legislation, Willard D. Rowland explains, 'references to democracy and to audience participation equated consumption with power,' and 'the myth of audience power, which rested on the myth of consumer choice, became reified and held up as evidence that Americans possessed unprecedented political and economic freedom.'[34] The broadcast reformers of the late 1960s and early 1970s inherited this confusion over the difference between democracy and consumer capitalism, and for this reason sowed the seeds of their own failure. Directing their critique towards the fact that programming options were limited by the network system, and calling for the creation of new options by means of the deregulation of new technologies, they reaffirmed their status as consumers and further facilitated the very concentration of media power that they had set out to challenge in the first place.

Regardless of these failures, the broadcast reform movement did attempt to challenge powerful, well-capitalized interests on behalf of minority groups and individual members of local communities. The fact that the movement seized upon exceptionalist rhetoric to achieve those ends highlights what Tom Byers has called the conscience of exceptionalism, and contradicts Joyce Appleby's characterization of American exceptionalism as an exclusively hegemonic ideology. There have been different strains of exceptionalism in American history, and certain of these have had much to do with movements towards progressive reform. Holding the nation to a democratic and communitarian ideal, exceptionalist rhetoric can produce salient critiques of American society in limited doses. In the case of the broadcast reform movement, however, it also ultimately served to accommodate the reformers themselves to the objects of their own criticism.

Joyce Appleby succinctly isolates both the downfall of the broadcast reform movement and the motivating principle behind Newt Gingrich's exceptionalist rhetoric when she notes that 'exceptionalism established a reciprocity between American abundance and high moral purposes.'[35] In the early years of the Republic, this plank of exceptionalist ideology undergirded the removal of the Native American population and the settling of the West, since as Appleby notes, 'taking up land in the national domain could become a movement for spreading democratic institutions across the continent.' In the context of communications deregulation, this has come to mean clearing bothersome regulations out of the way so that private corporations could develop (and profit from) what have become known as 'technologies of abundance.' Newt Gingrich carries this strain of thought to its logical conclusion, virtually conflating the virtues of participatory democracy with the luxuries of a consumer society and an open marketplace under the aegis of a technological revolution of world proportions. 'The coming of the Third Wave Information Age brings potential for enormous improvement in the lifestyle choices of most Americans,' he asserts. 'There is every reason to believe that this new era will see a revolution in goods and services that will empower and enhance most people' (55). To achieve this goal, Gingrich advocates an even more thorough program of privatization and deregulation. 'If we liberate entrepreneurs and make it relatively easy for them to discover and invent our new world,' he says, 'we will be rearing a generation that increases our wealth and improves our lives to a degree that we can now barely imagine' (61). Far from a ranting futurist, Gingrich sounds like his arch-political rival Bill Clinton signing the Telecommunications Reform Act. If the results of the wave of deregulation that began during the broadcast reform movement are any indication, Gingrich and Clinton's deregulatory designs will only carry them further away from the exceptionalist democratic idyll towards which they profess to strive.

## Notes

1.  Joan Didion, 'The Teachings of Speaker Gingrich,' *New York Review of Books*, 10 August 1995, 8.
2.  Didion, 7.
3.  Joyce Appleby, 'Recovering America's Historic Diversity: Beyond Exceptionalism,' *Journal of American History*, 79 (1992): 419–31.
4.  Appleby, 426.
5.  Newt Gingrich, *To Renew America* (New York: Harper Collins, 1995), 5. Subsequent page references to this work will be given in the text.
6.  Appleby, 423.
7.  Appleby, 424.
8.  Garry Wills, 'The Visionary,' *New York Review of Books*, 23 March 1995, 6.
9.  Didion, 8.
10. Didion, 8.

11. Newt Gingrich, 'Foreword: A Citizen's Guide to the 21st Century,' Alvin and Heidi Toffler, *Creating a New Civilization: The Politics of the Third Wave* (Atlanta: Turner, 1994), 14.

12. Newt Gingrich, 'Citizen's Guide,' 15.

13. Daniel J. Czitrom, *Media and the American Mind: From Morse to McLuhan* (Chapel Hill: University of North Carolina Press, 1982), 10. Quoting Donald Mann, 'Telegraphing of Election Returns,' *American Telegraph Magazine*, 1 (November, 1852): 76.

14. Czitrom, 10.

15. Stanley Frost, 'Radio Dreams that Can Come True,' *Collier's*, 69 (10 June 1922): 18; quoted in Susan Douglass, *Inventing American Broadcasting, 1899–1922* (Baltimore: Johns Hopkins University Press, 1987), 306.

16. Douglas, xv.

17. Quoted in Robert Britt Horwitz, *The Irony of Regulatory Reform: The Deregulation of Telecommunications* (New York: Oxford University Press, 1989), 178.

18. Richard Hofstadter, *The Age of Reform* (New York: Knopf, 1954), 213.

19. Rowland, 8.

20. Horwitz, *passim*.

21. Douglas, xxvi.

22. Erik Barnouw, *Tube of Plenty: The Evolution of American Television*, 2nd rev. ed. (New York: Oxford University Press, 1990), 20–23; Horwitz, 110; Douglas, 285–86, 290–91.

23. Horwitz, 114.

24. Czitrom, 79.

25. Quoted in Czitrom, 77.

26. E. Pendleton Herring, 'Politics and Radio Regulation,' *Harvard Business Review* (January, 1935): quoted in Barnouw, 28.

27. Horwitz, 114, 121.

28. Horwitz, 194.

29. Horwitz, 250.

30. Don R. LeDuc, *Cable Television and the FCC: A Crisis in Media Control* (Philadelphia: Temple University Press, 1973), vii.

31. See for example, *On the Cable: Television of Abundance: Report of the Sloan Commission on Cable Communications* (New York: McGraw Hill, 1971); 'Rand criticizes FCC's CATV approach,' *Broadcasting*, 26 October 1970, 46; 'Report Ties Profits to CATV Penetration,' *Broadcasting*, 15 February 1971, 56.

32. Rowland, 30.

33. Rowland, 30.

34. Rowland, 35.

35. Appleby, 424.

# Institutions

# 'A Divided Empire': African Americans, the South, and the Narrative of American Exceptionalism

*Peter W. Bardaglio*

American exceptionalism has been a mainstay of writing about US history since the nineteenth century, and it has virtually defined the field of American Studies since its founding in the twentieth century. The irony is that American exceptionalism is in many ways a European invention. 'In the reform-minded salons of Paris, at commemorative gatherings of London's Nonconformists, among emergent working-class radicals, the struggle for independence undertaken by thirteen of Britain's North American colonies was given ideological shape and weight and infused with magnetic force,' notes Joyce Appleby. Adopted by Americans, the vision of the United States as 'the hope of the human race' became the guiding light of new republic's political culture.[1]

Although the exceptionalist thesis came under fire in the 1970s and 1980s, the emergence of the United States as the only world superpower following the end of the Cold War revived the idea, leading to a new round of debate.[2] In response, several scholars have suggested that our time would be better spent analyzing the ways in which the nation's history has been 'different' from that of other countries rather than continuing to argue whether the American experience has been 'exceptional,' a term that implies superiority and transcendence.[3]

The chief advantage of such a reorientation is that it focuses attention on the ideology of exceptionalism itself. As Stephen Fender maintains, the first step in examining what he calls 'the American difference' is to recognize that the object of our inquiry 'is not an actual difference but the idea of one.' In his words,

*Marks of Distinction: American Exceptionalism Revisited*, ed. Dale Carter, *The Dolphin* 32, pp. 167–96. © 2001 by Aarhus University Press, Denmark. ISBN 87 7288 383 9; ISSN 0106 4487.

'Americans are different because they think they are.' Like other social values and attitudes, this ideology of American identity has had significant consequences. 'The discourse of difference,' for example, is part of what has moved so many people from other lands to come to the United States.[4]

Even one of the harshest critics of the exceptionalist position, Ian Tyrell, concedes that the belief in America as radically different continues to exercise a strong hold over American popular culture.[5] This essay sides, then, with those scholars who recognize the emotional and psychological reality of American exceptionalism and who argue that it forms a crucial component of the way that Americans define themselves. The notion that the United States has a unique destiny has also heavily influenced Americans' understanding of their past. How has the persistent adherence to the ideology of exceptionalism shaped the place of African Americans and the South in the American historical memory?

If America 'is a state of mind,' as Fender contends, then it follows that one isn't just born American; one becomes American. Adherence to a set of convictions about the promise of America and its transcendent character marks one as American, not where one is born. Inherent in this idea of becoming American, further-more, is the possibility that one can undo this process and become un-American. By dissenting from the consensus of American political culture in the 1950s, for example, one could become un-American. It is difficult, if not impossible, to imagine the British Parliament creating a select committee on un-British activities because a British subject is British by virtue of simply being born, not by a process of becoming.[6]

This notion of becoming also means that one can be deemed non-American, not because of anything that one *does* but because of who one *is*. Thus the US Supreme Court in the 1857 Dred Scott case affirmed that blacks were not citizens even though they had lived in America for generations. In comparison, newly arrived European immigrants in the nineteenth century met relatively little resistance in claiming an American identity and gaining their citizenship. American exceptionalism, in short, excluded people of African descent from fully participating in American society because the dominant culture decided that they did not embody the established norms.[7]

Excluded as citizens, blacks nonetheless became crucial to the construction of American identity, providing an 'Africanist presence' to contrast with the developing sense of Americanness. As Toni Morrison puts it, 'the process of organizing American coherence through a displacing Africanism became the operative mode of a new cultural hegemony.' The new republic set itself apart from the Old World by its claim to freedom, innocence, and the future. But the chance to start again with a clean slate generated its own unique anxieties. These included, according to Morrison, 'Americans' fear of being outcast, of failing, of powerlessness; their fear of boundarylessness, of Nature unbridled and crouched for attack; their fear of the absence of so-called civilization; their fear of loneliness, of aggression both external and internal. In short, the terror of human freedom – the thing they coveted most of all.' The presence of a resident black population that could serve as 'the racial other' offered white Americans an effective way to objectify their fear of freedom, a way to transfer 'internal conflicts to a "blank darkness," to conveniently bound and violently silenced black bodies.' In other words, the rise of liberty and equality in the United States was not just accompanied by the rise of slavery; black bondage was necessary to and even helped create the American concepts of liberty and equality.[8]

As Morrison's provocative analysis suggests, a narrative less concerned than American exceptionalism with imposing the norms of the dominant culture and meeting the particular needs of this culture would illuminate rather than obscure the ways in which African Americans have participated in the making of the nation's history and culture. It would make clear that the African-American experience belongs at the center, not the margins, of the national narrative. In their recent study of northern free blacks, James Oliver Horton and Lois E. Horton demonstrate how such a perspective dramatically alters our view of the historical landscape. 'The story of African Americans ... ,' insist the Hortons, '... both illustrates and contradicts the promise of America – the principles embodied in the nation's founding documents.' As the 'voice of America's conscience,' blacks between the American Revolution and the Civil War called on the United States 'to recognize all those who had helped create the nation and to be faithful to that nation's professions.' Telling the stories of the first free African Americans, *In Hope of Liberty* underscores the integral part that blacks have played in the United States right from the outset.[9]

Not only is it important to recognize how American exceptionalism as a cultural myth both includes and excludes parts of the past, we need to acknowledge the extent to which this narrative itself has a history. In particular, American exceptionalism – with its emphasis on the rise of liberty, equality, prosperity, and hope for the future – gained currency in the nineteenth-century United States because it helped to foster a more vigorous sense of national identity in the early republic and to repair the frayed sense of national unity following the Civil War. Reflecting Americans' ambivalence over the union's meaning before the Civil War, 'United States' was a plural noun: 'The United States *are* south of Canada and north of Mexico.' Not until after the defeat of the Confederacy in 1865 did the United States become a singular noun. The legacy of the Civil War, in other words, went beyond the preservation of the union to the forging of American nationalism. More than the Revolution, more than the Constitutional Convention, the Civil War put flesh on the bones of the American nation-state.[10]

But what sort of nation-state? The triumph of the Federal forces meant that, to a large extent, the North and the nation became identified as synonymous and the South was marginalized. One result of reunion taking place in this manner is that it reinforced the bias towards American exceptionalism, holding up the North as the model of what America stood for. Sorting through the southern experience, however, reveals the need to craft a more complex and nuanced understanding of the American past. Although often depicted as an outsider or antagonist, the South should be viewed, in Carl Degler's phrase, as 'a co-creator of the nation's history.' '[W]ithout the South,' Degler rightly points out, 'the history of the United States would have been quite different.' Therefore the focus should be not on whether the South or the North deviated from the mainstream of historical development but rather on how the South and North interacted to shape this development.[11]

Why has the South been portrayed for so long, and with such forcefulness, as outside rather than part of the flow of American history? As C. Vann Woodward has observed, the southern encounter with disaster, defeat, and poverty cast a shadow over any claim to new world innocence, any notion that the United States could transcend history.[12] The depth of commitment to the belief in American transcendence can be measured by the continued insistence of both northerners and southerners that the South is somehow a foreign place.[13] To accept that the South is an integral part of the nation's history, that it has played a crucial role in shaping American values and identity, undercuts the assertion of exceptionalism. The tragic dimension of southern history, in Eugene Genovese's words, reminds us 'of the corrupt and cruel tendencies inherent in our common humanity and the ease with which the social relations and institutions we sustain may encourage the most destructive aspects of our nature.'[14] Such reminders make it hard to maintain the illusion that Americans can escape the gravitational pull of history.

One of the little-known facts about the Civil War is that Mount Vernon – the home of George Washington – was proclaimed neutral ground by the Union and the Confederacy during the four-year ordeal.[15] That the North and South, in the midst of a wrenching and bloody civil war, could agree that Mount Vernon should be considered sacred reflects the power of Washington's image as the father of what had become a house divided. Despite the deep-seated differences that split northerners and southerners and drove them to war, they concurred that the Revolutionary tradition and its sense of high moral purpose should be protected in this symbolic fashion.

Of course, Mount Vernon was not only the residence of the first US president; it was also a plantation on which several hundred slaves lived and died. Mount Vernon thus embodies the ambiguity and contradictions that gave birth to the United States and that fueled its expansion. When the Civil War erupted, the land that saw itself as a shining beacon of liberty was also the largest slaveholding country in the world. As Morrison declares, 'it was a nation of people who *decided* that their world view would combine agendas for individual freedom *and* mechanisms for devastating racial oppression.'[16]

Ira Berlin, in his brilliant account of the first two hundred years of slavery in North America, draws a crucial distinction between '*societies with slaves* and *slave societies.*' In societies with slaves, slavery 'was just one form of labor among many' and slaves were not central to the productive processes. In slave societies, however, 'slavery stood at the center of economic production, and the master-slave relationship provided the model for social relations: husband and wife, parent and child, employer and employee, teacher and student.' The process by which societies with slaves became slave societies in North America differed from place to place, and the timing varied as well, but the distinguishing characteristic of 'the plantation revolution' was the seizure of political, economic, and cultural power by the slave-holders. 'The Great House, nestled among manufactories, shops, barns, sheds, and various other outbuildings ... dominated the landscape, the physical and architectural embodiment of the planters' hegemony,' writes Berlin. 'But the masters' authority radiated from the great estates to the statehouses, courtrooms, countinghouses, churches, colleges, taverns, racetracks, private clubs, and the like.'[17]

Having undergone the plantation revolution, the South on the eve of the Civil War had far more than the defense of slavery at stake. The intertwining of slavery and southern society meant that slavery shaped not only relations between blacks and whites, but also planters and yeomen, women and men, and parents and children. Consequently, a distinctive form of republicanism developed in the South, one based more on hierarchy and dependence than on egalitarianism and consent. It was this vision of republicanism and the social order that planters and yeomen sought to defend in 1860 when they called for secession from the union. As the North moved toward an increasingly contractual view of social relations, the white South saw itself as the defender of the organic ideal of the household and society.[18]

A closer look at the conflicting visions of social order that fueled the coming of the Civil War reveals more fully how the commitment to exceptionalism has shaped the place of blacks and the South in American historical memory. White southerners had little doubt during the 1850s about the seriousness of the differences that separated them from northerners at every level, even when it came to domestic governance. Northern reformers 'divide the household into separate interests; the domestic hearth is no longer a common property to the family,' declared *De Bow's Review* in 1855. In contrast, 'a very different idea of government prevails' in 'the slaveholding States.' The hierarchical character of 'the relations of parent and child, of husband and wife, of master and slave, and the right to property all go to make up the great corner-stone of the social edifice – the family.' This organic arrangement of 'institutions and rights' stemmed from 'the laws of nature, from God alone,' and existed 'independent of, and prior to, all government.' The overriding duty of government, the southern journal concluded, was 'to preserve these institutions in all their incidents, and all their derivative rights.'[19]

Slavery, in short, was not an institution that stood apart from the rest of southern society; it became, as LeeAnn Whites observes, 'an organic part of the southern household' and 'organic to the slaveowners' very conception of themselves as men and as women, as mothers and as fathers.'[20] A striking example of this interconnectedness can be found in the antebellum statutory codes from the southern states, where chapters on the law of what was called 'domestic relations' often included not only the headings 'husband and wife,' 'parent and child,' and 'guardian and ward,' but also 'master and slave.'[21] The interwoven character of slavery and the southern household helps to explain why all male heads of households, whether they owned slaves or not, experienced the attack of northern abolitionists on slaveholders as an assault on their independence. The Civil War, in this sense, was a domestic crisis at many levels.[22]

Elizabeth Fox-Genovese, in a 1983 essay, was among the first to emphasize the importance of viewing southern society as a network of households.[23] The reorganization of work away from home in the urbanizing and industrializing North led to the creation of separate spheres for men and women. The antebellum rhetoric of domesticity recast the home as a haven for nurturing, rather than a center of production, and empowered women to maintain the private sphere.[24] According to Fox-Genovese, because economic activities remained concentrated in the house-hold on southern plantations and farms, this rigid separation of home and work did not develop in the slave states. Furthermore, the traditional nature of the southern household meant that it did not become transformed into a woman's sphere and that patriar-chal control over the home remained firm.[25] White southerners adopted a broad conception of family, one that went beyond the nuclear unit to encompass non-nuclear kin, slaves, servants, and all other inhabitants of the plantation, in the house and slave quarters alike. As Eugene Genovese maintains, the incorporation of dependent laborers into the household and the identification of the 'household' with 'family' were not simply part of a proslavery propaganda campaign to disguise the exploitative character of bondage, but rather stemmed from the southern commitment to organic hierarchy as the basis of social order. Often referring to the residents as 'my people,' the planter considered it his God-ordained task to govern them all, black and white, with a firm but benevolent hand.[26]

The patriarchal ideal that ruled within the home also pro-vided the foundation for the exercise of public power in southern society. Subordination and stratification, rather than liberty and equality, shaped the social experience of slaves, women, and children. Employing a rationale that combined elements of protection and coercion, southern governing elites argued that these dependent groups could not survive the competitive and volatile world of the antebellum South on their own, and that granting them personal autonomy would lead to social chaos.[27]

The white male head of the household served as the link be-tween the exercise of public and private power. The subordinate members of the household, according to the southern ideal, were connected to the state only through the patriarch, who had the authority to represent the interests of all his dependents in the public arena. Planters and yeomen, Stephanie McCurry notes, thus shared 'a definition of manhood rooted in the inviolability of the household, the command of dependents, and the public prerogatives manhood conferred.'[28]

When it came to the daily exercise of power and authority within the household, legislators and judges in the Old South upheld the patriarchal prerogatives of white men, whether they were slaveholders or non-slaveholders. 'Despite the regional biases of local courts and differences of intellect and temperament among individual justices,' writes Victoria Bynum, 'the law recognized the privacy of the male-headed household and seldom intruded.'[29] The state intervened only when the male head of the household abused his rights or neglected his obligations in such an obvious and undeniable way that he posed a threat to the legitimacy of patriarchy as a social system. The goal, in other words, was the restoration of social order in the community rather than the extension of rights to subordinate groups.[30]

Planters felt strongly that the self-interest of slaveholders provided those held in bondage with adequate protection. By law and custom the master exerted enormous power over his slaves, who were required to show proper obedience and respect to him. The law stressed the character of the slave as property, but it also recognized, in a limited fashion, the humanity of the slave. Southern slave codes, in setting out various punishments for those who committed criminal acts, conceded that slaves had volition, will, and personality.[31] One southern court went even further, insisting that a slave was 'not in the condition of a horse or an ox' but was 'made in the image of the Creator.'[32]

The southern law of slavery, then, was deeply problematic. The slave codes sought to implement a system of social control that cut deeply against the grain of common-law and middle-class, republican values. Common-law doctrines emphasized a person's natural rights of life, liberty, and property; bourgeois republican ideology fostered a commitment to individualism and personal autonomy. The very basis of slave property challenged these principles. In particular, slaves had no right to marry and no right to custody of their children. Although the law may have ascribed to other families a near sacred status, it left the slave family outside the realm of legal protection.[33] Having inherited a legal and ideological tradition that it could not wholly embrace or wholly reject, the South found it impossible to clarify the ambiguities that permeated the law of slavery, resulting in a distinctive legal tradition and an understanding of republicanism that diverged significantly from that of the North.[34]

Although developments such as individualism and contractualism made inroads into southern domestic relations before the Civil War, most southern lawmakers and judges, as well as social theorists and writers, upheld the organic ideal of the household. As a South Carolina court maintained in 1858, 'a divided empire in the government of a family is not consistent with the welfare of the wife and children, and has not the sanction of law.'[35] Indeed, southern white elites felt compelled to defend the ideal of an undivided domestic empire, because it served as the governing metaphor not only for husbands and wives, parents and children, but also masters and slaves.

By 1860 planters and yeomen joined together to support secession in large part out of a perceived sense that only by making a strike for independence could they protect household patriarchy from the corrosive forces that threatened it.[36] The rise of individualism and contractual social relations in the North – which southern traditionalists saw embodied in such reforms as abolitionism, the expansion of married women's property rights, and the liberalization of divorce – endangered the entire 'domestic institution' as these white southerners understood it: not simply racial slavery, but a network of households grounded in dependency and inequality. Abolitionism, in particular, struck such a fearful chord in the South because of its insistence on the oppressive nature of patriarchal power in the slaveholding household.

Harriet Beecher Stowe, as much as any northern abolitionist, pursued this line of attack in her antislavery writings, especially the 1852 novel, *Uncle Tom's Cabin*. Her biting critique of slavery's deeply personal consequences for the family, both black and white, grew out of a flourishing ideology of domesticity that viewed the mother as the moral guardian of the home. Stowe deployed this ideology in her novel to focus on what she saw as slavery's greatest evil: the separation of mother and child. When asked why she escaped to freedom across the treacherous ice floes of the Ohio River, Eliza explains that her child 'was my comfort and pride, day and night; and, ma'am, they were going to take him away from me, – to *sell* him, – sell him down south, ma'am, to go all alone, – a baby that had never been away from his mother in his life!' Stowe's story achieved a remarkable level of resonance with her northern audience, in large part because slavery violated at its core the hallowed principles of the domestic order emerging in the North, an order that emphasized individualism, consent, and the mother-child bond.[37]

Although not as threatening as the abolitionist campaign against slavery, southern traditionalists also viewed divorce reform and the agitation for married women's property rights as significant challenges to the status quo. Indeed, they saw these three developments as part of a coordinated, sustained assault on the organic concept that undergirded the household order in the South. 'The danger to the South *in the Union* from the force of Northern example in these and other particulars, is imminent and cannot be exaggerated,' warned *De Bow's Review* in 1857. 'Already, the South, with the honorable exception of South Carolina, have adopted to a fearful extent, Northern ideas on the subjects of divorce and the independency of married women, through separate estates and exclusive revenues.' As a result of such developments in the North, 'family unity has become destroyed, and domestic life has been deteriorated, until few families remain united any longer.' In an earlier time, *De Bow's Review* cautioned, similar enactments had undermined Roman virtue, leading to the loss of civil liberty, the onset of civil war and anarchy, and eventually the fall of a great republic.[38]

The historical parallel was obvious. Unless the traditional domestic dominion could be sustained, the holy trinity of southern manhood – what McCurry has referred to as 'manliness, masterhood, and republican citizenship' – was imperiled.[39] A fullblown theory of constitutionalism, the compact theory of the union, had developed in the antebellum South to protect this distinctive conception of liberty. According to this theory, most powerfully espoused by John Calhoun, the states had acted as sovereigns in adopting the federal Constitution; in doing so, they had retained control over all their own 'domestic institutions,' and delegated only certain specific powers to the federal government. Now, with the election of Abraham Lincoln and the Republican party to the White House, it appeared as if the federal government would no longer refrain from interfering with the internal affairs of southerners, including the structure and governance of their households. Faced with mounting political conflict within the South, as well as an organic patriarchy under siege by individualism and antislavery Republicanism, southern conservatives maintained that secession was the only alternative.[40]

To the horror of those who led the South out of the union, the outbreak of war in 1861 accelerated the pace of change, setting in motion historical forces that hastened the demise of the old domestic and political order. The tumult of war and the over-throw of slavery put enormous stress on the interrelated hierar-chies of race, gender, and class, a process that began as soon as white men began to enlist in the Confederate military, leaving behind a world of white women, children, and slaves. As Drew Gilpin Faust contends, 'the very foundations of the South's paternalistic social order were necessarily imperiled by the departure of the men who served as its organizing principle.' White women struggled 'to do a man's business,' taking on unaccustomed and often unwelcome obligations: managing farms and plantations, coping with economic shortages, and supervis-ing slaves.[41]

The domestic crisis triggered by the Civil War reached a climax when the first slaves started heading for Union lines with the approach of the northern army.[42] Reverend Charles Colcock Jones, reporting on the many African Americans who began to flee the plantations along the Georgia coast in July 1862, had little doubt that such actions constituted an insurrection. 'They declare themselves enemies and at war with owners by going over to the enemy who is seeking both our lives and property,' he told his son. 'They are traitors of the worst kind, and spies also, who may pilot the enemy into your bedchamber.' A Virginia woman described the departure of the slaves as 'an entire rupture of our domestic relations.'[43]

Despite the dismay of white southerners at the rising number of runaway slaves, African Americans seized the opportunity to construct their own understanding of what it meant to be free. For most blacks, freedom meant more than anything else the right to marry, procreate, and nurture their families without white interference and control, although doing so was no easy matter. Indeed, as Wilma King points out, 'the parents' efforts to maintain the integrity of their families were often as strenuous as in days of slavery.'[44]

Emancipation overturned the traditional structure of power and authority in the households and larger society of the South. The most explosive development that took place as a result of this domestic reconstruction was the intertwining of sex and politics to an unprecedented degree. The end of bondage freed African Americans from their dependent status within the households of their masters and created the possibility for former slaves to become heads of their own households and actors in the political process. At the same time, white anxiety about black male sexuality skyrocketed, culminating in the myth of the black beast rapist. Recent work by Laura Edwards and Martha Hodes shows how white southerners viewed black political participation and black male sexuality as interrelated threats to the social order. The rape of white women by African-American men became a powerful symbol for the overthrow of an organic hierarchy that could never be restored and for the establishment of an egalitarianism that would, it was feared, result in the world turned upside down.[45]

The Civil War, in short, not only divided the national house; it also brought about the breakup of individual southern

households, transforming them in ways that left southern planters bewildered and frightened.[46] The social relations of a plantation society and slave system that had governed half the country
and dominated its national politics collapsed in a heap. White
masters, fathers, and husbands had failed to rescue what they saw
as the very essence of their reason for being: the traditional
patriarchal order that not only gave them power and authority
over all dependents – women, children, and slaves – but also
made possible their own freedom and autonomy in society at
large. The institutions and ideology of a free-labor market society,
with their emphasis on individualism, contractualism, and
egalitarianism, now dominated the entire nation, not just a part of
it.[47]

As Nina Silber argues, the process by which the North exerted
cultural hegemony during reunion took place in two stages. First,
following the defeat of the Confederacy, northerners viewed the
South in sentimental, feminine terms that allowed them to
celebrate the domestic harmony of reconciliation while at the
same time reiterating the subordinate and submissive position of
the South. Then, as the United States embarked in the last years of
the nineteenth century on a campaign of imperialist expansion,
northern culture fashioned 'a new and invigorated image of
southern white manhood,' one that embraced the military virtues
extolled in the Confederate legend of the Lost Cause.[48]

As the reunited nation acquired colonies and dominated
markets throughout the globe, at the same time imposing a harsh
regime of segregation at home, American exceptionalism placed a
new emphasis on patriotism and loyalty. The drive to expand
American power and influence necessitated the reconciliation of
North and South; the need to heal the sectional rifts, in turn,
meant that the management of race relations in the South would
be left to whites. The war with Spain in 1898, which many
Americans saw as a victory for Anglo-Saxons, underscored 'the
racial parallels between white control in the South and the new
position of the United States as a world power.'[49] The impulse to
conquer other lands thus facilitated the reintegration of the South

into the union on a basis consonant with American exceptionalism.

Consequently, what David Blight terms 'the emancipationist vision' lost out in the struggle over the memory of the Civil War. Reflected in the politics of radical Republicanism and the Thirteenth, Fourteenth, and Fifteenth Amendments, as well as in the African-American construction of the war's meaning, the emancipationist vision grasped the centrality of race in American life and stressed the importance of black citizenship as a national objective. The exceptionalist agenda of the late nineteenth century, however, overwhelmed the effort to promote this outlook. As Blight bluntly states, 'reunion trumped race in Civil War memory.'[50]

Antebellum white southerners had argued vociferously that a divided empire in their individual households would upset racial and gender hierarchies and lead to social turmoil. The fears of southern slaveholders and yeomen led them to secede from the union and precipitate a civil war that divided the American household. Now, in the interests of pursuing an overseas empire, postbellum northern elites acceded to the demands of southern white men that they be allowed to restore the old hierarchies that had come unglued during the Civil War and Reconstruction. The traditional organic arrangements could not be revived, however, so planters and policymakers in the South sought other means to accomplish their goals, turning to the state rather than the household as the basis for exercising their power.[51]

The irony and tragedy encompassed by these developments cannot be captured by the narrative of American exceptionalism, a vision preoccupied with what W. E. B. Du Bois refers to sardonically as 'Progress.' Only a more inclusive understanding of the Civil War and Reconstruction, such as that offered by Du Bois, can bring these events into proper focus. In *The Souls of Black Folk*, Du Bois depicts two characters who for him embody the legacy of these years:

one, a gray-haired gentleman, whose fathers had quit themselves like men, whose sons lay in nameless graves; who bowed to the evil of slavery because abolition threatened untold ill to all; who stood at last, in the evening of life, a blighted, ruined form, with hate in his eyes; – and the other, a form hovering dark and mother-like, her awful face black with the mists of centuries, had aforetime quailed at that white master's command, had bent in love over the cradles of his sons and daughters, and closed in death the sunken eyes of his wife, – aye, too, at his behest had laid herself low to his lust, and borne a tawny man-child to the world, only to see her dark boy's limbs scattered to the winds by midnight marauders riding after 'cursed Niggers.'[52]

As David Blight and Robert Gooding-Williams point out in a probing essay on Du Bois's classic book, the encounter described here is a long ways from the images of reconciliation promoted by the conventional narrative, one in which old soldiers from the Blue and Gray 'clasp hands in mutual respect.' What we have, instead, are the images of an old slaveholder and his former slave confronting each other in hate, both weighed down by burdens of the past. Du Bois, in other words, calls the exceptionalist narrative into question, underscoring his contention, as Blight and Gooding-Williams put it, that 'racial reconciliation, unlike sectional reconciliation, demands a serious confrontation with the hostility rooted in rape, lynching, and racism.' [53]

In the rush to put the past behind and stay focused on the unblemished promise of the American future, exceptionalism makes it nearly impossible to heal the wounds of race and gender that Du Bois's account brings to light. As a result, the opportunity for true recovery is lost. Over and against the exceptionalist narrative about the emergence of the American nation – an account that celebrates Mount Vernon as an emblem of freedom and plays down the dimension of moral ambiguity in human affairs – I would pose two counter-narratives in which very different kinds of households are portrayed: William Faulkner's *Absalom, Absalom!* and Toni Morrison's *Beloved*.

In Faulkner's novel, Thomas Sutpen moves west to Mississippi, seeking at all costs to build the great house of his dreams and to join the planter class. He is obsessed with the need to establish a perfect order over which he will exercise control. Seeking to escape the poverty of his mountain upbringing, Sutpen dreams of 'a country all divided and fixed and neat with a people living on it all divided and fixed and neat because of what color their skins happened to be and what they happened to own.'[54]

The unraveling of Sutpen's design for mastery begins with the appearance of Charles Bon, offspring of his first marriage with a Haitian woman. Sutpen, having abandoned his family, refuses to recognize Bon as his son because of his mixed-race heritage, precipitating a crisis in Sutpen's household that ultimately brings about his downfall. Unlike King David, who acknowledged his son Absalom even after Absalom's rebellion, Sutpen cannot exercise the imagination and sympathy necessary to affirm his kinship with Bon. In this sense, as Warwick Wadlington explains, Faulkner's novel 'dramatizes not so much the failure to know others as the failure to acknowledge and accommodate others adequately.'[55]

Sutpen believes that the failure of his grand scheme is due to an unforeseeable mistake, a miscalculation; he never understands that the inherent flaw in the design for his life, of which the house is the chief symbol, is his insistence on treating people as things.[56] Sifting through the wreckage of Sutpen's life years later, Quentin Compson comes upon the old house with Miss Rosa Coldfield, Sutpen's sister-in-law. Faulkner's description of the decaying structure leaves little doubt about the illusory nature of Sutpen's attempt to achieve self sufficiency and domination: 'It loomed, bulked, square and enormous, with jagged half-toppled chimneys, its roofline sagging a little; for an instant as they moved, hurried, toward it Quentin saw completely through it a ragged segment of sky with three hot stars in it as if the house were of one dimension, painted on a canvas curtain in which there was a tear.'[57]

Faulkner serves as a much-needed corrective to the dangers of American innocence embodied in the figure of Sutpen. *Absalom, Absalom!*, whose working title was 'Dark House,' underscores the impossibility of escaping the burden of history as well as the hazards of underestimating one's capacity for self-delusion. To see the South as Faulkner did is to recognize that the region and its culture are central to the national experience. It is to recognize that Sutpen, with his misguided conviction that he could begin anew, heedless of the pain and suffering that he inflicted on others, is not just a southerner but an American. It is to acknowledge that Sutpen's ruined mansion, built in violence and destroyed in violence, provides a more accurate signpost to the nation's past than the sanitized version of George Washington's Mount Vernon that today attracts thousands of visitors from all over the world.

Faulkner, in short, offers a tragic vision of individual men doomed by their ambitions and illusions. What about the women in *Absalom*? The male characters, for the most part, regard women as objects rather than as subjects. Mr. Compson, Quentin's father, sums up this perspective: 'Years ago we in the South made our women into ladies. Then the War came and made the ladies into ghosts.'[58] Such a view, however, does not represent the whole picture. As Diane Roberts points out, 'The stories they tell, these female ghosts, sabotage the stories put forth by the masculine narrators.' Miss Rosa's voice, for example, continually undercuts those of the men, 'correcting, amplifying, denying their vision of her as passive, weak.' Furthermore, it is Clytie, Sutpen's slave daughter, who sets fire to the big house, marking the final chapter in the fall of Sutpen. Despite the efforts of the men in *Absalom, Absalom!* to define and categorize women, to keep them in their place, Faulkner's women subvert these efforts, finding numerous ways to exercise agency.[59]

Female ghosts of a different sort haunt Toni Morrison's *Beloved*, a redemptive narrative of community in which women and men struggle to survive in the face of enormous obstacles. As in Faulkner's novel, the household is a key motif in *Beloved*, but for Sethe a house is not a symbol of achieved power and status, as it is for Sutpen. For her, a house, her house, is a place to be, not to do; indeed, the house is part of her. Paul D, though, perceives 124 Bluestone Road as a threat, sensing immediately that he is not welcome there by the spirit of Sethe's daughter, killed years before by her mother to prevent the girl's return to slavery. Paul D, not understanding Sethe's profound emotional attachment to the house, urges her to move out, 'to leave as though a house was a little thing – a shirtwaist or a sewing basket you could walk off from or give away any old time.'[60]

Of course, Sethe has walked off from one household, Sweet Home, where she had been held as a slave by Garner. After leaving, though, Sethe finds that Sweet Home continues to hold sway over her memory, despite the energy she expends on 'beating back the past':

[T]here was Sweet Home rolling, rolling, rolling out before her eyes, and although there was not a leaf on that farm that did not make her want to scream, it rolled itself out before her in shameless beauty. It never looked as terrible as it was and it made her wonder if hell was a pretty place, too. Fire and brimstone, all right, but hidden in lacy groves. Boys hanging from the most beautiful sycamores in the world. It shamed her – remembering the wonderful soughing trees rather than the boys. Try as she might to make it otherwise, the sycamores beat out the children every time and she could not forgive her memory for that.

Sethe speaks of Sweet Home so often, in fact, that her daughter Denver wonders, 'How come everybody run off from Sweet Home can't stop talking about it? Look like if it was so sweet you would have stayed.' Sethe never felt at home on the Sweet Home farm, she explains to Denver, but 'it's where we were [a]ll together.'[61]

It is this sense of interconnectedness that provides Sethe, Denver, Paul D, and the others with the necessary emotional resources to not only endure but live. *Beloved*, remarks Philip Weinstein, 'imagines a disowned community moving through the painful process of reclaiming itself, recovering its agency.' Baby Suggs's gatherings in the Clearing, where she holds forth as an 'unchurched preacher,' introduce a theme that threads its way throughout the novel, the importance of community. When the town blacks ostracize Baby Suggs, Sethe, and Denver for an elaborate feast that they put on, the pain of this rejection weighs heavily on Baby Suggs's soul. As Stamp Paid says, 'to belong to a community of other free Negroes – to love and be loved by them, to counsel and be counseled, protect and be protected, feed and be fed – and then to have that community step back and hold itself at a distance – well, it could wear out even a Baby Suggs, holy.'[62]

In the end, following Baby Suggs's death, only the support of the community that has cast out Sethe and Denver can rescue them. When the spirit of Sethe's murdered child assumes flesh as Beloved and nearly hounds her mother to death, refusing to let her forget the past, Denver reaches out to local blacks in an effort to save Sethe. In response, a group of women, all former slaves, come to 124 Bluestone Road. As Linda Krumholz puts it, these women seek to 'exorcise the ghost of her past preying on her life, because Beloved is in some sense their ghost, too.' The 'thirty neighborhood women' join their voices together, praying and singing in an effort to banish the 'devil-child':

For Sethe, it was as though the Clearing had come to her with all its heat and simmering leaves, where the voices of women searched for the right combination, the key, the code, the sound that broke the back of words. Building voice upon voice until they found it, and when they did it was a wave of sound wide enough to sound deep water and knock the pods off chestnut trees. It broke over Sethe and she trembled like the baptized in its wash.

The concerted spiritual power of the women's voices brings about Sethe's purification and rebirth, allowing her finally to lay aside the '[s]word and shield' that she had wielded to ward off the memories that had tormented her for years.[63]

While Sutpen's setbacks destroy him, the adversities encountered by Sethe, Denver, and Paul D make them stronger not just individually but collectively. Morrison's novel, Terry Otten asserts, enacts a version of the 'fortunate fall': 'the necessary and potentially redemptive passage from a garden state of debilitating innocence to painful self-knowledge and its consequences.' Instead of seeing such a fall primarily as a personal experience, as do the romantics, Morrison portrays it in the form of a 'communal myth.' According to Otten, 'The victorious end for her involves not only the escape from the white man's Eden but the discovery of the black consciousness muted in a white society.'[64]

*Beloved* thus concludes on a more hopeful note than *Absalom, Absalom!* Faulkner brings his story to a close with the burning of Sutpen's old house and a pained cry from Quentin that he doesn't hate the South. At the end of Morrison's novel, Denver announces her plans to become a teacher and Paul D, declaring his love for Sethe, tells her that he 'wants to put his story next to hers.'[65] By becoming more than passive victims and actively resisting their dehumanization, Sethe, Paul D, and the others become accountable for their actions and thus must look into their own hearts and minds. 'The true price of their humanity lay,' Elizabeth Fox-Genovese suggests, 'in their scarring acknowledgment of their responsibility – that is, in their willingness to claim the story of slavery as their own subjective experience, to claim southern history as their own.'[66] Mustering the courage to carry out a sustained effort at self-confrontation, in contrast to Sutpen, the former slaves in *Beloved* construct a sense of wholeness grounded in reality rather than evasion and self-delusion.

Proclaiming his hope for a shared future with Sethe, Paul D says to her, 'me and you, we got more yesterday than anybody. We need some kind of tomorrow.'[67] What *Beloved* and *Absalom, Absalom!* together teach us is that only if we keep our present rooted in a clearheaded understanding of our yesterdays can we experience the kind of tomorrows that make possible acts of humanity and acknowledgments of our connectedness to each other. For Morrison and Faulkner the presence of the past in the present is as thick as Sethe's love for her children, and both writers understand history as a ritual engagement with this entangling of past and present. Like Quentin, we all are 'a barracks filled with stubborn back-looking ghosts,' and like Sethe, we all have stories 'to pass on,' stories that must be remembered but also stories that we must get past if we are to survive and create a future for ourselves.[68]

We have paid dearly for the narrative of exceptionalism, Joyce Appleby reminds us, because it hinders a full comprehension of our yesterdays. Much of what really happened in American history has been left out of this account because it does not fit. Like Sutpen, who himself experienced early on the humiliation of having a door shut in his face, the master narrative has refused to grant the Bons of our past a place at the table. In Appleby's words, 'the idea of American exceptionalism projected onto the United States a future more significant than its past, encouraging a neglect of the historic diversity of the United States in deference to an imagined time when progressive, cumulative, irreversible processes of change would have worn away the variety in human experience.'[69]

The relevance of Appleby's insight to resituating African Americans and the South in American history is clear: the united state(s) of mind that the dominant national narrative demands forecloses a searching examination of the contested nature of the republic.[70] Faulkner and Morrison, in very different ways, reorient us to the ambiguity and complexity of American history and show us how the struggle over remembering and forgetting shapes the stories about the past that we tell and how we tell them. The narrative strategies of both *Absalom, Absalom!* and *Beloved* demonstrate that a chorus of conflicting voices rather than a single voice is necessary to recover all the past. Moving back and forth across time and introducing multiple narrators, these novels dramatize the constant ebb and flow of interpreting and reinterpreting the past, showing how each effort to make sense of the past becomes part of the past that we then have to make sense of again.[71]

Given their emphasis on the tragic dimension of the human experience, it is not surprising that Faulkner and Morrison, in different ways, illuminate the importance of forgiveness in achieving reconciliation as well as the virtue of patience in waiting for the right moment. The forgiveness they call for stems from a recognition that we are all capable of both self-awareness and self-delusion, and that, in Edward Ayers's words, 'moral struggles are located *within* individuals as well as *between* them.'[72] It is a forgiveness grounded in an appreciation of the realities of power, the inevitability of suffering, and the requirements of justice. Reconciliation, in other words, is not a matter of simply asking, as Cyril Fielding does at the end of E. M. Forster's *A Passage to India*, 'Why can't we be friends now?' As one of the colonized, Dr. Aziz understands that only when Indian independence is achieved, and he and Fielding are on an equal footing, can reconciliation take place. Fielding, taking for granted the privileges of power even if he doesn't always exercise them, insists, 'It's what I want. It's what you want.'

Forster concludes with one of the most haunting and heartbreaking passages in the literature of colonialism, a passage that resonates in some surprising ways with the American experience of racial and gender conflict:

But the horses didn't want it – they swerved apart; the earth didn't want it, sending up rocks through which riders must pass single file; the temples, the tank, the jail, the palace, the birds, the carrion, the Guest House, that came into view as they issued from the gap and saw Mau beneath: they didn't want it, they said in their hundred voices, 'No, not yet,' and the sky said, 'No, not there.'[73]

Sutpen's Hundred, Sweet Home, the Guest House: all outposts in the campaign to maintain an undivided empire, all projects that came to grief when the people they sought to control refused to play the roles assigned them and asserted their individual and collective humanity. Conflict, diversity, agency: all stuff out of which we can construct a more inclusive narrative, one that is both particular and yet connected. No easy task, but as the children in Toni Morrison's Noble Prize acceptance lecture tell the wise old woman, 'Narrative is radical, creating us at the very moment it is being created. We will not blame you if your reach exceeds your grasp. We know you can never do it properly – once and for all. Passion is never enough; neither is skill. But try.'[74]

## Notes

An earlier version of this essay appeared as '"A Divided Empire": Southern Households, Slavery, and the Narrative of American Exceptionalism' in *Annals of Scholarship*, 12, nos. 3 and 4 (1998), 63–82. I presented the original paper to the 'Americas Abroad' conference at Dartmouth College in June 1996. I would like to thank the participants for their comments and suggestions as well as Dale Carter for his thoughtful critique and steady encouragement that led to this latest effort. Thanks, too, to Wrexie Bardaglio for her close reading of all the drafts; as usual, she saved me from a number of errors and infelicities in my writing. The University of North Carolina Press has kindly granted me permission to use material from the preface, chapter 1, and chapter 4 of my book *Reconstructing the Household: Families, Sex, and the Law in the Nineteenth-Century South* (Chapel Hill: University of North Carolina Press, 1995) for the middle portion of this essay.

1.  Joyce Appleby, 'Recovering America's Historic Diversity: Beyond Exceptionalism,' *Journal of American History*, 79 (1992): 419; and Anne Robert Turgot, quoted in Appleby, 419.
2.  Michael Kammen, 'The Problem of American Exceptionalism: A Reconsideration,' *American Quarterly*, 45 (1993): 11–16, provides a brief overview of the exceptionalist critique mounted during the 1970s and 80s.
3.  See, e.g., Carl N. Degler, 'In Pursuit of an American History,' *American Historical Review*, 92 (1987): 4; Michael McGerr, 'The Price of the "New Transnational History",' *American Historical Review*, 96 (1991): 1061–62; and Kammen, 'Problem,' 32. Other recent contributions to the debate include Ian Tyrell, 'American Exceptionalism in an Age of International History,' *American Historical Review*, 96 (October, 1991): 1031–55; Byron E. Shafer, *Is America Different? A New Look at American Exceptionalism* (Oxford: Clarendon, 1991); and Seymour Martin Lipset, *American Exceptionalism: A Double-Edged Sword* (New York: Norton, 1997).
4.  Stephen Fender, 'The American Difference,' *Modern American Culture: An Introduction*, ed. Mick Gidley (London: Routledge, 1993), 7.
5.  Tyrell, 'American Exceptionalism,' 1032. Tyrell makes the important point that the idea of exceptionalism has a history and its power to persuade has varied over time (1049–50).
6.  Fender, 'American Difference,' 2–3.
7.  See James Oliver Horton and Lois E. Horton, *In Hope of Liberty: Culture, Community, and Protest Among Northern Free Blacks, 1700–1860* (New York: Oxford University Press, 1997) for a recent analysis of African-American exclusion in early America.
8.  Toni Morrison, *Playing in the Dark: Whiteness and the Literary Imagination* (Cambridge, MA: Harvard University Press, 1992), 6, 8, 37, 46, 38.
9.  Horton and Horton, *In Hope of Liberty*, ix, xi.
10. James M. McPherson, 'A War That Never Goes Away,' *American Heritage*, 41 (1990): 47–48.
11. Carl N. Degler, 'Thesis, Antithesis, Synthesis: The South, The North, and the Nation,' *Journal of Southern History*, 53 (1987): 3–18. James McPherson has suggested that, from a global perspective, it was the North that was outside the mainstream of historical development. Given the South's experience with poverty, military defeat, and skepticism about progress, it 'shared a bond with the rest of humankind that other Americans did not share.' See

'Antebellum Southern Exceptionalism: A New Look at an Old Question,' *Civil War History*, 29 (1983): 242.

12. C. Vann Woodward, *The Burden of Southern History*, 3rd ed. (Baton Rouge, LA, 1993), 3–25, 187–211.

13. John Egerton, *The Americanization of Dixie: The Southernization of America* (New York: Harper's Magazine Press, 1974) may, at first glance, seem to contradict the notion of the South as a foreign place, but Egerton's extended complaint about the degree to which the South and the nation have begun to mirror each other stems from his commitment as a native of the region to maintaining the South as a place and state of mind outside the American mainstream. The standard work on the persistence of southern distinctiveness is John Shelton Reed, *The Enduring South: Subcultural Persistence in Mass Society* (Lexington, MA: Lexington Books, 1972).

14. Eugene Genovese, *The Southern Tradition: The Achievement and Limitations of Southern Conservatism* (Cambridge, MA: Harvard University Press, 1994), xiii.

15. Paul Wilstach, *Mount Vernon: Washington's Home and the Nation's Shrine* (Garden City, NY: Doubleday, Page, 1916), 262; and Ernest B. Furgurson, 'Introduction,' Dorothy Troth Muir, *Mount Vernon: The Civil War Years* (Mount Vernon, VA: Mount Vernon Ladies' Assoc., 1993), 28. Thanks to Margie Simon of the Julia Rogers Library at Goucher College for tracking down these references for me.

16. Morrison, *Playing in the Dark*, xiii. On the close relationship between American slavery and freedom before the American Revolution, see Edmund S. Morgan, 'Slavery and Freedom: The American Paradox,' *Journal of American History*, 59 (1972): 5–29; and Edmund S. Morgan, *American Freedom, American Slavery: The Ordeal of Colonial Virginia* (New York: Norton, 1975). On the early national and antebellum periods, see William J. Cooper, Jr., *Liberty and Slavery: Southern Politics to 1860* (New York: Knopf, 1983); and Eugene D. Genovese, *The Slaveholders' Dilemma: Freedom and Progress in Southern Conservative Thought, 1820–1860* (Columbia: University of South Carolina Press, 1992).

17. Ira Berlin, *Many Thousands Gone: The First Two Centuries of Slavery in North America* (Cambridge, MA: Belknap, 1998), 8, 97.

18. Among other works, see Elizabeth Fox-Genovese, *Within the Plantation Household: Black and White Women of the Old South* (Chapel Hill: University of North Carolina Press, 1988); Victoria E. Bynum, *Unruly Women: The Politics of Social and Sexual Control in the Old South* (Chapel Hill: University of North Carolina Press, 1992); LeeAnn Whites, *The Civil War as a Crisis in Gender: Augusta, Georgia, 1860–1890* (Athens: University of Georgia Press, 1995); Stephanie McCurry, *Masters of Small Worlds: Yeoman Households, Gender Relations, and the Political Culture of the Antebellum South Carolina Low Country* (New York: Oxford University Press, 1995); and Peter W. Bardaglio, *Reconstructing the Household: Families, Sex, and the Law in the Nineteenth-Century South* (Chapel Hill: University of North Carolina Press, 1995). Joel

Williamson discusses the southern ideal of the organic society in *The Cruci-ble of Race: Black-White Relations in the American South Since Emancipation* (New York: Oxford University Press, 1984), 24–35. As Eugene Genovese argues in *The Southern Tradition*, the southern tradition of conservatism, one that calls for 'a society of orders based on a hierarchy that recognizes human inequality,' is still a force to be reckoned with.

19. 'The South and the Union,' *De Bow's Review*, 19 (July 1855): 47, 43.

20. Lee Ann Whites, 'Civil War as a Crisis in Gender,' *Divided Houses: Gender and the Civil War*, ed. Catherine Clinton and Nina Silber (New York: Oxford University Press, 1992), 6.

21. See, e.g., Alabama, *Code* (Ormond, Bagby, and Goldthwaite, 1852), 375; Georgia, *Code* (Clark, Cobb, and Irwin, 1861), 330; and Tennessee, *Code* (Meigs and Cooper, 1858), 480.

22. Whites, *Civil War*, 17–18.

23. Elizabeth Fox-Genovese, 'Antebellum Southern Households: A New Perspective on a Familiar Question,' *Review: A Journal of the Fernand Braudel Center*, 7 (1983): 248. Fox-Genovese warns against the dangers of 'reducing households to family or co-residence'; she defines households as units that 'pool income in the interests of consumption, reproduction, or possibly production.' Such an approach recognizes the importance of non-kin members of the household and also makes clear that not all household members need reside under the same roof (222).

24. On the ideology of separate spheres and domesticity in Victorian America, see Barbara Welter, 'The Cult of True Womanhood, 1820–1860,' *American Quarterly*, 18 (1966): 151–74; Carroll Smith-Rosenberg, *Disorderly Conduct: Visions of Gender in Victorian America* (New York: Knopf, 1985); Nancy Cott, *The Bonds of Womanhood: Women's Sphere in New England, 1780–1835* (New Haven: Yale University Press, 1977); Kathryn Kish Sklar, *Catharine Beecher: A Study in American Domesticity* (New Haven: Yale University Press, 1973); and Mary P. Ryan, *Cradle of the Middle Class: The Family in Oneida County, New York, 1790–1865* (New York: Cambridge University Press, 1981).

25. Fox-Genovese, *Within the Plantation Household*, 61–63, 66–68, 98–99. On gender roles in the households of southern townspeople and yeomen, see Jean E. Friedman, *The Enclosed Garden: Women and Community in the Evangelical South, 1830–1900* (Chapel Hill: University of North Carolina Press, 1985), 21–38; Stephanie McCurry, 'The Politics of Yeoman Households in South Carolina,' in *Divided Houses*, 22–38; and McCurry, *Masters of Small Worlds*.

26. Eugene Genovese, '"Our Family, White and Black": Family and Household in the Southern Slaveholders' World View,' *In Joy and in Sorrow: Women, Family, and Marriage in the Victorian South, 1930–1900*, ed. Carol Bleser (New York: Oxford University Press, 1991), 69–87. For a contrasting view that downplays the extent to which planters considered slaves as part of their

family, see Jane Turner Censer, *North Carolina Planters and Their Children, 1800–1860* (Baton Rouge: Louisiana State University Press, 1984), ch. 7.

27. Peter Wallenstein, *From Slave South to New South: Public Policy in Nineteenth-Century Georgia* (Chapel Hill: University of North Carolina Press, 1987), 86–88.

28. McCurry, *Masters*, 304.

29. Bynum, *Unruly Women*, 87. See also McCurry, *Masters*, 85–86.

30. For discussions of the dilemmas faced by antebellum southern courts as they sought to define the limits of patriarchal power in cases involving incestuous sexual assault and the physical abuse of wives and slaves, see Bardaglio, *Reconstructing the Household*, 39–40; and Bynum, *Unruly Women*, 70–72.

31. Judith Kelleher Schafer, *Slavery, the Civil Law, and the Supreme Court of Louisiana* (Baton Rouge: Louisiana State University Press, 1994), 21–27; Eugene D. Genovese, *Roll, Jordan, Roll: The World the Slaves Made* (New York: Pantheon, 1974), 28–29; and Mark Tushnet, *The American Law of Slavery, 1810–1860: Considerations of Humanity and Interest* (Princeton: Princeton University Press, 1981), 111–21. The most thorough and balanced study of slave law in the South as a whole is Thomas D. Morris, *Southern Slavery and the Law, 1619–1860* (Chapel Hill: University of North Carolina Press, 1996). See Melton McLaurin, *Celia, A Slave* (Athens: University of Georgia Press, 1991) for a fascinating analysis of the predicament faced by southern legal authorities in prosecuting a female slave who killed her master following years of sexual abuse.

32. Quoted in Arthur F. Howington, '"Not in the Condition of a Horse or an Ox": *Ford v. Ford*, the Law of Testamentary Manumission and the Tennessee Courts' Recognition of Slave Humanity,' *Tennessee Historical Quarterly*, 34 (1975): 258.

33. Maxwell Bloomfield, 'Law and Southern Society,' in *Encyclopedia of Southern Culture*, ed. Charles Reagan Wilson and William Ferris, 4 vols (New York: Anchor, 1991), 2: 669–70; and Margaret A. Burnham, 'An Impossible Marriage: Slave Law and Family Law,' *Law and Inequality*, 5 (1987): 187–225. On the difficulties and challenges faced by slave parents in bringing up their children, see Wilma King, *Stolen Childhood: Slave Youth in Nineteenth-Century America* (Bloomington: Indiana University Press, 1995), ch. 1.

34. Tushnet, *American Law of Slavery*, 157–58, 229–31; and Eugene D. Genovese and Elizabeth Fox-Genovese, 'Slavery, Economic Development, and the Law: The Dilemma of the Southern Political Economists, 1800–1860,' *Washington and Lee Law Review*, 41 (1984): 1–29.

35. *Ex parte* Hewitt, 11 Rich. 326 (S. C. 1858), 329–30. On developments in antebellum domestic relations law, see Bardaglio, *Reconstructing the Household*, 31–34, 79–112.

36. McCurry, *Masters*, 304.

37. Document no. 54, *The Limits of Sisterhood: The Beecher Sisters on Women's Rights and Women's Sphere*, ed. Jeanne Boydston, Mary Kelley, and Anne

Margolis (Chapel Hill: University of North Carolina Press, 1988), 173. For an astute discussion of how the ideology of domesticity shaped Stowe's approach to slavery, see 'Harriet Beecher Stowe: "My Life's Blood",' *Limits of Sisterhood*, 155–65.

38. 'The Relative Moral and Social Status of the North and the South,' *De Bow's Review*, 22 (March, 1857): 246, 242, 230–33.

39. McCurry, 'Politics of Yeoman Households,' 35.

40. William M. Wiecek, '"Old Times There Are Not Forgotten": The Distinctiveness of the Southern Constitutional Experience,' in *An Uncertain Tradition: Constitutionalism and the History of the South*, ed. Kermit L. Hall and James W. Ely, Jr. (Athens: University of Georgia Press, 1989), 169; Randall C. Jimerson, *The Private Civil War: Popular Thought during the Sectional Conflict* (Baton Rouge: Louisiana State University Press, 1988), 12–18; and Michael P. Johnson, *Toward a Patriarchal Republic: The Secession of Georgia* (Baton Rouge: Louisiana State University Press, 1977), xx–xxi, 85–101. On the political and constitutional principles of nineteenth-century southern conservatives, see also Genovese, *Southern Tradition*, 41–67.

41. Drew Gilpin Faust, *Mothers of Invention: Women of the Slaveholding South in the American Civil War* (Chapel Hill: University of North Carolina Press, 1996), 35, 6, 54. For a discussion of how wartime mobilization reshaped the gender roles of southern women in a town setting, see Whites, *Civil War as a Crisis in Gender*, ch. 2.

42. Leon F. Litwack, *Been in the Storm So Long: The Aftermath of Slavery* (New York: Knopf, 1979), 52–59; C. Peter Ripley, *Slaves and Freedmen in Civil War Louisiana* (Baton Rouge: Louisiana State University Press, 1976), 14, 16–21; Clarence L. Mohr, *On the Threshold of Freedom: Masters and Slaves in Civil War Georgia* (Athens: University of Georgia Press, 1986), 72–75; and Jimerson, *Private Civil War*, 61–62, 65–67.

43. Robert M. Myers, ed., *The Children of Pride: A True Story of Georgia and the Civil War* (New Haven: Yale University Press, 1972), 935; and Faust, *Mothers of Invention*, 74.

44. Litwack, *Been in the Storm So Long*, 229–31; and King, *Stolen Childhood*, 141. For a contemporary discussion of the issues raised in Reconstruction courts by the legalization of slave unions, see 'Slave Marriages,' *Virginia Law Journal*, 1 (November 1877): 641–52.

45. Laura F. Edwards, *Gendered Strife and Confusion: The Political Culture of Reconstruction* (Urbana: University of Illinois Press, 1997); and Martha Hodes, *White Women, Black Men: Illicit Sex in the Nineteenth-Century South* (New Haven: Yale University Press, 1997), chs. 7–8.

46. See James Roark, *Masters without Slaves: Southern Planters in the Civil War and Reconstruction* (New York: Norton, 1977) for a vivid portrayal of slaveholders struggling to come to grips with the consequences of emancipation.

47. Eric Foner, *Reconstruction: American's Unfinished Revolution, 1863–1877* (New York: Harper & Row, 1988) provides a detailed discussion of Reconstruction as a social and economic process as well as a political transformation.

48. Nina Silber, *The Romance of Reunion: Northerners and the South, 1865–1900* (Chapel Hill: University of North Carolina Press, 1995), 9–10, 12.

49. Silber, *Romance*, 161–62, 181.

50. David W. Blight, 'Reunion and Race: Did the South Win the Struggle Over the Memory of the American Civil War?' (paper delivered at the Commonwealth Fund Conference on 'The Two Souths,' January 1999, University of London), 1–2.

51. For a detailed discussion of how southern elites constructed new modes of domestic governance that relied on the paternalistic state, see Bardaglio, *Reconstructing the Household*, ch. 7.

52. W. E. B. Du Bois, *The Souls of Black Folk*, ed. David W. Blight and Robert Gooding-Williams (Boston: Bedford, 1997), 73, 54–55.

53. Blight and Gooding-Williams, 'The Strange Meaning of Being Black,' in Du Bois, 15.

54. William Faulkner, *Absalom, Absalom!* (New York: Vintage, 1990), 179.

55. Warwick Wadlington, *Reading Faulknerian Tragedy* (Ithaca, NY: Cornell University Press, 1987), 218.

56. Hyatt H. Waggoner, *William Faulkner: From Jefferson to the World* (Lexington: University of Kentucky Press, 1959), 159–60, 166–67.

57. Faulkner, 293. For a fine discussion of how the image of a house in crisis shapes Faulkner's narrative in this novel, see Eric J. Sundquist, *Faulkner: The House Divided* (Baltimore: Johns Hopkins University Press, 1983), 100–30.

58. Faulkner, 7.

59. Diane Roberts, *Faulkner and Southern Womanhood* (Athens: University of Georgia Press, 1994), 28, 167, 96–101.

60. Toni Morrison, *Beloved* (New York: Knopf, 1987), 22. Steven Weisenburger provides a compelling account of the actual events that inspired Morrison's novel in *Modern Medea: A Family Story of Slavery and Child-Murder from the Old South* (New York: Hill and Wang, 1998).

61. Morrison, *Beloved*, 73, 6, 13, 14. For an interesting analysis of 'the myth of Sweet Home' in the context of African-American folk traditions, see Trudier Harris, *Fiction and Folklore: The Novels of Toni Morrison* (Knoxville: University of Tennessee Press, 1991), 175–83.

62. Philip M. Weinstein, *What Else But Love? The Ordeal of Race in Faulkner and Morrison* (New York: Columbia University Press, 1996), 179; and Morrison, *Beloved*, 87, 177.

63. Linda Krumholz, 'The Ghosts of Slavery: Historical Recovery in Toni Morrison's *Beloved*,' *African American Review*, 26 (1992): 402; and Morrison, *Beloved*, 261, 86.

64. Terry Otten, *The Crime of Innocence in the Fiction of Toni Morrison* (Columbia: University of Missouri Press, 1989), 3–4.

65. Morrison, *Beloved*, 273.

66. Elizabeth Fox-Genovese, 'Slavery, Race, and the Figure of the Tragic Mulatta; or, The Ghost of Southern History in the Writing of African-American Women,' *Haunted Bodies: Gender and Southern Texts*, ed. Anne Goodwyn Jones and Susan V. Donaldson (Charlottesville: University Press of Virginia, 1997), 467.

67. Morrison, *Beloved*, 273.

68. Faulkner, 7; Morrison, *Beloved*, 275.

69. Appleby, 'Recovering America's Historic Diversity,' 430.

70. William Chaloupka explores the various levels of meanings of the phrase 'united states' in his review of Thomas L. Dumm's *United States* (Ithaca, NY: Cornell University Press, 1994): 'Tales of Unity, Frustration, and Violence in these United States,' *American Quarterly*, 48 (1996): 535–41.

71. Bernard W. Bell, '*Beloved*: A Womanist Neo-Slave Narrative; or Multivocal Remembrances of Things Past,' *African American Review*, 26 (1992): 7–15; Marilyn Sanders Mobley, 'A Different Remembering: Memory, History and Meaning in Toni Morrison's *Beloved*,' in *Toni Morrison*, ed. Harold Bloom (New York, 1990): 189–99; and Waggoner, *William Faulkner*, 148–55.

72. Edward L. Ayers, 'Narrating the New South,' *Journal of Southern History*, 61 (1995): 565.

73. E. M. Forster, *A Passage to India* (New York: Harcourt, Brace, 1952), 316.

74. Toni Morrison, *Lecture and Speech of Acceptance, Upon the Award of the Nobel Prize for Literature, Delivered in Stockholm on the Seventh of December, Nineteen Hundred and Ninety-Three* (New York: Knopf, 1995), 27–28. Thanks to Marie-Rose Logan of Temple University for bringing this lecture to my attention.

# A College Upon a Hill: Exceptionalism and American Higher Education

*John Halsey and W. Bruce Leslie*

Governor John Winthrop famously proclaimed that newly settled Massachusetts Bay Colony would be a model, 'a City upon a Hill.' Remarkably, only a few years after his audacious proclamation, the Puritans established a college, if not on a hill, on higher ground in New-Town, quickly renamed Cambridge after the university that educated, and sometimes oppressed, so many Puritan intellectuals. Within this surprising commitment to higher education on the edge of the frontier lies the contradictory relation of American higher education to exceptionalism. On one hand, it sought to replicate Cambridge, directly borrowing its curriculum and statutes. On the other hand, once planted the seed sprouted like bamboo, taking on structures and cultural roles not dreamed of then, nor for centuries, in Europe. Few American institutions began life so consciously, indeed filiopietistically, based on European models, yet few developed so distinctively, even exceptionally. And today arguably no area of American life is as international as academic scholarship, with disciplines, especially the sciences leaping national borders with ease.[1] Yet, until recently, the system that nurtured that scholarship remained remarkably unique. This stark contrast makes higher education a particularly useful test of American exceptionalism.

American Exceptionalism, as Dale Carter notes, has shown remarkable longevity.[2] It is a protean idea, with three central components:

a) that America is different (although, as Appleby sternly reminds us, this is not sufficient since everywhere is different);[3]

*Marks of Distinction: American Exceptionalism Revisited*, ed. Dale Carter, *The Dolphin* 32, pp. 197–228. © 2001 by Aarhus University Press, Denmark. ISBN 87 7288 383 9; ISSN 0106 4487.

b) that this difference entails a break from the previous patterns that prevailed elsewhere, especially Europe. As Appleby puts it, in that sense Exceptionalism 'is America's peculiar form of Eurocentrism',[4] and
c) further, that this difference stems from, and reflects, a cultural or structural element which is central to and characteristic of the United States.

The idea dates back to De Tocqueville. Visiting the United States in 1832, during the Presidency of Andrew Jackson, Tocqueville was fascinated with the United States as a laboratory in which democracy, freedom and equality were being tested. Not that these values were confined to America, but '[t]he great advantage of the Americans is that they have arrived at a state of democracy without having to endure a democratic revolution, and that they are born equal instead of becoming so.'[5]

Andrew Jackson was, of course, the first President elected by electors who had been selected in most states by universal white male suffrage. (He was also instrumental in gaining Florida for the United States. In the aftermath of the 2000 election there may have been some who regretted both these achievements.) The slogan he adopted after losing in 1824, 'Let the People Rule,' may have been self-serving, but given America's sense that equality was at the heart of what made it distinctive, it was hard to argue against. And, as Richard Heffner wrote, in the introduction to his edition of *Democracy in America*, 'the roaring mobs that pushed and fought their way into Andrew Jackson's inaugural reception, that knocked over punch bowls and smashed glasses, and trod in muddy boots on White House tables and chairs, made it abundantly clear that at long last equality had become the hallmark of American life.'[6]

The conservative Tocqueville had doubts about the desirability of this phenomenon, but not about its importance or that it represented the future.

The thesis argued here is that, except at its inception and in the final decades of the twentieth century, American higher education was exceptionally inclusive, unsegmented and diverse. These characteristics reflected values in American institutional life which were themselves exceptional. Byron Shafer calls two of these values 'democratization' and (perhaps rather awkwardly) 'market-making.'[7] Democratization is the idea that 'major social institutions ... should be run so as to be directly responsive to their ... publics.' Market-making is the notion that organized alternatives – in products and services, but also in occupations, entertainments and even lifestyles – ought to appear or disappear as there is (or is not) sufficient demand to sustain them. These two ideas are linked by the idea of consumer sovereignty. Americans assume that there is a limited role for government: institutions are always coming and going, and those that meet people's needs will survive, and the ones that don't won't. Democracy is both Jacksonian (the people do rule) and Jeffersonian (the role of the central government is limited).

For higher education, the argument here is that what developed in America was unique because it was steeped in the democratic values of inclusiveness and accountability. But times change, and those values are now less foreign to European societies, or to the higher education to be found within them. To that extent, American higher education is far less exceptional. At first, this distinctiveness did not extend to higher education. The early days illustrate Appleby's argument that the concept of American exceptionalism fails to give due weight to the continuities between America and the European societies from which most of its people had stemmed. For higher education, what she calls 'the invidious distinction between the talented few and the vulgar many' is particularly significant.[8] However, as it developed it took on quite different structures and cultural roles. Recent convergence with other systems of higher education, and especially the English one that spawned it, offers a suggestive case study of the effect of social change on cultural distinctiveness. Thus higher education is a particularly useful test of American exceptionalism.

## Evolution of American Higher Education

To establish our claims of exceptionalism, we must examine the
forces that shaped American higher education and their enduring
effect. Harvard's founders were not intentional educational
pioneers. They wished to transplant the Cambridge (and especially the Emmanuel College) they had known to a more godly
and congenial setting. Given that they launched their enterprise
on a frontier, they achieved remarkable success. One of their
tutors, Thomas Brattle, even made an observation of the 1680
comet which was cited by Newton in *Principia*.[9] But Harvard did
not become Cambridge. The seed of a Cambridge college planted
at Harvard self-propagated in America as it had not done at
home. Religious and colonial rivalries dispersed higher education.
An Anglican college, William and Mary, fitfully struggled in
Virginia. More vigorously, Calvinist schisms yielded Yale in
Connecticut (1701) and then, in the gales of the first Great Awakening, Princeton in New Jersey (1746). Five other foundings
occurred before the Revolution. Baptists created Brown in Rhode
Island and Congregationalists founded Dartmouth in New
Hampshire. Calvinists and Anglicans contested Kings College in
New York City and the University of Pennsylvania in Philadelphia. Only New Jersey spawned more than one colonial college,
foreshadowing the role local rivalries would play in post-Revolutionary American higher education. Princeton was founded in
Elizabeth, moved to Newark, and then encouraged a bidding war
between New Brunswick and Princeton for money and land as
inducements to move again. The loser then found common cause
with Dutch Reformed ambitions and founded Queens (Rutgers)
College. Thus by the revolution, nine colleges across eight
colonies looked to Oxbridge for a model, but already responses to
the physical and social conditions in the colonies foreshadowed
forces that were to create a remarkably different system.

Independence brought further institutional diversity, as state
governments sought to widen religious and social inclusiveness.
The first was Georgia, which established a state college in Athens
in 1785 to include those excluded by the dominantly Anglican

and Calvinist colonial colleges. Similarly, Thomas Jefferson, who was swayed by the Enlightenment and its Deism, urged the foundation of the University of Virginia (1819) as a direct alterna- tive to [Anglican] William and Mary. Daniel Levy sees a political dimension to this. As Jefferson's Republicans overtook Federalists in more state houses, they sought to promote democratization, public opportunities, and accountability as against private elitism, and the new state colleges were part of that.[10] Although the new state governments added another type of college, their power over existing ones was soon restricted. In 1816 the New Hamp- shire state legislature sought control over Dartmouth College, on the basis of having previously granted public funds to the institution. The College trustees resisted all the way to the Supreme Court where Daniel Webster melodramatically pleaded that although it was a small college, 'there are those who love it.'[11] Whether or not the justices shared such sentiments, their *Dart- mouth College Case* ruling established the inviolability of charters. Once granted state charters, private colleges would henceforth be virtually autonomous.

Evangelicals, mostly Baptists and Methodists, found existing colleges sterile or repugnant. Although revivals repudiated educated, overly cerebral clergy, many of the new sects soon themselves adopted the model of a learned clergy and their middle class members wanted educational institutions for their children. The result was a war for control of existing colleges, with some taken over by those demanding more piety, and a spate of new foundations. Thus intensified denominational rivalries were added to the existing mix of colonial (now state) rivalries and local boosterism. The story of Thomas Jefferson's University of Virginia epitomizes the situation: a campus plan with no place for religion, hostility from many Virginians, subsequent take-over, and the re-establishment of religious traditions.

While religion, localism, and social class were central to the way higher education developed in America, the lack of a guiding role by central government especially distinguished American developments from those in Europe. A national university was a logical extension to the new national identity, and one for which George Washington left provision in his will. But the money is untouched and the 'Father of His Country' did not become the Father of a College. As the Constitution did not mention the word 'education' no legal sanction counteracted state and local initiative.

Ethnicity added another layer of collegiate diversity from the mid-eighteenth century, contrary to Appleby's implication that colonial institutions were culturally monolithic. Princeton's connection with Scottish Presbyterianism led it to call John Witherspoon from Paisley, Scotland to become President in 1768. Rutgers's Dutch Reformed connection was echoed in Pennsylvania by the creation of German colleges, Reformed and Lutheran, in the post-Revolutionary decades. Successive immigrants groups saw college founding as an important expression and vehicle of their culture. Scandinavians were no exception. Danes created Dana College (1878) in Elk Horn, Nebraska and Grand View (1895) in Des Moines, Iowa. Norwegians founded St. Olaf's (1886) in Minnesota. Swedish Lutherans created Augustana (1860) in Illinois. Even many institutions that eventually wound up as state colleges, began at the intersection of denominationalism and localism. For instance, in the 1830s western New York Baptists had no institution reflecting their denominational affiliation with reasonable distance. Enticed by an offer of land and cash from local leaders of Brockport, a boom town on the Erie Canal, the Baptist Convention built an impressive structure and started classes. It soon went bankrupt. In a few years it re-opened, and after another financial crisis, accepted affiliation with New York State. Meanwhile the Baptists tried again in a nearby city, successfully founding the University of Rochester. Their original effort became the State University of New York College at Brockport.

It is difficult to imagine a pattern more distinct from Europe, where universities tended to be founded nationally, usually under the sway of an established church. In the United States, higher education was from its earliest days shaped by the intersection of denominationalism, local boosterism, and state support. And although its initial membership was largely confined to

White, Protestant, males, the American college had become a vehicle of ethnic, denominational, state, and local identity. Before long it proved to be a flexible structure which enabled colleges to become important to most groups.

The ambitions of the Catholic hierarchy posed the most significant alternative form of higher education, based on a venerable Jesuit model with significant curricular and social differences. Georgetown, the first Catholic College, was founded in 1789, but Catholic higher education grew very slowly. Not only did it take several generations before significant numbers of Catholics sought higher education, but the majority of them attended Protestant colleges. Leo XXIII's rejection of the 'Americanizers' in 1899 guaranteed continuation of the Jesuit model. It proved to be a Pyrrhic victory for traditionalists as the majority of Catholic students continued to attend non-Catholic colleges, attracted by their potential for enhancing social mobility and/or greater social freedoms. The mainstream Protestant colleges were so open to Roman Catholics, especially the second and third generation Irish and German middle class, that the Church attacked them as 'secular' institutions. Indeed, the most widely read chronicler of the 'Protestant' collegiate tradition, F. Scott Fitzgerald, was raised Catholic.

Catholic colleges had to meet the demand for a Catholic higher education that would meet the rising admission standards of mainstream professional schools. Thus Catholic colleges had to meet the standards of accrediting bodies, enforcing partial conformity to mainstream curricular patterns. Soon, the demand among Catholic women for an education which would give them access to white collar jobs, especially teaching, led to an extensive parallel system of female Catholic colleges. By the 1920s, Catholic colleges and universities had acculturated organizationally. The legendary football prowess of Notre Dame and Fordham demonstrated the compromises made with the mainstream to attract even a respectable minority of college-bound Catholics. Catholic colleges offered a somewhat more disciplined variation on the national model and the prospect of marriage within the faith. After World War Two, upwardly mobile Italians and Poles added to enrollments, but the hierarchy's hope of a distinctive parallel system lost out to the pressures to attract an increasingly Americanized youth.

The relative openness to women also distinguished American colleges from their European counterparts. The first higher educational institutions for women (called 'seminaries') offered piety, domesticity and no degrees. One pioneer, Emma Willard (1819), wrote of 'the absurdity of sending ladies to college,' guaranteeing that her seminary would be 'as different from those appropriated to the other sex, as the female character and duties are from the male.'[12] Normal schools, which prepared teachers, also offered women non-degree bearing advanced education within conventional roles. Outside the South, seminaries were soon replaced either by coeducation or by women's colleges committed to an essentially androgynous curriculum. Vassar (1865), Wellesley and Smith (both 1875), and Bryn Mawr (1884) all took the liberal arts route, while some former seminaries like Holyoke, Rockford, and Mills became colleges in 1880s. These 'Seven Sister' and other leading women's colleges replicated the curriculum of male colleges. In the Midwest and West, coeducation soon became the norm. By 1870 eight state universities (mostly Midwestern 'Big Ten') accepted women. In the 1890s Chicago and Stanford Universities opened as co-educational institutions. The proportion of co-educational institutions soared from 9% in 1870, to 43% in 1890, to 69% in 1930. Women constituted one-third of college enrollments by 1880 and nearly one-half by 1920. At the same time the percentage of young women who attended college rose from 2% to 8%. In the 1920s, although the number of women in higher education rose further, changing sex roles led to a relative decline proportional to men that continued into the 1950s:

| | % of students who were female | % of females age 18–22 in higher education |
|------|------|------|
| 1880 | 33 | 2 |
| 1920 | 47 | 8 |
| 1930 | 44 | 11[13] |

Fritz Ringer estimates that in Europe the proportion of women in universities in 1930 ranged from about 26% in France and Great Britain, to 18% in Germany, 15% in Italy, and 7% in Spain.[14]

An extensive African-American college system also developed with surprising speed after the Civil War. The Black colleges emerged in the North in the decades before the Civil War, the product of Black and White Protestant efforts. With the defeat of the Confederacy came a spate of college foundings, again sponsored largely by northern Protestant denominations. Most prestigious historically Black colleges and universities began in the post-bellum years, including Fisk, Talladega, Tougaloo, Morris Brown, and Morehouse. The struggle between Booker T. Washington and W. E. B. DuBois brought to a head Black educators' debates over the usefulness of a classical college education. Eventually DuBois's belief in the importance of educating a 'Talented Tenth' won out. By the 1920s there was a true Black college system that, while always under financial and social pressures, began generating the leadership class Dubois promoted.

American Jews followed a different path. Unlike Catholics, women, and Blacks, many of whom chose or were forced to adopt a parallel system, there was little interest in separate institutions of higher education among American Jews. German Jews who migrated to the United States in the mid-nineteenth century assimilated rapidly. Reform Judaism and liberal Protestantism shared many sensibilities. Although they faced anti-Semitism, German Jews also found educational opportunities. Leading university presidents such as Woodrow Wilson and William Raine Harper hired Jewish faculties. Many Jewish students gained admission to the most prestigious historically Protestant colleges.

In the 1920s they faced admission quotas, though these were set at levels well above the Jewish proportion of the population. The later generations of eastern European Jews, facing more discrimination and feeling less comfortable in traditionally Protestant colleges, made their mark in urban colleges. After World War Two, with anti-Semitism in retreat, Jewish-Americans' success in higher education reached legendary proportions.

Ironically Protestant Fundamentalists, true descendants of the founders of the college system, by the 1920s were feeling excluded. Changing student life styles and liberal Protestantism drove them to dig in their heels and try to maintain control, especially in the Southern Baptist and Methodist colleges. Elsewhere, after briefly withdrawing, they initiated a new round of college founding. Faith-based Protestant colleges experienced a remarkable resurgence in late twentieth-century America.

Thus, successive American groups adopted, and adapted, a higher education system whose roots reached back to colonial America. It was one supported and differentiated by denominational, ethnic, racial, gender, state, and local identities. By the dawn of the twentieth century, a system originally developed in Protestant, pre-industrial America was successfully adapting to a society being transformed by urbanization, industrialization, and immigration.

But invoking the words 'higher education' and 'system' is misleading. To understand the structural evolution we must return to the late nineteenth century. Few colleges were free-standing. Most were part of multipurpose institutions that also provided secondary 'academies' and even elementary education. The pre-collegiate 'academies' mixed public and private support, and attracted local and boarding students. The college was often an appendage, a luxury financed by the lower grades. Governments were in no position to impose a rational system. The only significant Federal initiative, the Land Grant College Act of 1862, handed the funds and responsibility to the states with minimal oversight. State governments primarily interested themselves in supporting teacher training, first through grants to academies and then by creating 'normal schools' (this odd, seemingly self-deprecating label derived from the French École Normale Supérieure). State universities languished and were virtually indistinguishable from 'private' colleges. Thus in the 1880s about 1,000 multipurpose 'colleges' averaged about 100 collegiate level students and 15 faculty, awarding about 15 degrees annually. Students shared a common curriculum that ranged widely across the Classics and science with some modern language and the rudiments of social science. This chaotic non-system was ripe for rationalization and convergence with Europe. When the 1890s brought near systemic breakdown, convergence with Europe seemed probable.

Germany particularly offered a model. Beginning with four recent Harvard graduates setting sail in 1819, 10,000 American students and scholars followed over the next century. There they imbibed the wonders of post-Napoleonic educational revival, with its stress on specialization, student curricular choice, and specialized faculty freed of *in loco parentis* duties and introductory courses. Most educational leaders of the coming decades, including such diverse figures as Daniel Gilman, M. Carey Thomas, and W. E. B. DuBois imbibed what seemed to be the future. The temporary émigrés brought home scholarly values that inspired creation of discipline-based professional organizations, pedagogical innovation, and incipient concepts of academic freedom. New and reconstituted research universities inspired by the German model drove late nineteenth-century developments. The first, Johns Hopkins University, was founded in 1876 and initially only served graduate students. Its early graduates became academic leaders such as Richard Ely, Frederick Jackson Turner, John Dewey, Woodrow Wilson, and G. Stanley Hall. Harvard scrambled to compete, creating new professional schools and abandoning much of its curriculum and *in loco parentis* controls. Around 1890 came a flood of new universities, including Clark, Chicago, Catholic, and Stanford, which threatened to drown the college.

From below loomed another threat to the traditional American college. Academies, with their *ad hoc* mixture of public and private funding, were being replaced by publicly funded high schools. Some academies metamorphosed into high schools, some closed leaving lovely buildings across the landscape, and a few converted into elite 'prep' schools. Simultaneously the Catholic hierarchy was trying to create the Jesuit-based education system that had no place for the American-style college. Potentially these institutions could produce students equivalent to those in Europe who could proceed directly to specialized 'university' studies. Traditional colleges were on the defensive. They opened unsustainable professional schools and rashly tried to grant PhDs, earned and honorary. They experimented with various parallel curricula and with plentiful electives. Columbia sociologist John Burgess commented in 1884 that 'I am unable to divine what is to be ultimately the position of Colleges which cannot become Universities and which will not be Gymnasia. I cannot see what reason they will have to exist.'[15] Logical, but wrong. Why did this uniquely American form survive and prosper?

The answer is that the colleges successfully re-invented themselves, fitting the predilections of the 'new' (i.e., white-collar) middle class. Advocates of the collegiate way and education for 'the whole man' found an alternative foreign model to compete with Germanic tendencies, the English. The admiration for things British in the American elite and upper middle class boosted its credibility. Books like Chas Astor Bristed's *Five years in an English University* (1852) and John Curtin's *An American at Oxford* (1902) and laudatory articles in leading upper middle class journals like *Saturday Evening Post* familiarized many with a style of education that seemed leisurely, contemplative, and within bounds of genteel propriety. Reflecting a romanticized view of Oxbridge, 'collegiate gothic,' first introduced at Trinity College in Connecticut, became the architecture of choice in the Northeast and Midwest. Its foremost proponent, Ralph Adams Cram, became resident architect at Princeton. Yale and Harvard followed, creating their Oxbridge-style colleges in the 1920s, complete with Collegiate Gothic quadrangles.

Despite this Oxbridge nostalgia, the contrast between the exclusiveness of British higher education and American inclusiveness remained. American higher education was a broad church while the English moved away from their narrow conception of suitability only reluctantly. Indeed the Oxbridge commitment to a narrow church was literal: non-Anglican students were not admitted until 1856 and all Oxbridge lecturers had to be members of the Church of England until 1871. Bertrand Russell suggested that the concept of the gentleman was an idea invented by the British upper class to keep the middle class in order. By encouraging the bourgeoisie to adopt their definition of what constituted an educated man, the English upper class maintained its hegemony at the cost of co-opting more sons of the aspiring middle class into its ranks. The American elite could not, and may not have been inclined to, control higher education in the same way.

Not that they were indifferent to their children's career opportunities; members of the emerging American upper middle class were as keen to pass on their privileged position to their children as their European counterparts were. But they adopted a different means. De Tocqueville said that in France anxiety about status produced high rates of suicide, whereas in America it produced high rates of insanity.[16] It actually produced high American rates of higher education, because there was less concern than in Europe to exclude others from higher education. On the contrary, the underlying idea, as Trow puts it, remains that there must be room, somewhere, 'for everyone who wants an education beyond higher school.'[17]

Alan Ryan's discussion of the ideas of liberal education held by John Stuart Mill and John Dewey illustrates Anglo-American differences nicely.[18] Dewey would have had no quarrel with Mill's wish to live in a society 'with none but a working class,' because Mill meant that he wanted a community 'that was reflective and broadly cultivated, as well as liberally educated in the usual sense.'[19] Dewey and Mill shared an anxiety about the brutalization of the poor without education. But Mill remained a voice outside educational policy-making, by contrast with Dewey. Dewey was committed to 'democratic communitarianism' and he defined democracy as 'free and equal communication and co-operation.'[20] His was an American inclusiveness; there was no

British counterpart to Albert Barnes, John Dewey's close friend, who used his collection of post-impressionist paintings to teach the formally uneducated how to see the world as Renoir and Matisse saw it. In Europe, higher education was seen as something like a lifeboat; if too many people clambered into it, its very purpose would be defeated. But in America, as we have seen, inclusiveness was a key value, and the response to a feeling of exclusion was to create new colleges and universities. Higher education was regarded as rather like the United States itself. If it didn't seem big enough you could pay for some more (the Louisiana Purchase, for example).

In any case the American borrowing of the English model was hardly literal. Partly it drew on a mythical view of Oxbridge that exaggerated its stability and confused new architecture for a venerable Gothic past. And many borrowings were incomplete. Woodrow Wilson launched influential reforms at Princeton on the basis of a brief visit to Oxford. The Claremont Colleges unwittingly copied the University of Toronto rather than Oxbridge. The English model was a myth modelled on a myth that became a powerful argument for perpetuating and reforming an essentially American tradition and defending a broad education for 'the whole man.' President Garfield could proclaim that the best education was 'Mark Hopkins on one end of a log and a student on the other.'[21] Germanic professionalism might carry the day among leading faculty, but not among most trustees, alumni, prospective students, or the public.

The American colleges were creating their own mythology, inventing their own traditions. Few had been able to afford the dormitories, dining halls, and chapels that would have fulfilled their self-image and operationalized the control they statutorily claimed over students' lives. Not only had they shared facilities with secondary and even elementary classes, but even many of their collegiate students had often been in their early teens or late twenties and even thirties. Post-bellum affluent students desired something more genteel. After the Civil War a gentlemanly self-image (soon followed by a female equivalent) appeared persistently in student newspapers. Intercollegiate contact, especially through athletic contests, spread the collegiate self-image. Colleges seeking to attract such students needed to provide facilities to support the appropriate lifestyle. In addition to dining halls, dormitories, classrooms, and laboratories, gymnasiums and stadia were required. The colleges could now truly act *in loco parentis*, but in a different style. Piety was out and the physical exuberance of 'muscular Christianity' was in. Multipurpose institutions shed their academies to eliminate the presence of younger scholars who undercut the collegiate lifestyle. The romantic collegiate life might interfere with academic excellence at times, but it paid substantial financial benefits. Alumni began to offer a dependable source of largesse that would enable colleges to live in a style to which they wished to become accustomed. For state universities, alumni in the legislature became important allies.

If a largely American social model survived among undergraduate students, Germanic specialization was sweeping the academic profession and threatened the place of liberal education in the curriculum. The college found a uniquely American niche in the new system by successfully modernizing liberal education. Woodrow Wilson, borrowing on his experiences at Bryn Mawr, introduced the concept of a 'Chinese menu' first two years guaranteeing sampling the major areas of knowledge (while dropping prescribed courses and attempting comprehensive coverage) in the first two years, followed by two years of a 'major' in a discipline. There would be depth, but also breadth, maintaining a significant difference from European curricula.

College survival alongside research universities required new lines of demarcation. Most colleges gave up their professional schools and attempts to award PhDs. Those functions would henceforth be performed by a small number of research universities. In turn, professional schools came to require bachelors degrees for entry to theology, medicine, law, and doctoral studies. Theological seminaries were the first to require bachelors degrees for admission. When Johns Hopkins Medical School opened in 1893, it required a bachelor degree for admission. The Flexner Report of 1909, backed by Carnegie money, assured victory for that model, which was also adopted in law. Only engineering, among the highest paid professions, would be studied as a first degree.

Below the colleges, the emerging high schools failed to become German-style gymnasia. Instead, most high schools sought to fit their advanced curricula to college requirements and concentrated on attracting a broader range of students rather than offering advanced courses. Pressure for systematic articulation between secondary and higher education led to the codified measures of 'Carnegie Units' and exams administered by the College Board, founded in 1901. By World War One a true system of education had been shaped, with colleges in a central role. They had become the goal for academically talented high school students, the gatekeeper for the leading professions, and a staple of the popular culture via novels, magazines, movies, and athletics.

But why did colleges, bred as they were in a localistic, agrarian society, manage the transition into an urban, industrial America so well? Certainly institutional inertia helps explain their survival, but their remarkable transformation into prosperous omnipresence is best explained by the symbiosis between colleges and the new upper-middle class that was growing in numbers and wealth around the turn of the century. Dramatic class reformation bifurcated the 'old' middle class as the old professions grew and new white collar professions emerged demanding advanced skills and credentials. Engineering, accountancy, public administration, science research, marketing, public relations and advertising, among others grew rapidly. Their dawning professional consciousness was implemented in organizations such as the American Society of Mechanical Engineers (1880), the American Association of Public Accountants (1897), and promoted in journals such as *Printers' Ink* (1888).[22]

A slowly emerging class consciousness and lifestyle emerged in a class looking for an identity and a way to pass their advantages and values to their children. The growing divide between work and home was translated into providing a refuge from the world presided over by a full-time mother. Raising children and adolescents would be extended, expensive, and carefully planned. The urban middle class was having fewer children and their education was lasting longer, ensuring credentials that separated them from the heavily immigrant working class. Crudely stated, in the 1880s high school diplomas provided that separation. In the 1890s participation in the new academic track of high schools provided a firewall. In the new century college increasingly differentiated the upper middle class from the rest. The upper class might depend on 'prep schools,' wealth, and social connections; the upper middle class depended on educational credentials. Colleges became the conduit of choice, fitting many upper-middle class predilections. The 'traditional' college offered relief from urban pressures on bucolic campuses. Its pan-Protestantism provided a respectable but undemanding religion and, while making room for assimilated Irish Catholics and German Jews, offered separation from the millions of 'new' immigrants pouring into the country. Colleges offered relief from Victorian piety and restraints within the careful restraints of the 'new woman' and 'muscular Christianity.'[23] Freed of the annoying preparatory students, 'college democracy' thrived within a relatively homogeneous society of affluent 18 to 22 year olds. The symbiotic relationship of colleges and the emerging upper middle class promoted imagined communities at the intersection of colleges' desires, professions' ambition, parents' hopes, and youth culture.

## American Exceptionalism

By 1906, then, when the German sociologist Sombart posed his famous question about American political exceptionalism – *Why is There No Socialism in America?* – the United States was an exceptional society with an exceptional system of higher education.[24] The scale and shape of its higher education reflected the value of social inclusiveness and the belief that no social group should be left outside. And so did its political culture. In his 1979 discussion of Sombart's question, Karabel (echoing De Tocqueville's remark that Americans had never had a democratic revolution) argued that what set American workers apart from their European counterparts was that they had been denied the experience of exclusion. In America, white men, at least, had always felt that they were part of the social and political system, and had not had to struggle for recognition and the right to vote. Americans lacked social class consciousness. Not, of course, that the United States was a particularly equal society: indeed in economic terms it was rather more unequal than a number of European societies. But it did not have the legacy of a feudal past. It lacked an hereditary proletariat, and ethnic and religious divisions cut across socioeconomic lines. It perceived itself as socially mobile, and although the evidence about comparative levels of social mobility is mixed, there could be no doubting Americans' geographical mobility.[25]

## The Emergence of Mass Higher Education

Thus even before the development of mass higher education in America, a peculiarly American form of higher education had developed, designed to give a large segment of the population the feeling that they were part of a competition in which they had as many options and as much chance as everyone else. This system survived at the same time as American research universities increasingly became part of an international academic world. The latter remained largely invisible to the public, for many of whom the student life and collegiate anthems and totems made higher education seem accessible. By 1930 the system was serving a swath of society unimagined in Europe. Konrad Jarausch's figures below suggest the proportional and absolute differences. Other scholars adjusting for different definitions of higher education have estimated lower differentials. But it is safe to say that three to four times the proportion of the age cohort attended higher education in the United States than in Western Europe before World War Two. The sheer magnitude of American higher education was unrivalled. By 1930 nearly half a million American students were attending about 1,400 different institutions of higher education.

| 1930 | Students | Institutions | Students as % of 20–24-year-olds |
|---|---|---|---|
| Great Britain | 37,255 | 16 | 1.9 |
| Germany | 97,692 | 23 | 2.6 |
| United States | 489,500 | 1,400 | 11.3 |

Rather than open the floodgates, many private colleges chose to curtail growth, thereby raising their admission standards and prestige. The burden fell on the states which created co-ordinated systems. Old state universities presided at the top; former teachers colleges morphed into multipurpose colleges; and a new species, the community college, took the largest share of students. Many of their students transferred to four-year colleges, taking the credits they had achieved at community colleges with them. To use Fritz Ringer's term, state systems of higher education were impressively *unsegmented*. He defines a segmented education system as 'one in which parallel courses of study are separated by institutional or curricular barriers, as well as by differences in the social origins of their students.[26]

Thus both the size and the unsegmented structure of American higher education reflected a history of social inclusiveness and a belief that no social group should be left outside. If existing private and public provision did not cater for a racial, ethnic, religious or social group then it could create its own colleges. Once in a college, a student had the option of transferring to another one. Like the social structure, there were to be no clear divisions. Such inclusiveness was a widely-shared social goal, even though the federal government had little or no role in achieving it as far as higher education was concerned. Indeed so widely held was the value of inclusiveness that very few American voices attacked the breadth of access. It would seem both elitist and irrational to believe, as Trow puts it, that 'our modest state colleges offering modest degrees to students of modest

capacities in any way threaten the academic standards of Princeton or Berkeley, or Michigan.[27] There were no American 'Black
Papers,' as there were in Britain, decrying the very idea of even a
modest expansion of higher education, with proud elitists
fulminating that, as Kingsley Amis put it 'more means worse.'

The basis was established for mass higher education in
America. It was perhaps indicative of the social and psychological
role of higher education in America that college financing was
one of the principal benefits offered to World War Two veterans.
Whether the 'GI Bill' boosted the number attending significantly
is debated, but it certainly increased the sense that higher education was accessible. And when the massive post-war 'baby boom'
hit the campuses in the 1960s, mass higher education became a
reality. With participation rates approaching 50%, the world's
first attempt to provide mass higher education was well and truly
launched as America stumbled into Vietnam and campuses
captured headlines. Structures begun as vehicles of ethno-reli-
gious identity for an agrarian society had morphed into another
exceptional venture.

## Mass Higher Education: Initial Divergence

In the 1980s or 1990s, then, a European looking at higher education in the United States would readily accept the idea that, with
its scale, diversity and relative lack of segmentation, there was a
great deal that was exceptional about it. Ten years after his
discussion of the weakness of a socialist tradition in America,
Karabel took his argument further. Not only can the absence of a
class-based socialist party be understood as a function of the
pattern of social class relations, but the unsegmented character of
American education, too, reflects United States perceptions of
social inequality, specifically the perceived seamlessness of the
United States social class system.[28] Indeed the relationship
between educational structures and class patterns is mutually
reinforcing, since education helps sustain those patterns by a twin
process of obscuration and legitimation. Obscuration, because the
perceived equality of opportunity encouraged the belief that

America was a uniquely open society, where inherited position was relatively unimportant. Legitimation, because the same perception gave a meritocratic sheen to those in positions of power.

Divisions between the kinds of education received by secondary age students who were perceived to have different aptitudes and abilities were accepted, but only with careful provision to reduce the impact of, for example, tracking or accelerated programs. In higher education, too, colleges and universities were linked, both in principle and at least to some extent in reality, within a system which allowed students to move between institutions. Brint and Karabel attach great importance to the role of Community Colleges, and argue that although few students actually transfer from, say, East Los Angeles Community College to Berkeley, the fact that the system is constructed to make such a movement possible is hugely significant. Those few economically poor students who make the transfer are disproportionately important, because they carry the message that both the educational system, and the social class system, are unsegmented. The principle of portability of American academic credits means that a student may transfer several times during the process of gaining a degree. This applies to a greater extent to public higher education in the United States than to the private sector, but even there, portability means that there is movement both within the private sector of higher education, and between the private and public sectors. And the sense that the system of higher education is accessible is a key factor in mobilizing support for public expenditure on universities in the United States.

The social inclusiveness of the United States system of higher education in the late twentieth century was a marked contrast to European systems. This can be illustrated by taking one example, the United Kingdom.

At the heart of the postwar model for British education was the idea that different sorts of people needed different sorts of education. There should be an educational separation which was parallel to the social class separation which all foreign observers noted. The segmented character of education in Britain reflected perceptions of social inequality in a society with a high level of social class consciousness. A brief account of a student's journey through the educational system indicates how much educational segmentation there was in postwar Britain. At the age of 11 most children faced a selection process, usually based on a combination of intelligence testing and examinations, which resulted in the segregation of secondary students into different schools. The fifth or quarter perceived to have greater academic potential went to the grammar schools. These had a traditional academic style, which one apologist, Robin Davis, described as '... a "sit down and think" school for "sit down and think" children.' Those not selected, the '11+ failures,' went to schools which most left at the statutory leaving age of 15 or 16, never to return to education. At the age of 14 students started a two year course in preparation for public examinations taken at 16. Once again there were diverging paths: more academic students took 'Ordinary Level' General Certificate of Education, while the others either took no exams at all, or took the less traditionally academic Certificate of Secondary Education. Most students had left full-time education by the age of 16, but for those who had not, there was, once again a sharp distinction between those on university and non-university tracks.

The society whose educational system had such diverging paths was stable, but there was little sense of fellow-feeling across class lines. Ralph Dahrendorf described British social structure as being like a layer cake: the strata were sufficiently separate to be easily distinguishable.[29] As Ralph Turner put it in his classic discussion of modes of upward mobility in Britain and the United States, the British system sought to inculcate a sense of inferiority and deference among those who were destined for low status.[30] The fact that this did not alienate them, indeed that it helped to legitimate the structures of inequality in Britain, indicates the traditional shape of British society. David Lockwood, describing traditional patterns of images of social inequality held by manual workers in Britain, indicates that traditional working class people saw themselves as separated from non-manual workers.[31] For some, this was because nature had endowed their betters with superior qualities. For others, their bosses simply had greater access to power. But, whether on the one hand they were conservative and deferential, or on the other saw society as dichotomous, and sought to organise to defend 'us' against 'them,' traditional manual workers assumed that their world had few points of contact with that of the white-collar worker.

All societies need to pacify the disadvantaged, to give them the sense that they are better off accepting the way things are rather than rejecting it, but according to Turner the United States secured the quiescence of its less educated members differently. They were encouraged to perceive themselves as essentially the fellows of those in superior positions. They were also expected to be future oriented and to hold unrealistic aspirations. But Brint and Karabel add an interesting twist to Turner: in the United States the less advantaged were offered the prospect of higher education. In Britain, by contrast, there was a welfare state. To oversimplify this argument: a society with an unsegmented class system (United States) has an unsegmented education system which was inclusive because of its size and diversity. Britain, by contrast, had both a segmented class system and an education system which was not only segmented, but also relatively small, and nationally homogeneous.

It seemed to a number of distinguished observers that this contrast would remain. In 1989 Martin Trow argued that the attitudes and values that had characterised British policy and practice in higher education since World War Two were 'incompatible with the provision of mass higher education to much more than the 15% of the age grade currently enrolled in British higher education.'[32] Since those beliefs were 'widely accepted by the people who make the decisions' a significant expansion was unlikely. In 1987, Gary Rhoades had suggested that the key to understanding American higher education was that the American academe was able to respond flexibly to the demands made by its consumers. The comparatively weak influence of American political structures on higher education was important. 'In Europe, academic structures and organization tend to inhibit flexibility; in America they make the higher education system more willing to supply what various customers demand

Gary Rhoades also argued that British educational values were so deeply embedded, and so thoroughly supported by the university establishment, that changing the exams taken by secondary students, for example, was almost impossible.[33] Although only a small proportion of the age group went to degree-awarding institutions of higher education, the universities had a good deal of influence on the content of secondary school curriculums, because of their control of the examinations at 16 and 18. The sponsorship norms described by Ralph Turner were intact. Writing from an American perspective Rhoades said of Britain: 'Secondary schools were designed not to include, assimilate and prepare all students for common citizenship, as they were in the United States, but to exclude, select and prepare the elite in a special way for their natural station.'[34]

## Convergence in the 1990s

What is striking about educational changes in Britain in the years leading up to the end of the twentieth century, however, is how radical they were, and how wrong these observers turned out to be. In Britain, universities came to resemble American ones more than ever before. From the growth in numbers of both students and universities, to the introduction of semesters, the increased student concern about grades, the growth of consumerism (as evidenced, for example, by the use of student evaluations), to the development of credit transfer, the introduction of student loans and tuition fees, and the reduction in the amount of individual teaching contact, the British system of higher education grew more like a United States state system. There was a parallel shift from a manpower-planning model (which despite the Thatcher government's scepticism about planning and faith in markets, was still to be found in British higher education policy as late as the mid–1980s) to a market-led model. Individual decisions by students about courses increasingly came to dominate management decisions in universities. And the locus of management itself shifted: the role of central administration grew, and power moved away from the departmental level.

Let us examine the changes in Britain in terms of the three factors we identified as characterizing American higher education. First, *scale*. In 1962 the number of full-time students enrolled in British institutions of higher education was 216,000. 'By 1989–1990, including home and overseas students, part-timers in universities, the Open University, the polytechnics, and other colleges offering advanced courses, it was 1,086,300.'[35] In 1998–99 the total figure was 2,081,664. The Age Participation Index (the number of entrants to full-time higher education as a percentage of the 18–22 year old population), which was less than 8 at the beginning of the 1960s, reached 33 by the end of the century, and was expected to continue to rise. The scale of this change is so great that it represents not only a qualitatively different phenomenon, but also a radical shift away from the values held in the past. Within a few years of Trow's description of the strength of 'the Robbins Trap,' the 15% hurdle had been left far behind.

Second, *diversity*. There is a paradox in the way the diversity within British higher education grew during the period when the polytechnics became designated universities, and the sector appeared to become unitary instead of binary. But the range of courses available within the rubric of higher education increased in variety at the same time as the huge increase in the number of students. The Dearing Report recognised this as a strength, and argued that 'the diversity of programme provision and of students' would continue to be important.[36] It did, however, discuss the twin problems of convergence and quality. One the one hand, pressures of funding and of reputation might lead all universities to value the same kinds of activities. Conversely, how could a system based on mutual assurance of quality be effective if institutions were doing very different things from one another? As Roger King put it, 'to establish first-class credentials on the world stage requires institutions to understand clearly and strategically what are their distinctive strengths and weaknesses.'[37] But despite these problems, the range of academic experiences available within British higher education became greater than ever, as did the number of partnerships between institutions. There was also a new emphasis in many institutions on links with the local community, and the desirability of responsiveness to local needs – yet another source of diversity.

Third, *non-segmentation*. The British system sought to minimise segmentation, subjecting few of its 11 year olds to a selection process to determine whether they attended a more academic secondary school or not. The modal high school became comprehensive. The only constraint faced by most students was space, and gaining admission to an oversubscribed school was largely a matter of geography. Once in the secondary school, students followed a common curriculum, and took a common examination, the GCSE, at 16. No longer did most leave school at 16. For those who remained in education beyond 16 there was a wide range of courses and examinations available, in addition to the traditional 'A' levels. Most important of all, several non-'A'-level routes to university were developed. The British educational values that had seemed so fixed to Rhoades in 1987 did not prevent the creation of a non-segmented system a decade or so later. Even the distinction between Higher and Further education, a hitherto unbridgeable gulf, narrowed. The student figure of more than two million for 1998–99 cited above included 235,907 who were taking higher education courses offered in the Further Education sector. Many universities came to regard local colleges of Further Education as 'partner institutions,' and local partnerships and consortia, enabling students at one institution to take a course at another, became common. Some of these were long-distance partnerships, making use of the internet.

In Britain, then, there was a quiet abandonment of the idea that there should be different sorts of education for different sorts of people. This is not to deny, of course, that there are still significant aspects of American higher education which are different. The presence of private colleges, the importance of religious institutions, the absence of a significant role for central government, the liberal arts core requirement, the greater power of the college president in the United States, and the role of lay boards are all quite different from higher education in Europe.

But the differences are fewer, and the similarities greater, than in the past.

We have drawn from the British example, because it is the most dramatic illustration of the adoption of American patterns. A higher education system that was more unlike the American one than most changed rapidly, and came to resemble it to a degree that seemed impossible a few years previously. Our argument is that this did not happen in a vacuum, but reflects fundamental changes in British society. The British are less class conscious than they were. At the top, the hereditary principle for membership of the House of Lords has been rejected, and re-spectable newspapers are even advocating the abolition of the monarchy. More generally, the British increasingly hold (to use Lockwood's term) a 'pecuniary' model of society: they think of one another, and of the society in which they live, as a matter of having more or less money, rather than membership of one layer or another of a hierarchical society. Deference is not dead, but is terminally unwell.

Although we have focused on Britain, a similar case can be made for other higher education systems. According to an article in the OECD publication *PEB Exchange* in 1996, most industrial countries will soon have an age participation rate of 50% or more.[38] The huge growth in enrolment throughout the developed world reflects demand as much as deliberate expansionary policies. 'We know this because in many countries there is no tight government control over numbers of places.... In France ... more than half the students now go on to some form of higher education. In Australia, between 1939 and 1999, as the country's population increased less than threefold, university enrolments went up from 14,000 to 681,000 – almost a fifty-fold increase.' And the Japanese government, faced with growing demand for higher education but knowing that they face a projected population decline after 2011, decided to hold the participation rate at the current 50% rather than expand too far.[39] Similarly, the decline in class consciousness is not confined to Britain, even if it is most noticeable there. As Dahrendorf says, 'in contemporary OECD societies there is no class conflict in the classical sense of the term.'[40] The language of class conflict is still sometimes employed, but even where there are wide gaps between north and south, as in Italy or Britain, 'class in the old sense is not the dominant basis of conflict.' In such societies it is unsurprising that systems of higher education are also changing.

## Conclusion

This convergence with American patterns of higher education is not a response to implacable political demand: indeed when the British Conservative government first raised the possibility of expansion and imposing some parental fees it backed down because of rumblings of discontent within what was perceived to be their natural middle-class, middle-England constituency. However, when change happened, it was accepted smoothly. There were no riots in Tunbridge Wells, and the attitude survey by Rootes and Heath found that there was widespread support within Britain for further expansion.[41]

Our explanation is threefold. First, convergence in higher education reflected growing similarity in distribution of wealth and political ideology. Despite echoes of the class divisions of the past, the structure of social inequality in Britain, and elsewhere, has come to resemble that in the United States to a significant extent. This has led to political changes. To return to the British case, the postwar Labour Party depended for its support on a sense of class consciousness and segmentation which is no longer available. 'Tax and Spend' has become a political liability, and the Labour defeat in 1992 is widely interpreted as evidence that the British electorate will no longer vote for higher taxes. Indeed before winning the election in 1997, the party renamed itself New Labour, a change that reflected reduced support for the welfare state. Social welfare spending was originally seen as creating inclusive programs which would achieve a sense of social integration among British citizens. The decline in universal welfare provision coincided with the introduction of mass higher education, exactly as Brint and Karabel would have predicted.

Secondly, once the decision was taken to expand the scale of its higher education system, Britain really only had one model of mass higher education available to it: the United States. Nowhere else made higher education accessible to such a wide section of its young people. Quite apart from the common language, and the fact that so many of its academics had spent time in America, it was inevitable that a British mass higher education system would resemble patterns in the United States rather than those of any other society.

Finally, it is increasingly difficult to discuss any national system of higher education in isolation. There is a global higher education market. Faculty, administrators, students and policy-makers all have greater international awareness, and almost every week a new international higher education partnership is announced. Few doubt that this globalization will grow. Already Britain's University and College Admission Service is discussing offering other countries its expertise in using the university admission process to widen participation.[42] And Student Unions (like the labour unions) have created a European Student Union to give a supra-national voice to students.[43]

We do not know the shape of things to come. De Tocqueville thought he spotted the way things were going:

The more I advanced in the study of American society, the more I perceived that the equality of conditions is the fundamental fact from which all others seem to be derived, and the central point at which all my observations constantly terminated.

I then turned my thoughts to our own hemisphere, where I imagined that I discerned something analogous to the spectacle which the New World presented to me. I observed that the equality of conditions is daily progressing towards those extreme limits which it seems to have reached in the United States, and that the democracy which governs the American communities appears to be rapidly rising into power in Europe.[44]

Convergence in access to higher education has taken a long time. And the trajectory has not been linear: much that characterises American higher education is not to be found in other systems. But the scale, diversity and relative lack of segmentation of higher education in America are no longer exceptional. Moreover it is reasonable to believe that this change is a permanent one. With higher education, as with trial by jury, the vote, and government pensions, it is easier for governments to give than to take away. The coming of mass higher education outside America, was, of course a shock to traditional elitists, who interpreted the arrival of the muddy boots of the newly-enfranchised as a sign that educational standards had been betrayed. What had in fact happened was that those societies had become less rigidly segmented. And with that change, American and European institutions were converging, dramatically reducing the uniqueness of one of America's most 'exceptional' ventures.

## Notes

1. Martin Trow, 'American Higher Education: "Exceptional" or just Different?' *Is America Different? A New Look at American Exceptionalism*, ed. Byron E. Shafer (Oxford: Clarendon, 1991), 138–39.
2. Dale Carter 'American Exceptionalism: An Idea That Will Not Die,' *American Studies in Scandinavia*, 29 (1997): 76–84.
3. Joyce Appleby, 'Recovering America's Historic Diversity: Beyond Exceptionalism,' *Journal of American History*, 79 (1992): 419–31.
4. Appleby, 420.
5. Alexis De Tocqueville, *Democracy In America* (New York: Vintage, 1945), 2: 108
6. Alexis De Tocqueville, *Democracy in America: Specially edited and abridged for the Modern Reader*, ed. Richard D. Heffner (New York: New American Library of World Literature, 1956), 10.
7. Byron E. Shafer, 'What is the American Way? Four Themes in Search of Their Next Incarnation,' in Shafer, ed., *A New Look*, 234–35.
8. Appleby, 425.
9. Samuel Eliot Morison, *The Intellectual Life of Colonial New England* (Ithaca, NY: Cornell University Press, 1956), 252–53.
10. Daniel Levy, 'The Rise of Private Universities in Latin America and the United States,' *The Sociology of Educational Expansion, Take-off, Growth and Inflation in Educational Systems*, ed. Margaret S. Archer (Beverly Hills: Sage, 1982), 102–03.
11. Richard Hofstadter and Wilson Smith, ed., *American Higher Education: A Documentary History* (Chicago: University of Chicago Press, 1961), 212.

12. Barbara M. Solomon, *In the Company of Educated Women* (New Haven: Yale University Press, 1985), 14.
13. Solomon, 63–64.
14. Fritz Ringer, 'Patterns of Access to Modern European Universities: Rates of Enrollment,' *History of Higher Education Annual*, 14 (1994): 113.
15. Frederick Rudolph, *The American College and University* (New York: Random House, 1962), 330.
16. Robert Nisbet 'Alexis de Tocqueville,' *International Encyclopedia of the Social Sciences*, 16: 92.
17. Trow, 'American Higher Education,' 139.
18. Alan Ryan, *Liberal Anxieties and Liberal Education* (New York: Hill and Wang, 1998).
19. Ryan, 59, 60.
20. Ryan, 135, 128.
21. Rudolph, 243.
22. See Olivier Zunz, *Making America Corporate, 1870–1920* (Chicago: University of Chicago Press, 1990).
23. See especially Lynn Gordon, *Women and Higher Education in the Progressive Era* (New Haven: Yale University Press, 1990), and Paula Fass, *The Damned and the Beautiful* (New York: Oxford University Press, 1977).
24. Werner Sombart, *Why Is There No Socialism in the United States?* (White Plains, NY: International Arts and Sciences Press, 1976; first published in German in 1906).
25. The question of American political exceptionalism has been widely discussed, of course, especially by Seymour Martin Lipset, *American Exceptionalism: A Double-Edged Sword* (New York: Norton, 1996), and Seymour Martin Lipset and Gary Marks, *It Didn't Happen Here: Why Socialism Failed in the United States* (New York: Norton, 2000).
26. Fritz Ringer, *Education and Society in Modern Europe* (Bloomington: Indiana University Press, 1979), 29.
27. Trow, 'American Higher Education,' 63.
28. Steven Brint and Jerome Karabel, 'American Education, Meritocratic Ideology, and the Legitimation of Inequality: The Community College and the Problem of American Exceptionalism,' *Higher Education*, 18 (1989): 725–35.
29. Ralph Dahrendorf, *On Britain* (London: British Broadcasting Corporation, 1982), 55.
30. Ralph Turner, 'Sponsored and Contest Mobility and the School System,' *American Sociological Review*, 25 (1960): 855–67.
31. David Lockwood, 'Sources of Variation in Working Class Images of Society,' *Sociological Review*, 14 (1966): 249–67.
32. Martin Trow, 'The Robbins Trap: British Attitudes and the Limits of Expansion,' *Higher Education Quarterly*, 43 (1989): 55–75.
33. Gary Rhoades, 'Folk Norms and School Reform: English Secondary Schools,' *Sociology of Education*, 60 (1987): 44–53.

34. Rhoades, 48–49.
35. A. H. Halsey, 'Opening Wide the Doors of Higher Education,' *Education Economics*, 1 (1993): 85.
36. National Committee of Inquiry into Higher Education, *Higher Education in the Learning Society* (London, HMSO, 1997), paragraph 10, 102.
37. Roger King, 'World Class Means Domestic Diversity,' *Times Higher Education Supplement*, 12 September 1997.
38. David Jobbins, 'Planning and Designing Higher Education Facilities,' *PEB Exchange*, 27 (March, 1996).
39. Tony Tysome, 'Japan Faces Number Crunching Future,' *Times Higher Education Supplement*, 25 October 1996.
40. Ralph Dahrendorf, *The Modern Social Conflict: an Essay on the Politics of Liberty* (London: Weidenfeld and Nicolson, 1988), 159.
41. Chris Rootes and Anthony Heath, 'Differences of Degree: Attitudes towards Universities,' in *British Social Attitudes: The 12th Report*, ed. R Jowell et al (London: Dartmouth Publishing Company, 1995).
42. Harriet Swain, 'Net Opens Way to Global Admissions System,' *Times Higher Education Supplement*, 27 September 1996.
43. Jane Marshall, 'European Students Secure Lang's Backing for a Role in Making Policy,' *Times Higher Education Supplement*, 10 November 2000.
44. De Tocqueville, 1: 3.

# Laws

# 'They Came to Lawyers, You Know, What Can You Do?'[1] American Exceptionalism and Judicial Activism

*Helle Porsdam*

The concept of American exceptionalism has recently been the target of heavy criticism. Implicit in 'exceptionalism,' critics claim, is an attempt to characterize American society as a unified whole, and in a completely multicultural society such as the American any talk of a national character makes little sense. Historian Joyce Appleby is one critic who has taken issue with American exceptionalism. In her presidential address to the Organization of American Historians in the spring of 1992, she described it as a version, or rather perversion, of European Enlightenment ideas. The grand narrative of American exceptionalism, she argued, has been 'America's peculiar form of Eurocentrism.' It has ignored the 'original and authentic diversity' in America's past, especially the Colonial past, and has foreclosed 'other ways of interpreting the meaning of the United States.' It has cast into the shadows experiences of people whose errand has not been self-promotion and autonomy, and it has imbued with universality particular social traits – virtually all white and male. When looking at the American past and present through the lens of American exceptionalism, therefore, American historians and others have been blinded to the importance of the multicultural agenda, and the time has now come to move beyond exceptionalism 'to recover the historic diversity of our past.'[2]

For fashioning out of American exceptionalism an ideology that would unite all Americans, Appleby blames the country's lawyers. At the time of the Revolution, the few things that all

*Marks of Distinction: American Exceptionalism Revisited*, ed. Dale Carter, *The Dolphin* 32, pp. 231–56. © 2001 by Aarhus University Press, Denmark. ISBN 87 7288 383 9; ISSN 0106 4487.

Americans actually did have in common were British in origin
and consequently had to be redefined. Among ordinary Americans, moreover, there existed no great wish to form 'a more
perfect union.' What mattered to most people were local ties, local
politics. When therefore nationalist leaders, most of whom were
lawyers, took it upon themselves to turn American exceptionalism into a unifying ideology, they did not enjoy the support of the
people:

The case for a 'more perfect union' was made in a lawyerly fashion by
nationalist leaders, most of them lawyers. Outside of their circles, there
were abroad in the land few common sentiments, fewer shared assumptions operating at the intimate level of human experience, and a paucity
of national symbols recognizable from Georgia to Maine.[3]

Joyce Appleby is not the only critic to point to the role of law
and lawyers in the creation of an exceptional United States. Nor is
she alone in criticizing the general unwillingness to deal with
America's multicultural histories. Unlike some of her colleagues,
however, Appleby fails to point out that American common law
and judicial activism are an important part of the legacy of
America's colonial past.[4] The very multiculturalism that she
celebrates in her presidential address has been fostered by activist
lawyers and judges, most notably in the Civil Rights movement.
Down through American history, the law and the courts, by
providing social definitions for events and transactions, and by
extending citizenship to previously 'unwanted' groups of people
have constituted one of the few fora or 'things' all Americans
have in common. 'Can a multicultural nation of nearly a quarter
of a billion people be a community?,' asks Kenneth Karst in
*Belonging to America*. His answer is a resounding yes; being an
American essentially means adhering to the American civic
culture and to behave according to that culture's norms. Karst's
civic culture is made up of five elements: individualism, egalitarianism, democracy, nationalism, and tolerance of diversity, and
what ties these elements together is an ideology, 'a creed that is
both manifested in our constitutional doctrine and shaped by it.'[5]

In Karst's version of American exceptionalism, that is, it is the law which translates ideology into behavior.

Lawrence M. Friedman has talked about an 'American legal culture,'[6] Sanford Levinson about an American 'faith community' centered around the Constitution, and Mary Ann Glendon about American 'rights talk' and 'law-riddenness' – others have referred to American legalism or legalization. Like Kenneth Karst, these commentators on American culture and society tend to see the law and its practitioners as protectors and translators into actual day-to-day behavior of American exceptionalism. This chapter will argue that any discussion about American exceptionalism will have to take into account the role of law and lawyers in American culture. Section one will focus, in a general and speculative way, on judicial activism – how it has been used, particularly since *Brown v. Board of Education of Topeka* in 1954, in the service of national community, to make America more inclusive, and how its emphasis on a protection of rights and due process originates in the common law.

As illustrations or case studies of how judicial activism works in practice, I shall then turn, in section two, to Melissa Fay Greene, *Praying for Sheetrock* (1991), and David L. Kirp, John P. Dwyer, and Larry A. Rosenthal, *Our Town. Race, Housing, and the Soul of Suburbia* (1995). The former is a study of how civil rights came to McIntosh County, Georgia in the 1970s, and the latter tells the story of the creation of something like a right to fair housing in New Jersey over a period of two decades. In both books, judicial activism markets 'a very new commodity: Law. For the poor'[7] – a commodity that seeks to de-segregate, to include those who have hitherto not been seen as welcome additions to American society. The assumption will be throughout that the arguments advanced by Kenneth Karst and other believers in American exceptionalism are ultimately more persuasive than are those of Joyce Appleby.

## Judicial Activism: The Theory

In an interesting article on 'The 'Hegelian Secret': Civil Society and American Exceptionalism,' Daniel Bell argues first of all that it does make sense to talk about American differentness and secondly, that this differentness has to do with the United States being a 'complete *civil society*, perhaps the only one in political history.' By civil society Bell means a society in which individual self-interest and a passion for liberty reign supreme. In such a society, no institutional structures – no state in a European sense – have been created 'to shape and enforce a unitary will over and above particular interests.' What has taken the place of a state in the United States, Bell argues, is a government or political marketplace, 'an area in which interests contended (not always equally) and where deals could be made.' The foundation for the American civil society has been inalienable, naturally endowed rights inhering in each individual rather than in a group or a community of people, and institutions have been created for the purpose of protecting these rights. Among such institutions, the Supreme Court has played a very special and very important role:

Fortuitously, for it was not planned (nor were these powers specified in the Constitution), the Supreme Court became the final arbiter of disputes, and the mechanism for the adjustment of rules, which allowed the political marketplace to function, subject to the amendment of the Constitution itself – which then again was interpreted by the court. The Constitution and the court became the bedrock of civil society.

The Constitution, Bell suggests, has provided a social contract, 'a contract initially between the several states, yet transferred over time as a social contract between the government and the people. It may be the only successful social contract we know in political history, perhaps because the state was so weak and often non-existent.'[8]

Americans have remained committed to constitutionalism and judicial activism. From the Supreme Court down, courts have generally been perceived to have a special responsibility as arbiters, even legitimators, of change. The degree of authority which American judges exercise is unparalleled among modern Western nations. Americans tend to take this for granted, writes Gordon S. Wood:

> but any foreign observer is immediately overwhelmed by the extent to which the courts not only set aside laws passed by popularly elected legislatures but also interpret and construe the law in such a way as to make social policy. It is not simply the power of the Supreme Court, which tends to be the focus of our attention, but the power of all courts, both federal and state, to interpret the law in accordance with either written constitutions or fundamental principles of justice and reason that is impressive. Nowhere else in the modern world do judges wield as much power in shaping the contours of life as they do in the United States.[9]

Law professors and political experts engage in lengthy and complicated discussions from time to time as to the desirability for a modern democracy such as the American of having the courts resolve issues that are essentially political.[10] In other modern democracies issues concerning for example racial desegregation, abortion or the relationship between religion and the government would be looked upon as political matters which ought to be determined by parliamentary legislation.[11]

When legal and political commentators criticize this exercise of judicial authority as unwarranted and issue warnings against judicial encroachment or usurpation, however, their criticism does not seem to meet with too much approval from the general public. The staying power of judicial activism as well as of the most important 'tool' with which the Supreme Court pursues its activist course, judicial review, 'is an undeniable historical fact,' according to Kenneth Karst. He claims that we can talk about an American 'natural-rights mentality' – a mentality that, 'accompanied by a receptiveness to judicial review, has stayed rooted in the popular folklore for reasons only indirectly related to democracy, either economic or political.'[12] As we shall see shortly, natural-rights doctrines such as substantive due process and its modern offshoots in the equal protection field have their origins in the common law.

The Supreme Court first claimed the power of judicial review in *Marbury v. Madison* (1803). The practice of judicial review has been 'so extraordinary, so pervasive, and so powerful,' however, claims Gordon Wood, that we have to look beyond this particular decision to the history of American jurisprudence and American legal culture as a whole to discover its origins. In colonial America, old beliefs in law as something discovered, not made lingered on long after such beliefs had been effectively discredited in the mother country by positivist thinkers such as John Austin. The colonists 'were much more conscious than their English cousins of the distinctiveness of the common law – as something set apart from statutory law and even from current English judicial decisions and precedents,' and persisted in identifying the common law with 'right reason or natural justice – with principles that existed apart from current English statutes and judicial decisions.'[13]

The continued American preoccupation with the morality of law was a result of the ambiguities and complexities of colonial law. Judges had to take into consideration before handing down their decisions not only English legal sources (common-law reports, new judicial interpretations, and parliamentary statutes) but also local colonial statutes and judicial customs. Often, conditions would be so different in the New World that no suitable precedents could be found in English law, or local customs so undeveloped that judges had to take recourse to the immutable maxims of reason or justice. The extraordinary degree of judicial discretion that was needed under these circumstances paved the way for judicial review:

Amidst the confusion and disorder of colonial law, lawyers and judges found that they had really no other basis except reason and equity for clarifying their law and for justifying their deviations from English practice. By resting their law on some principle beyond statutory will or the technicalities of the common law – on justice or common sense or utility – the colonists prepared the way for what we came to know as judicial review.[14]

With the exception of the infamous *Dred Scott* case in 1857, the Court made little use of its power to declare statutes unconstitutional until the late nineteenth and early twentieth centuries. At this point, judicial review was mainly used to uphold old forms of privilege. It was only after the Second World War and in particular with *Brown v. Board of Education* that the Court started concentrating on the rights of the underprivileged:

The truth is, that where rights pertaining to fair criminal procedure, equal legal treatment, free expression, or privacy are concerned, the United States Supreme Court has only a slightly longer experience than a great number of other nations. For us, too the great expansion of personal liberties and civil rights began in the post-World War Two period.[15]

The *Brown* decision, says Kenneth Karst, is 'our leading authoritative symbol for the principle that the Constitution forbids a system of caste.' With the Warren Court's decision in favor of racial equality, the principle of equal citizenship was revived. That principle had become formal law when the Fourteenth Amendment was ratified in 1868. For almost a century, the Court had been reluctant to realize its potential, however, for fear of fundamentally changing the relation between the federal government and the states. When, after the Second World War, political leaders as well as the population at large showed a certain willingness to reconsider matters concerning race and equal citizenship, the Supreme Court responded. In the late 1940s and early 1950s, the Court handed down a number of decisions that had been unimaginable only a few years earlier.

The Justices who decided *Brown v. Board of Education* perceived the Fourteenth Amendment's guarantee of liberty and equality in the way every one of us perceives: through the filters created by the perceiver's acculturating experience. The Justices understood that the whole system of racial segregation was a betrayal of the central values of American civic culture. And political action, from the Niagara movement to the threatened march on Washington, had helped the Justices to understand.[16]

The revival of equal citizenship in *Brown* amounted to a formal redefinition of the national community. When Chief Justice Warren wrote the opinion for the Court in the *Brown* cases, he recognized 'the strong connection between the meaning of the Constitution and the national community of meaning that is the American civic culture.' Of the five elements that make up Karst's civic culture, the most interesting – at least for the purposes of this paper – is nationalism. The civic culture defines the national community, Karst claims, and nobody has done more to uphold and protect that community than the country's judges. When activist, these judges, and especially the justices on the Supreme Court, have been nation-builders – the prime example being *Brown*, which expanded the meaning and actual contents of belonging. 'Validation of a claim of equal citizenship is not merely important to the individual claimant. It also forms part of the social cement that makes the nation possible.' When legislatures have defaulted, courts and lawyers have reacted, thereby providing a 'cultural glue,' a frame that may hold all Americans together, however uneasily.[17]

Courts have been in a better position than have legislatures to defend the principle of equal citizenship. Not subject to majoritarian domination, courts have generally been insulated from partisan politics. Their point of departure being concrete cases, moreover, judges have acquired a way of thinking that emphasizes prudence or practical wisdom. The training in practical wisdom starts in the country's law schools where students are exposed to the case method of instruction. What the case method essentially consists of, Anthony Kronman has argued, is forced role-playing. In reenacting concrete disputes by playing the roles of the original parties and their attorneys, students learn to be sympathetic to a whole range of different points of view. Ultimately, it is the role of the judge that is given priority. This has the effect, according to Kronman, of emphasizing the need to reach a 'reasoned' and 'publicly justifiable' conclusion to the problems at hand, thereby encouraging student interest in civic-mindedness.[18] In American civil society or political marketplace where individual interests contend, it would thus seem, it has fallen to lawyers and judges to defend the public good. 'If there are possibilities for some realization of the republican vision in today's polity, they appear to lie with the judiciary.'[19]

The use of law as an instrument of 'policy' and social engineering is a reconstruction of the common law.[20] Naturally preoccupied with the most basic requirements of the law, the common law has provided from the very outset a useful vocabulary in which to talk about conceptions of individually-centered justice. 'As against the continental legal system with its powerful inquiring magistrates, Anglo-American legal procedure has been an adversarial one, with an emphasis on rights.'[21] The common law and common-law judges have always been held in high esteem. Even though by far the majority of cases that reach the nation's courts are statute-law rather than common-law cases, American lawyers still tend to consider the common law the truest expression and repository of the most basic legal rights and principles. 'Not even the most learned treatise can do justice to the fertility, variety, and ambiguity of the case law, its surprising ability to put out new shoots, or to turn an old theme to a fresh purpose. American judges at their best have been virtuosos of practical reason,' as Glendon puts it.[22]

The common law dates back to the twelfth century and possibly beyond. Its boundaries have always been defined by prevailing community standards. What gave authority to the common law as a legal order entitled to the highest respect was the belief that it embodied centuries of human wisdom. Emphasizing continuity and peaceful incorporation of change rather than sudden and violent reform, and residing in the customs of the community rather than in the political system, the common law understood law as developing out of and along with the people. 'Law by and large evolves; it changes in piecemeal fashion. Revolutions in essential structure are few and far between. That at least is the Anglo-American experience. Some of the old is preserved among the mass of the new.'[23]

What all common lawyers share is 'an emphasis on the ongoing cultivation of a concrete historical tradition.'[24] This ongoing, dynamic, and incomplete tradition encompasses both theory and practice. The common law does not consist only of the legal doctrines derived from binding official legal sources such as statutes and precedents. Under the institutional principles that govern the common law, what Melvin Eisenberg calls 'social propositions' – propositions of morality, policy, and experience – are relevant in all cases. One of the key questions in common-law reasoning concerns precisely the interaction of social and doc-trinal propositions, and it is not difficult, Eisenberg claims, to see why such propositions must necessarily play an important part in common-law reasoning:

The common law is heavily concerned with the intertwined concepts of injuries and rights, and moral norms largely shape our perception of what constitutes an injury and a right. Judicial considerations of policies furthers the courts' function of enriching the supply of legal rules: if the courts are to establish legal rules to govern future social conduct, it is desirable for them to consider whether those rules will conduce to a good or a bad state of affairs. Experiential considerations are necessary to mediate between policies and moral norms on the one hand and legal rules on the other.[25]

Not any and every social proposition is acceptable, however. Only 'applicable social propositions' that it is 'proper for a court to employ' will do.[26] Unfortunately, the consensus as to what constitutes 'proper' social, non-legal propositions is no longer as stable as it used to be. For some, e.g. the legal positivists, social propositions ought to be discarded altogether, whereas for others, such as the members of the Critical Legal Studies and Critical Race Theory Movements, legal doctrines are hardly worth considering entities in and of their own right but only make sense in connection with social propositions. More often than not, though, the question is one of degree rather than kind – what weight to give to each of the respective propositions. What concerns us here is the fact that the common law is, in its very nature, both material and ideological.

That the common law is not merely fact, but also inevitably has an intellectual and moral dimension, has to do with law being 'custom transformed, and not merely the will or reason of the lawmaker. Law spreads upward from the bottom and not only downward from the top.'[27] What happens at the grass-roots level carries importance for decisions made at the top. Reflecting and defending on the one hand the interest of the ruling class, the law has provided protection against the misuse of power of that very class on the other.

Law not only expresses and creates power but also serves to limit power – Law expresses community norms and it applies them to particular situations by interpreting the norms in the light of community morality and other community understandings. The essence of a norm is that it constrains behavior, including the behavior of the powerful.[28]

It is in this doubly dualist nature of the common law, as it were – its being material but also ideological, and its spreading upward from the bottom and not merely downward from the top – that we may find the origins of judicial activism. In many ways, contemporary judges are merely doing what generations of common-law judges have done before them: making law with the self-conscious goal of bringing about social change.

## Judicial Activism: The Practice

### (a) Praying for Sheetrock

Joyce Appleby would not find much support for her attack on American exceptionalism among the general public. As already mentioned, most Americans find in the very notion of American exceptionalism – and especially in its legal underpinnings – a viable path to effective inclusion in American society. This is reflected in the nation's cultural life. From the works of Scott Turow, John Grisham and countless other writers of detective novels, via television series such as 'The People's Court' and 'L. A. Law,' to the works of 'serious' writers such as William Gaddis and Margaret Atwood, the sacred principles of personal freedoms and rights as outlined in the Constitution are invariably invoked above or beyond the actual plots. A person's decency and human worth are tested against whether or not he or she still – deep-down – believes in the American civic culture. If and when the average American stops believing in American exceptionalism and stops wanting to fight for it, these cultural works suggest, then things do not look good.

One revealing example is the story of a small Southern community's awakening to civil rights in the 1970s – a story told in *Praying for Sheetrock* by Melissa Fay Greene. The development that takes place within just one generation is one from church to court. As the book unfolds, the devoutly Christian black community of McIntosh County, Georgia, who have been 'blind and deaf to issues of civil equality, equal employment, and local corruption,' discover that the law and its practitioners may actually be of more help to them in their fight for justice and equality than may their church leaders.[29]

In the early 1970s, McIntosh County is a completely segregated community. Tom Poppell, the white sheriff, wields all power; he controls everyone and everything. He has been sheriff since 1948, when he inherited the office from his father, Sheriff Ad Poppell, and he rules McIntosh in much the same way that George Washington Plunkitt once ruled New York's Tammany Hall: by 'honest graft.' In return for votes, he protects and takes care of his constituents. He is famous all over the South, for example, for allowing the local population to loot the cargo spilled onto old U.S. 17 through McIntosh County whenever trucks collide or suffer the mishaps of heavy interstate traffic. Oftentimes, such mishaps will be caused by Sheriff Poppell himself and his deputies, who will take possession of the scene and call in the locals once the truck driver has gone off in search of help. 'Such redistribution of wealth,' we are told, 'invariably put the sheriff in an excellent mood' and earns him 'ever-widening circles of supporters' (3, 241).

Like most successful political bosses, Tom Poppell is a wealthy man. He has acquired his wealth in a number of illegal business transactions over the years. During his reign, McIntosh County has been converted into 'a mini-Las Vegas, a mini-Atlantic City, a southern Hong Kong or Bangkok where white men came looking for, and found, women, gambling, liquor, drugs, guns, sanctuary from the law, and boats available for smuggling' (14). The locals do not condone Poppell's activities; indeed, most are sorry for the bad reputation these activities bring to McIntosh. Yet, by playing Robin Hood from time to time and tossing the occasional bonus to law-abiding whites and blacks alike, Poppell has managed to stay in power, thereby continuing one of the longest-running sheriff's dynasties in the state's history.

Between the black and the white communities of McIntosh, there are 'close and long-time connections – unlike anything in the North.' Half of the population are white and for the most part they live in Darien, where they own all the major shops and businesses and occupy all the important offices. All the menial tasks are performed by the blacks, the majority of whom still inhabit slave or sharecropper shacks to the north of Darien between the shoreline and the pine woods. They live their lives much as they have since emancipation, trusting in the Lord to provide for their needs and relying on the sheriff to maintain the racial equilibrium.

The historic black community of McIntosh lived in a sort of pale outside a century of American progress and success. They survived by raising vegetables and keeping chickens and pigs, by working menial jobs in Darien, and by fishing the network of tidewater rivers and blackwater swamps. They lived without plumbing, telephones, hot water, paved roads, electricity, gas heat, or air-conditioning into the 1970s. (16–17, 20)

When finally the call for civil rights disrupts the silent understanding between blacks and whites in McIntosh, everybody – blacks and whites alike – has a hard time understanding how acquaintances, people they have known all their lives, now turn into adversaries. It all starts when Thurnell Alston, an uneducated and unemployed black man with a keen sense of justice, has finally had it. Years before he first hears about Martin Luther King and his fight for racial equality, Thurnell starts becoming conscious of the systematic attacks on his own dignity and that of his black brothers. In 'a series of rude awakenings' – one of which consists of his overhearing Sheriff Poppell remarking how the 'only way you can control the Negroes is to keep them hungry' – Thurnell undergoes a gradual, but effective 'education,' 'until the day he had heard and seen enough and could not, in good conscience, remain passive any longer' (38).

What turns Thurnell's passive knowledge of racial discrimination into an active will to fight for change is the senseless shooting of a black man named Ed Finch by Darien's white chief of police, Guy Hutchinson. Annoyed at Finch, who is engaged in a drunken and loud quarrel with his girlfriend on the front porch of her house and refuses to be quiet when Chief Hutchinson tells him to, the Chief simply sticks his revolver into Finch's mouth and fires. He then takes Finch, bleeding, to the jail, charges him with aggravated assault and drunk and disorderly conduct and leaves him without any medical attention. What chiefly upsets the black community is not so much the fact that a violent act is committed by a white person against a black neighbor – after all, the black community is used to far worse! – but rather the fact that all of this happens in broad daylight within a residential area.

Clearly an attack such as Hutchinson's upon Finch was not allowed: the blacks were not, after all, to be slaughtered like hogs; the fiction was to be maintained of two separate societies living rather gingerly side-by-side, each with its own hub of social and business life. Such a vicious and unprovoked attack by the chief of police against a citizen was a violation of the unspoken social contract that allowed the whites and the outcast blacks to live in peace. (122)

The night Chief Hutchinson shoots Ed Finch, black McIntosh gathers around Thurnell Alston and from now on it is Thurnell to whom they turn for advice and leadership. Thurnell teams up with two old pals, Reverend Nathaniel Grovner and Sammie Pinkney. Together, these 'Three Musketeers' set out to *do* something. For various reasons, all three of them have independent sources of income and thus need fear no economic reprisal from the sheriff and the rest of white McIntosh. They hold meetings, around Thurnell's kitchen table, but also in church where they try to raise the political consciousness of their devoutly Christian black brothers and sisters. At some point, Sammie Pinkney, who as a former New York City policeman with experience of the American West and of Europe knows about the ways of the world, becomes impatient, however. Alston and Grovner's reiterating every evening in church 'the same half-dozen painful facts' which are then swept away by the congregation 'with another mighty hymn,' does not get them anywhere (151). Outside intervention is needed, Pinkney decides, so he contacts Georgia's controversial legal aid network, the Georgia Legal Services Program and hires a lawyer.

Alston and Grovner are not immediately persuaded that the move from church to court is a wise one. Not long after their first appointment at the Brunswick Legal Services office, however, they find themselves commuting back and forth between McIntosh and Brunswick nearly every day. The meeting with the young legal aid lawyers, whom they initially view with much skepticism, turns out to be a revelation:

The amazing thing, to Thurnell, was how quickly and easily the young white lawyers had named the ill health of the county; how they had listened as the three McIntosh men tumbled out their tales of poverty, underemployment, and a sense of being the untouchables in McIntosh's caste system – It was as if he'd come to them delirious, a feverish child, and they had smoothed his hair, laid a cold cloth on his forehead, and explained to him that he had the mumps and this was the cherry syrup he must sip from a spoon to be all better. (178–79)

Time and again, Thurnell and his fellow-Musketeers hear the white lawyers talk about and refer to one particular document: the American Constitution. This document, the lawyers promise, has something to say about every fight for equality – even when that fight occurs in such a far-away and seemingly insignificant place as McIntosh County, Georgia. The Constitution, the black men soon come to understand, 'was the white boys' Bible; and the lawyers quoted it often, chapter and verse, taking secular pleasure in its ornate language every bit as much as the rural people relished the antiquated resonance of biblical thou shalts and wherefores and cometh and goeths' (180).

For their part, the young white lawyers rejoice in the chance to leave their offices in Brunswick and do some active service in the black community. Fresh out of the nation's best law schools, these 'young, upper-middle-class, mostly urban, mostly Yankee lawyers' have no idea what awaits them in the South. They are taken aback by the Third World conditions under which people, white and black, are still living and consider the challenges they meet in Georgia 'akin to those of their friends who had joined the Peace Corps instead of VISTA and who now dwelled in Asian or African villages. The exoticism and foreignness of the surround-ings were vivid, and they themselves were looked upon as bizarre implants.' Their social commitment is genuine and deep-felt. They had gone to law school in the first place out of a desire to perform public service, and consider a legal career the best instrument for creating social change. Their will to a judicially activist life is founded on an understanding of law as 'self-evident truths about fundamental human rights,' and when they set up shop in the small rural towns, they are 'prepared to work heroic hours' (161, 156).

The course upon which the lawyers decide to embark is to bring suit in federal court, contending that the electoral system for electing city and council officers presently in operation in the city of Darien and McIntosh County, respectively, dilute the votes of black citizens. *The NAACP v. McIntosh County* is resolved with a consent order, which divides McIntosh into five voting precincts. As for the second voting rights suits, *The NAACP v. The City of Darien*, the Georgia Legal Services Program lawyers fail to convince Judge Alaimo of the Southern District that anything is wrong with the way the city of Darien runs its elections, and the judge dismisses the suit. The legal aid lawyers decide to try their luck a second time and appeal their loss. This time they win; in October, 1979 the U.S. Court of Appeals for the Fifth Circuit reverses, 'and Darien, like McIntosh before it, was sliced into districts, including a majority-black district' (219).

The way is now paved for black citizens to run for both city and council officers. The first to benefit from the court order that has created a majority-black district is Thurnell Alston. Running, at age forty-one, for county commissioner for the fourth time, he finally succeeds in placing himself squarely in the midst of McIntosh County politics. Politically, he is a success, forcing the white commissioners to dedicate the sparse budget to the most fundamental needs of the poor. What Thurnell has not anticipated, however, is that after his election, the black community, tired of fighting and wishing merely to go back to their lives, lose interest in him and his continued struggles with the white commissioners.

In a strange collapse of vision, the election of Thurnell Alston to the County Commission now appeared to everyone to be the chief thing they had worked for, the ultimate victory. He became, to the black people, simply the Commissioner; not the Barber, not the Undertaker, not the Preacher, but the Commissioner, as if the larger community had no more vested interest in his daily work than in anyone else's. (253)

Without the support of the close-knit black community, Thurnell is lost. None of what he has fought so hard for over the past years, seems worth it. When furthermore he and his wife suffer the loss of a favorite son, Thurnell feels so alienated, so tired and depressed that he starts loafing and drifts in the direction of the criminal milieu in McIntosh. He is indicted on charges of accepting bribes and possessing and distributing drugs and eventually has to go to jail.

'What might have happened differently,' muses one of the young white lawyers as the two voting rights suits are about to be filed, 'if Sammie and Thurnell and Reverend Grovner – had contacted say, political organizers, the national NAACP or SNCC. There might have been a different approach to this stuff. But they came to lawyers, you know, what can you do?' (175). The question as to whether the course of events would have been a different one, had the Three Musketeers decided to fight in the political rather than the legal arena, is never addressed by Melissa Fay Greene. In fact, the author of *Praying for Sheetrock* does not even seem to find it a relevant one. The reader cannot help wondering if the backing of a political group or organization might not have prevented Thurnell's sad fall from grace. As far as

Greene is concerned, however, the real heroes are the lawyers whose judicial activism makes it possible for Thurnell to embark on a political career in the first place. As the book closes, a black man has replaced Thurnell as county commissioner, a black woman is elected to the post of superintendent of education, another black woman runs the tourism office, and yet a third black woman teller works in Darien's bank. Of course, says Greene, 'it is not enough, but it is a beginning' (175, 335).

## (b) Our Town. Race, Housing, and the Soul of Suburbia

Like *Praying for Sheetrock*, David L. Kirp, John P. Dwyer, and Larry A. Rosenthal's *Our Town. Race, Housing, and the Soul of Suburbia* is about the use of law to make America more inclusive. As the title implies, the issue discussed in the more recent book is zoning and its implications for the racial make-up of America's suburban landscape. We are in Mount Laurel, New Jersey – a state, we are told, which is the most suburbanized state in the nation, and in which judicial activism is 'the byword,' New Jersey's Supreme Court Justices having been 'more openly political and politically strategic in their decrees than other states' judges.'[30]

The story of Mount Laurel – the township and the landmark case – begins on a Sunday in 1970, when the congregation of the all-black African Methodist Episcopalian Church has invited the Mayor of Mount Laurel to announce the town's response to a housing proposal which will open up suburban Mount Laurel to local, poor and mostly black families. After praising the new prosperity that is fast changing small rural Mount Laurel into a booming suburb the Mayor comes to the point: the township has no intention of ever approving the proposed housing project. Indeed, he goes on, '"if you people" – *you poor and black people, that is* – "can't afford to live in our town, then you'll just have to leave"' (2). These words are like a slap in the face to the blacks present; the Mayor as good as tells them that for them and their families, whose roots in Mount Laurel after all go back to before the

American Revolution, there is no room. This leaves them no option but to move to the riot-torn slums of nearby Camden.

Appalled at Mount Laurel's rejection of the idea of housing for the poor, the minister of the African Methodist Episcopalian Church approaches Camden's radical Legal Services lawyers. Upon hearing about the Mayor's message to the black population of Mount Laurel, the Camden lawyers decide 'to bring their equalitarian agenda to the suburbs.' Like their colleagues in *Praying for Sheetrock*, these lawyers

had gone to law school in the sixties, not with the intention of becoming partners in some stuffy Wall Street firm, but instead meaning to accomplish a quiet social revolution in the nation's courtrooms. These children of the Warren Court era regarded the law almost as a secular religion, and they had faith in its power to undo injustice. (3, 70)

With the involvement of the Camden Legal Services lawyers, the housing controversy ceases to be a matter for the citizens of Mount Laurel to settle among themselves. For the lawyers, affordable housing is a matter of simple justice, and they see in the Mount Laurel controversy a potential 'frontal challenge to the ever widening divisions between blacks and whites, as well as between the poor and everyone else.' Together with local community organizers they decide to take the controversy to the courts, contending that Mount Laurel's zoning ordinance unconstitutionally excludes poor and minority citizens from affluent neighborhoods. Among the local organizers, it is especially a black woman by the name of Ethel Lawrence with whom the lawyers deliberate, as they pursue their legal course. Ethel Lawrence is the Thurnell Alston of *Our Town*. The book is dedicated to her for, as the authors put it, without her it 'would have been simply an account of how policy gets made, not a textured human drama as well.' It is Ethel who first educates the authors on 'the folk-ways and law-ways' of New Jersey, just as it is her constant presence in court which serves to remind attorneys and judges that real people, not just legal principles, are involved (70, ix).

When the lawyers file *Southern Burlington County NAACP et al. v. Township of Mount Laurel* in May 1971, they have no idea that *Mount Laurel*, as the zoning litigation comes to be collectively known, will continue to be argued in court for a decade and a half, and will become 'the *Roe v. Wade* of fair housing, the *Brown v. Board of Education* of exclusionary zoning.' The first to hear the case is trial court judge Edward Martino. Judge Martino is so overwhelmed by the stories told in court by the township's poor of neglect and abuse on the part of Mount Laurel's politicians, that he pronounces Mount Laurel's zoning ordinance unconstitutional on grounds of economic discrimination. Writing his opinion, Martino has to do some creative legal thinking as he has no New Jersey precedent to rely on. Instead, he 'cobbled together an opinion that relied on dissents, decisions from other states, and law review commentary' (3, 75).

Judge Martino's opinion, delivered in May 1972, is bold, though not as bold as the judgment delivered three years later by Justice Frederick Hall for a unanimous New Jersey Supreme Court. Upon the township's appeal of the trial court's ruling, the Supreme Court decides to hear the case directly, skipping the intermediate appellate court. Picking up on Judge Martino's notion of economic discrimination, Justice Hall speaks of a moral obligation on the part of America's suburbs toward the poor and homeless and demands that 'developing towns across the state rewrite their zoning laws so that private developers, taking advantage of federal subsidies and market forces, could build homes for a "fair share" of the region's poor and moderate-income families' (77). As had been the case for Judge Martino before him, Justice Hall has no specific text other than the New Jersey Constitution's vaguely formulated concern for the general welfare to rely on in his call for constitutionally mandated municipal obligations.

The politicians are enraged at Justice Hall's demand for an ordinance providing 'realistic opportunity' for affordable housing. They refuse to play this game of 'judicial dictatorship' and submit a 'farcical document, every bit as defiant of the judiciary as southern school districts' responses to desegregation in the

1950s and 1960s.' To the lawyers' dismay, the trial court approves of the town's sham zoning changes, and they decide to mount a new Mount Laurel lawsuit. In *Mount Laurel II*, as the suit comes to be known, they are defeated at the trial court level, but vindicated by the New Jersey Supreme Court in 1983. The opinion delivered by Chief Justice Robert Wilentz himself gives 'developers, lawyers, and poor families eager to prise open the suburbs expansive declarations of rights, detailed remedies to make those rights real, and even the apparatus of a new mini-administrative system to enforce them' (86–87, 93).

The lawyers rejoice in Chief Justice Wilentz' public interest-oriented call for each town to take affirmative responsibility for its 'fair share' of the state's poor. As it turns out, they rejoice too soon, however. Prodded into action by Wilentz' specific warning in *Mount Laurel II* that the Supreme Court will continue its judicial activism until the Legislature acts, members of the State Legislature start negotiating a compromise. After several failed attempts at reconciling liberal hopes of preserving in legislation the most central elements of *Mount Laurel II* and conservative plans of aborting the court's ruling, the Legislature finally produce the 1985 Fair Housing Act. Along the way, Republican Governor Thomas Kean has done his best to transform 'the fair-share problem *Mount Laurel II* had addressed into another kind of problem – runaway judges' (101, 123).

The 1985 Fair Housing Act, it is generally understood, sends an unequivocal signal to the New Jersey Supreme Court that further judicial activism is neither needed nor wanted. It takes the high court barely six months to respond. In February 1986, in a case formally known as *Hills Development v. Bernards Township* but more commonly called *Mount Laurel III*, the Supreme Court unanimously upholds the new law. To some, this is a realistic, even pragmatically wise peace offering from the bench; to Ethel Lawrence and the Legal Services lawyers, who have made the cause of affordable housing central to their lives over the years, *Mount Laurel III* amounts to retreat, even capitulation on the Justices' part.

In the assessment of the authors of *Our Town*, neither response is entirely fair. The New Jersey Supreme Court must be commended first of all for forcing the Legislature to recognize the state's responsibility to solve the housing needs of the poor, and secondly for knowing exactly how far to pursue a legally activist course without losing its autonomy and integrity. Unlike what has happened in other states where justices have been forced to resign for being too openly political, New Jersey's justices 'have continued to be legal innovators, and appointments to the Supreme Court still stress professional competence, not partisan politics.' On the other hand, *Mount Laurel III* raises questions about the high court's willingness and ability to keep a reform agenda going. Just as the court had demonstrated, in *Mount Laurel II*, a willingness to 'craft broad remedies for systemic social problems and transcend the limitations of traditional litigation,' it draws back and leaves the issue of affordable housing in the hands of New Jersey's politicians for whom the needs of the prosperous middle class have always been more important than those of the poor. The unfortunate result has been that Justice Hall's talk, in *Mount Laurel I*, of a moral obligation toward Mount Laurel's poor, essentially black population, has been conveniently forgotten, and that 'there has been relatively little low- and moderate-income housing built in New Jersey since the Fair Housing Act was passed in 1985' (147, 113, 159).

For a brief moment, it looks as if a handful of judicially activist justices may succeed in forcing Middle America to commit itself to the principle of fair shares for the Haves and the Have-Nots alike. But then the justices retreat from 'that bold new conception of the commonweal,' allowing Middle America to slip back into its old beliefs in the power of a free market economy to resolve America's problems. *Our Town* is very much about judicial activism – its potential for 'defining and enforcing newly created social rights and obligations.' Above and beyond the issue of whether affordable housing is a matter for the judiciary or for the legislature, however, it is the actual – and very real – needs of the poor, the human problem, that concerns the authors. At a time when 'the very idea of our being a "good society," a city on a hill, commands little credence,' and when 'compassion, once a byword, has become a political liability,' Kirp, Dwyer and Rosenthal ask, to whom are the poor going to look for support? Until Middle America finally wakes up and recognizes that help is needed, 'it is vital that the idealists keep talking the talk' (173, 79,174). And for the time being there seem to be more idealists among America's judges than among its politicians.

## Concluding Remarks

For Thurnell Alston and Ethel Lawrence, the black protagonists of *Praying for Sheetrock* and *Our Town*, respectively, the fight to be included into American society is a long and arduous one. Not knowing at first where to turn for support and understanding, they approach the Legal Services Programs of their respective states. The idealism and willingness to fight for a better and more just society that characterize the young white lawyers who man these programs, impress the two protagonists. As they befriend these lawyers, they cannot help but being swept along by the lawyers' belief in the law to do good. The law of the land, they come to believe, is there for them too.

Central to the authors of *Praying for Sheetrock* and *Our Town* is the belief in judicial activism – the belief that in a civil society such as the American, the courts will have to step in to protect the rights of the underprivileged. Both books illustrate how intimately American exceptionalism is related to the role of law and lawyers in American society. Ever since the Republic was founded, nobody has been more instrumental in extending the rights of citizenship to previously unwanted groups of people than the country's judges. When activist, these judges have reminded the nation and its politicians that what makes America exceptional are not only certain constitutional rights and liberties, but also the very idea that such rights are for everybody – high and low, white and non-white, man and woman. To the extent that there is a republican tradition in America, it has been promoted or honored by judges rather than politicians. When therefore critics such as Joyce Appleby attack the notion of

American exceptionalism for *excluding* down through American history all that is non-white and non-male, they miss the point.

## Notes

1. Melissa Fay Greene, *Praying for Sheetrock* (New York: Fawcett Columbine, 1991), 175.
2. Joyce Appleby, 'Recovering America's Historic Diversity: Beyond Exceptionalism', *Journal of American History*, 79 (September, 1992): 420, 431.
3. Appleby, 422.
4. See, e.g., Gordon S. Wood, 'The Origins of Judicial Review,' *Suffolk University Law Review*, 22 (1988).
5. Kenneth L. Karst, *Belonging to America: Equal Citizenship and the Constitution* (New Haven: Yale University Press, 1989), 182, 31.
6. Lawrence M. Friedman, 'American Legal Culture: The Last Thirty-five Years,' *Law and Society: Readings on the Social Study of Law*, ed. Stewart Macauley, Lawrence M. Friedman, and John Stookey (New York: Norton, 1995), 271–77 (his legal culture is defined as 'the attitudes and expectations of the public with regard to law'); Sanford Levinson, *Constitutional Faith* (Princeton: Princeton University Press, 1988); Mary Ann Glendon, *Rights Talk: The Impoverishment of Political Discourse* (New York: Free Press, 1991).
7. Greene, 158.
8. Daniel Bell, 'The "Hegelian Secret": Civil Society and American Exceptionalism,' *Is America Different?: A New Look at American Exceptionalism*, ed. Byron E. Shafer (New York: Oxford University Press, 1991), 60, 66, 62.
9. Wood, 1293.
10. Cf. Geoffrey C. Hazard, who notes, 'In case no one has noticed, it should be reported that these days some very intense debates are going on in political and legal philosophy. These debates concern what our society should be like and how decisions about it should be made, and particularly who should make those decisions. One of the primary issues of those debates is the legitimacy of what lawyers and judges do, particularly appellate judges and more particular Supreme Court justices' ('Rising Above Principle,' *University of Pennsylvania Law Review*, 135 [December, 1986]: 153).
11. For an interesting recent attack on judicial activism see Susan V. Demers, 'The Failures of Litigation As a Tool for the Development of Social Welfare Policy,' *Fordham Urban Law Journal*, 22 (1995): 1009–50.
12. Karst, *Belonging to America*, 222.
13. Wood, 1296, 1299.
14. Wood, 1302–03.
15. Glendon, 163.

16. Karst, *Belonging to America*, 74, 73. On the Court's reluctance to embrace the potential of the Fourteenth Amendment, see Karst, *Belonging to America*, ch. 4.

17. Karst, *Belonging to America*, 18, 10, 29. See also the conclusion to Kenneth L. Karst, 'Myth of Identity: Individual and Group Portraits of Race and Sexual Orientation,' in *UCLA Law Review*, 43 (1995): 263–369: 'In other words, not every form of "legal universalism" threatens to undermine the nation's subcultures. To one who self-identifies within a culture or a social group partly or wholly defined by race or sexual orientation, equal citizenship implies that she can belong to America and at the same time keep that par-ticularized identification if she wants it. An increasing recognition of the mythical qualities of racial or sexual orientation identity should make no difference at all to the anti-discrimination component of the guarantee of equal citizenship. Nor should the recognition of race as a myth be taken to undermine the constitutional or statutory foundation for race-conscious group remedies that are appropriate for group-based harms. In the end, both the anti-discrimination principle and race-conscious remedies should be seen as the instruments of integration. Not "assimilation" in the sense of an identity lost, but integration in the sense of a reality renamed, an identity renewed, a myth retold.'

18. Anthony T. Kronman, *The Lost Lawyer: Failing Ideals of the Legal Profession* (Cambridge, MA: Harvard University Press, 1995), 117.

19. Karst, *Belonging to America*, 225.

20. See e.g. Harry H. Wellington, *Interpreting the Constitution* (New Haven: Yale University Press, 1990); and Lawrence H. Tribe and Michael C. Dorf, *On Reading the Constitution* (Cambridge, MA: Harvard University Press, 1991) for recent statements to the effect that modern, activist judicial review is an inevitable (and by and large desirable) effect of the common-law method of adjudication.

21. Bell, 59.

22. Glendon, 169.

23. Lawrence M. Friedman. *A History of American Law* (New York: Simon and Schuster, 1973), 14.

24. Bruce Ackerman, *We the People: Foundations* (Cambridge, MA: Harvard University Press, 1993), 24.

25. Melvin Aron Eisenberg, *The Nature of the Common Law* (Cambridge, MA: Harvard University Press, 1988), 1–2.

26. Eisenberg, 1–2, 43.

27. Harold J. Berman, *Law and Revolution: The Formation of the Western Legal Tradition* (Cambridge, MA: Harvard University Press, 1983), 556.

28. Karst, *Belonging to America*, 194.

29. Greene, 3. Subsequent page references to this work will be given in the text.

30. David L. Kirp, John P. Dwyer, and Larry A. Rosenthal, *Our Town: Race, Housing, and the Soul of Suburbia* (New Brunswick, NJ: Rutgers University

Press, 1995), 65. Subsequent page references to this work will be given in the text.

# 'Against Any Winds that Blow': American Exceptionalism, Multiculturalism, and Judicial Review

*Jody Pennington*

> Under our constitutional system, courts stand against any winds that blow as havens of refuge for those who might otherwise suffer because they are helpless, weak, outnumbered, or because they are non-conforming victims of prejudice and public excitement.
>
> Justice Hugo Black, for the Court, *Chambers v. State of Florida*.[1]

The concept American exceptionalism has been found wanting in a number of ways. Two significant – and interrelated – critiques have questioned whether the concept remains viable in light of international comparisons (the comparative critique) or whether it provides an accurate, representative account of the sociocultural matrix of the United States (the multicultural critique). Both critiques proffer evidence to counter the claim that American history differs significantly in any respect from that of European democracies. The comparative critique has tended to question American exceptionalism's veracity by comparing certain parameters claimed within the discourse of American exceptionalism to be *exceptional*, *unique*, or *different* to the United States with those in another country. This has been necessary because, Laurence Veysey argues, 'American history has been viewed far too often as if it were autonomous, a theme entirely unto itself, rather than in enormous measure a reflection of forces operating throughout the modern world.'[2] Comparative research, Veysey and others have maintained, would separate the exceptionalist chaff from the wheat, either salvaging something uniquely American or revealing that the United States differs in no

*Marks of Distinction: American Exceptionalism Revisited*, ed. Dale Carter, *The Dolphin* 32, pp. 257–81. © 2001 by Aarhus University Press, Denmark. ISBN 87 7288 383 9; ISSN 0106 4487.

fundamental way from European democracies.[3] The multicultural critique is concerned with the accuracy of the historical representation of the American experience in and of itself. Multicultural critiques argue that the mainstream of American history traditionally ignored the experiences of minorities and women, resulting in an idealized – and false – representation of American history and national identity.

While the comparative critique informed Professor Joyce Appleby's 1992 presidential address to the Organization of American Historians, Appleby mainly made a multicultural case against American exceptionalism.[4] Appleby's multiculturalist objection to American exceptionalism can be summarized as the 'foreclosure thesis,' which basically argues that American exceptionalism created an illusionary national identity and an exclusionary national history that foreclosed historical accounts of marginal regional, ethnic, racial, or gender-based identities and experiences within the United States. By so doing, American exceptionalism shaped a 'grand narrative' of American history that 'stands in the way of a different understanding of our past, one that foregrounds those experiences that were earlier cast into the shadows.'[5] Once the door had been slammed shut on alternative understandings of an American national identity, it would take two hundred years before a generation of social historians would uncover the foreclosed and begin revising American history. Furthermore, Appleby would have it, American exceptionalism underlay the discomfort among historians in particular and Americans in general with multiculturalism in the early 1990s.

Employing a standard opening gambit meant to discredit American exceptionalism by suggesting that the qualities claimed to distinguish the United States from European nation-states are not even American in origin, Appleby delineates the European origins of American exceptionalism as an intellectual import during the eighteenth century, which originally was 'America's peculiar form of Eurocentrism.'[6] American exceptionalism was an imported construct of 'the European reform imagination' of 'Continental *philosophes*, English Dissenters, and radical pamphleteers.'[7] This social and discursive construction was readily imported, according to Appleby, because the former colonists had little to bond them to one another.[8] Indeed, the only thing holding the colonies together were the fragile bonds created by 'language, law, and institutional history,' which, in Appleby's view, offered precious little in terms of forging a common national identity.[9] By positing shared national traditions and values where there had been numerous local traditions and values, American exceptionalism concealed sociocultural diversity beneath a veneer of hegemonic socially and discursively constructed commonalities shared in reality only by propertied white males who turned a blind eye to the injustices and inequalities surrounding them. They then proceeded to promote their exceptionalist ideology as a set of tenets adhered to by all Americans, their experiences as analogous to those of all Americans, and their understanding of freedom and equality as that reflected in the natural order of things. Accordingly, the ideology of American exceptionalism asserted that liberal political ideals expressed in the Declaration and the Constitution defined the national identity of Americans and as such functioned as ideological shorthand for those ideals.

Unfortunately, in Appleby's view, the shorthand account of the grand narrative of American exceptionalism was detrimental to American historiography by being succinct to the point of ignoring the attitudes, values, beliefs, and experiences of Native Americans, African slaves, and white women, who became invisible. This invisibility was discursive (the experiences of Native Americans, African slaves, and white women were excluded from historical narratives). Furthermore, Native Americans, African slaves, and white women did not have the same legal or political rights as propertied white males. Thus, both in shaping the narratives of American history and in defining the national identity of Americans, those who defined American exceptionalism failed to include Native Americans, African slaves, and women in the extension of that concept and hence the applicability of its liberal ideals to members of those groups. Without being invisible, the exclusivity that denied Native

Americans, African Americans, and women the same rights as propertied white males would have been blatantly incongruous with the grand narrative and political ideals of American exceptionalism. Even though the exclusion of Native Americans, African Americans, and women from the conception of American exceptionalism was wrong, Appleby's assertion that American exceptionalism led to narrow, monolithic representations of American history that presented a false image of a shared national culture is not warranted. That Appleby proceeds to draw on the historical record molded by American exceptionalism to show that there was as much conflict as consensus in the colonial and revolutionary periods suggests that such a claim is too broad. Furthermore, Appleby grossly underestimates the significance of the bonds created by 'language, law, and institutional history' in laying the foundation for an American national identity. At least one aspect of American exceptionalism is to be found in the American conception of and practice of judicial review and the role of the Constitution in shaping American national identity.

Indeed, American history begins with conflicts resolved by a revolutionary war. Accounts of the founding of the nation are also accounts of conflicts resolved not of insipid consensus. The need to hammer out compromise after compromise at the Constitutional Convention of 1787 has long been common historical knowledge.[10] Appleby's argument that '[n]either the constitutional debates nor the state ratifying conventions produced the stuff of culture in appeals to cherished sentiments and references to visceral convictions' suggests that ordinary Americans were either uninterested in political and legal debates or too ignorant to follow them. This follows from Appleby's argument that the Constitution interested only the elite that wrote it and worked for its ratification: 'Outside of their circles, there were abroad in the land few common sentiments, fewer shared assumptions operating at the intimate level of human experience, and a paucity of national symbols....'[11] If the attitudes, values, and beliefs that animated debates among lawyers over the Constitution were confined to closed elite circles, as Appleby would have it, then those circles were large and overlapping, given that the texts of the state constitutions suggested that there was much shared. That much was shared can be seem in the general consensus that was reached in each state in devising a state constitution and eventually at the Constitutional Convention in 1787 in devising the legal frameworks for the states and the nation. Donald S. Lutz notes the lack of interaction between the colonies but emphasizes nonetheless the development of a common legal and constitutional culture manifested in the numerous covenants, state constitutions, and ultimately in the United States Constitution.[12] Underlying the American faith in political pacts was another tradition that the colonies had in common, the common law, one of the chief sources of early American law. The common law had been recognized throughout the colonies 'as a guarantor of personal liberty' and later would be perceived as 'a foundation of republican liberty after the American Revolution.'[13]

Both the common law and conceptions of rights were brought by colonists when they migrated to what would become the United States. Nonetheless, crucial differences in the understanding of rights, a constitution, and limits on the sovereignty of the legislature distinguished American legal theory from British. During the colonial period, law was British law, but it was British law as it was practiced and understood across the distance of the Atlantic. Colonists in New England, for example, 'produced a layman's version of English legal institutions,' writes Daniel Boorstin. 'The half-remembered and half-understood technical language of English lawyers was being roughly applied to American problems.'[14] 'An interplay between inherited legal culture and the New World environment molded law in early America,' writes Kermit Hall. In that new environment, 'the very act of creating new societies provided both the opportunity and the necessity for inventing or adapting legal institutions' to that environment.[15] The novel experiences in the New World led to new conceptions of both the common law and constitutionalism. Gordon Wood suggests that by the time the Declaration of Independence was written 'Americans had produced out of the polemics of the previous decade a notion of a constitution very different from what eighteenth-century Englishmen were used to

– a notion of a constitution that has come to characterize the very distinctiveness of American political thought.'[16] The uniqueness of American constitutional thought was expressed in the creation of a written constitution, a federal system of government, and an insistence on the rule of law, on limits on government power, and the interrelationship between the latter two heretofore not known in political science.

The ideal of the rule of law in the United States was influenced by Calvinism, which had been widespread during the colonial era and which had influenced the American understanding of higher law and of written compacts to govern the community. As Donald S. Lutz argues, this 'fact is essential when trying to explain the surprising similarity to be found in state constitutions and colonial documents written throughout America.'[17] In Lutz's view, 'It is very difficult to read covenant after covenant, used by 1645 to establish political communities from Massachusetts to Delaware, and not conclude that this was an explosion in political culture of major importance.'[18] The most important document to emerge out of that cultural movement was the United States Constitution, a national political document unique at the time. The American conception of constitutional law – of constitutional supremacy – was implemented in the United States Constitution 'at a time when the Blackstonian concept of legislative supremacy was dominant' in England.[19] For the Framers, the choice was between positions staked out by Sir Edward Coke, Chief Justice of the Common Pleas, in *Bonham's Case* (1610),[20] which lay the theoretical groundwork for judicial review, and by Sir William Blackstone in the eighteenth century, which 'maintained that Parliament was sovereign and no judge could declare an Act of Parliament void, because he would be usurping the legislative function.'[21] The Framers followed Coke rather than Blackstone, but they did so implicitly.

The Constitution does not explicitly state the Supreme Court's right to carry out judicial review of legislative enactments. Judicial review, as constitutional scholar Edward S. Corwin testified before the United States Senate Committee on the Judiciary in 1937, 'is a matter of inference.'[22] Determining that the framers had intended that inference to be drawn, Corwin told the Committee, was a matter of 'great uncertainty.'[23] Leonard W. Levy finds few precedents for judicial review in case law up to the Constitutional Convention and concludes that judicial review 'was nowhere established, indeed that it seemed novel, controversial, and an encroachment on legislative authority.'[24] Nonetheless, Levy continues, the 'idea of judicial review was ... rapidly emerging.'[25] Its emergence was stimulated by a number of factors, including the Supremacy Clause in Article VI of the Constitution; the Judiciary Act of 1789, especially Section 25, which allowed the Supreme Court's jurisdiction to hear appeals from state supreme courts concerning the constitutionality of state or federal laws; the debates over the ratification of the Bill of Rights, during which James Madison, Thomas Jefferson, and others pointed to the judiciary as the guarantor of those rights; and party politics, since in their first years of existence, political parties established the American tradition of debating the validity of laws in terms of their constitutionality.[26] Judicial review emerged in practice, of course, with the Supreme Court's decision and Chief Justice John Marshall's opinion for the Court in *Marbury v. Madison* (1803).[27] In his opinion, the Chief Justice ruled that 'an act, repugnant to the constitution' was void because the Constitution was 'superior, paramount law, unchangeable by ordinary means' of the legislative process available to Congress.[28] Not only was the Constitution unique; so too was American constitutionalism, the supplementing of the brief text of the United States Constitution by the judiciary through its interpretations.

Judicial review has thereby served to shape a legal system that has provided a forum within which disputes over the meaning and extent of individual rights were debated and settled (although never finally). Within that forum, individuals and groups have had the possibility to challenge the dominant understandings of codified individual rights such as the right to freedom of expression that supported the liberal elements of American society and culture that, rather than suppressing multiculturalism, allowed it to develop. It has done so furthermore because judicial review has institutionalized the right to defend individual rights against government action and because it has provided protection for individual rights so important to liberals despite the fact that the decisions of the Court have been at times expansive, at times restrictive or that access to the courts has been unevenly distributed. In the American legal system, the individualist tradition of the adversary system and the ability to seek remedy for perceived violations of constitutional rights has served to foster a rights-consciousness in the United States that has only recently begun to develop in Europe. As Ellen Sward argues, 'judicial law-making and adversarial adjudication go hand in hand.'[29] Although the degree to which the adversary system might be said to have contributed to Americans' tendency to litigate will not be examined here, it is nonetheless worth noting, as does Sward, that the establishment of the adversary system in England and the United States was advanced by 'the rise of democratic principles and institutions,' the most important of which was individual autonomy: '[w]ithout a democratic ideal that honored the dignity and autonomy of the individual, the adversary system could not have worked.'[30] Similarly, conceptions of individual autonomy have had a symbiotic relationship with judicial review. Importantly, judicial review can be said to have institutionalized the notion that remedies to perceived infringements on individual rights by one branch of government could be found in the judicial branch. What is crucial to American national identity is the common belief that numerous actions by various governmental bodies can and should be challenged by individuals or groups through litigation.

Neither American national identity nor judicial review have been static; conceptions of individual autonomy and individual rights have changed throughout American history. Because judicial review was seldom used to support individual civil rights before 1937, many scholars, such as Mary Ann Glendon, reject the notion that judicial review had been significant enough in the United States before the rights revolution of the postwar era to constitute a unique American phenomenon. Noting the infrequent use of judicial review before the twentieth century, she notes 'that where rights pertaining to fair criminal procedure, equal legal treatment, free expression, or privacy are concerned, the United States Supreme Court has only a slightly longer experience than a great number of other nations.'[31] Glendon notes that one of the earliest periods of judicial review activity was the *Lochner*-era Court's use of the right of contract to void progressive social legislation by the states.[32] It is not clear why the protection of property rights should not count in terms of giving the Court as an institution – and perhaps more importantly, American citizens as litigants – experience with the process that other countries first began to acquire much later. The Supreme Court's caseload in itself indicates a degree of experience that other countries simply cannot attain over the course of a few years. It seems that the outcome of any particular act of judicial review is irrelevant to the exercise of judicial review. (This assertion must be qualified by the caveat that it would hold only as long as litigants were successful frequently enough to sustain the institution. It is conceivable that had the Supreme Court never or rarely handed down liberal decisions then the institution would not have played the role it has, especially since 1937.) Furthermore, many of the cases before 1937, most of which did not involve decisions that expanded individual rights, contained dissents (by Justices Holmes and Brandeis, often as not) that often informed later majority opinions that did expand individual rights.

In the twentieth century, following a lengthy period of germination and as most of the rights protected by the Bill of Rights were gradually incorporated into the Fourteenth Amendment, during the postwar era, judicial review came to function, as Daniel J. Solove rightfully notes, 'as an institution that furthers the values of liberalism'; because of that, 'most modern liberals see judicial review as a potentially positive instrument of liberalism and as a necessary check on the discretion of government officials.'[33] The liberal faith in judicial review was strengthened in large part by the brand of judicial activism practiced by the Warren Court, which showed that judicial review 'can serve as a powerful tool of liberalism.'[34] While acknowledging that there is no universal support of judicial review (or the manner in which the Warren Court exercised its power), Solove rightfully argues that 'despite their differences, liberal theorists of judicial review generally support a vigorous judicial scrutiny when fundamental constitutional rights are involved.'[35] During the postwar era, judicial review has pitted an expansive liberalism continually at odds with, competing with, and developing in symbiosis with a more or less equally dominant conservatism in the United States and shaping American national identity. Despite debates between liberals and conservatives about the legitimacy of the institution itself, 'judicial review has historically tended to transmute general or ambiguous constitutional language into loci of national contestable ideals.'[36]

Judicial review offers an excellent example of unity despite diversity and the fostering of diversity through unity. Americans do not agree on the legitimacy of judicial review but they accept the power of the Court to exercise it. In 1958, in the wake of *Brown v. Board of Education* (1954),[37] and faced with Southern politicians intent on not complying with the ruling in *Brown*, the Supreme Court reasserted its role within the constitutional framework in *Cooper v. Aaron* (1958), holding that 'the federal judiciary is supreme in the exposition of the law of the Constitution, and that principle has ever since been respected by this Court and the Country as a permanent and indispensable feature of our constitutional system.'[38] That 'indispensable feature' has been a crucial factor in defining the basic rights of Americans and thereby creating the sociocultural structure within and by which American identity has been shaped. It has provided Americans with a national ethos by allowing Americans from all walks of life, including those such as Gideon,[39] who must file their writs of certiorari *in forma pauperis*, to contribute to the broad definitions of the political ideals championed by American exceptionalism and embedded in the United States Constitution:

These values range from those of federalism (associated with the text of the Eleventh Amendment), to those of substantive equality (implied by the Equal Protection Clause), to those of fairness (as embodied in the Due Process Clause), to those of liberal humanitarianism (typically located in the text of the Eighth Amendment). Most instances of lively constitutional adjudication involve the effort to peer 'behind the words of the constitutional provisions' to discern the 'postulates which limit and control.'[40] These postulates ultimately root themselves in 'constitutional ideals,'[41] which is to say, in interpretations of the historically fundamental norms of the national community. Taken together, these ideals comprise what may be called a national ethos.[42]

This national ethos has been influenced by the development of American constitutionalism because of 'the enormous achievements and awesome responsibility of the judicial branch of government.'[43] One of the centerpieces of American national identity, perhaps the core material cultural artifact in shaping that identity, is then the United States Constitution. Just as that document cemented thirteen disparate states into a single nation-state, it has served to cement Americans in their national identity. 'So enthralled have Americans become with their idea of a constitution as a written superior law set above the entire government against which all other law is to be measured,' argues Gordon Wood, 'that it is difficult to appreciate a contrary position.'[44] Americans have broadly accepted – and long lived with – the counter-majoritarian idea expressed by Justice Robert Jackson for the majority in *West Virginia State Board of Education v. Barnette* (1943):

The very purpose of a Bill of Rights was to withdraw certain subjects from the vicissitudes of political controversy, to place them beyond the reach of majorities and officials and to establish them as legal principles to be applied by the courts. One's right to life, liberty, and property, to free speech, a free press, freedom of worship and assembly, and other fundamental rights may not be submitted to vote; they depend on the outcome of no elections.[45]

One of the subjects withdrawn 'from the vicissitudes of political controversy' and one that has been the subject of numerous Supreme Court decisions is freedom of expression. Freedom of expression insured that narratives of American history written before the 1960s and 1970s – as well as other elements of mainstream public discourse – were not as monolithic as Appleby wants to argue they were. Indeed, when she touches on issues of freedom of expression, she contradicts herself. At one point, she decries the effect of 'a language of uniformity and standardization' only to complain, in the very next sentence, of the effect of the 'many mixed messages about the freedom to be different' in that narrative.[46] The statement is paradoxical since the freedom to be different entails mixed messages. First Amendment jurisprudence, as developed through judicial review in the postwar era by Justices Hugo Black, William Douglas, and William Brennan, who drew on Justices Oliver Wendell Holmes and Louis Brandeis, among others, was meant to foster and protect those 'many mixed messages about the freedom to be different.' The diversity of those messages was not racial or ethnic but ideational, a plurality of ideas. Indeed, the development of First Amendment jurisprudence through the Supreme Court's liberal exercise of judicial review during the postwar era has been fueled in part by recognition of the sociocultural diversity of the United States. Without freedom of expression, the broadening of American historiography brought about by social history in the 1960s and 1970s could not have happened. Without access to archives, government documents, and the freedom to publish, contemporary scholars could not have told histories of oppression. Without the liberal expansion of conceptions of freedom of expression that contributed significantly to the democratization of culture that Appleby elsewhere acknowledges as an important impetus to the widening of scholarship, there might be little chance of alternative versions being published at all.[47] Freedom of expression does not exist *a priori* or outside of a given society and culture which has recognized it as a right and which enforces that right against government infringement. Since *Marbury*, constitutionalism and judicial review have not only contributed to what can be viewed as an important element of American exceptionalism; they have, as freedom of expression jurisprudence became more expansive during the twentieth century, also helped make possible any expression of diversity that Appleby seeks.

Multiculturalism errs in focusing too closely on racial and ethnic difference while ignoring or downplaying the significance of viewpoint difference. As David Hollinger points out, multi-culturalism 'was never about "diversity" as such. If it were, campuses would make a concerted effort to increase the number of Promise Keepers in their midst. Multiculturalism was about certain kinds of diversity and not others.'[48] It is difficult to see why groups demarcated along the lines of ethnic or racial self-identification are more important or crucial to American history than groups demarcated by religious, political, or other attitudes, values, and beliefs. To borrow the argot of post-structuralists, why should one demarcation be privileged above another? While an individual's membership in some community of descent might be important in some contexts, his or her political allegiances might be more important in others. Focusing on ethnic or racial elements of self-identification is a demarcation that flows from a political argument put forth to advance some particular version of American national identity or the lack of a national identity. As with all political statements, such demarcations blend descriptive and prescriptive elements. Political debates are debates over facts *and* values. American exceptionalism has at times involved value choices that by today's widely accepted understanding of the liberal values at the core of American exceptionalism were wrong or that construed the topics worthy of inclusion in the writing of American history too narrowly. American exceptionalism need not avert attention from the many failures throughout American history for Americans in general, or even Supreme Court justices particularly, to live up to the political ideals its ideology espouses.

For example, multiculturalists often question the integrity of the United States Constitution because of its failure (or rather the failure of the men who wrote it) to eliminate slavery or extend suffrage universally. There is sufficient evidence that supports accounts of the United States as a racist and sexist country that has largely only paid lip service to its political ideals when minorities and women evoked those ideals. Indeed, as the decisions in *Plessy v. Ferguson* (1896)[49] and *Bradwell v. State of Illinois* (1872)[50] indicate, the Supreme Court was at times an accomplice in maintaining that racial and gender-based subordi-nation. Does the widespread presence of racism and sexism throughout the history of the United States – despite the constant pronouncement by white male political elites of political ideals that reasonably could have been (and today are) understood to be incompatible with and contrary to racism and sexism – mean that those ideals were themselves to blame, that they were simply false, or that they simply were not lived up to? Any answer to this question is political since the political ideals referred to and the historical and sociocultural circumstances being 'measured' by them must be interpreted. Appleby's – and others' – multicultural (and comparative) critiques are as much political as they are historiographic. Debates over American exceptionalism are, then, political debates over what *counts* in American history. Appleby rightly notes the interrelationship between the theoretical, the factual, and the political when she argues that choosing which details to research or present 'involves deciding in advance which human lives and whose social enactments will be counted as significant. And this is an act of authority, not research design.'[51] The historical record is immense and always viewed aspectually, perspectivally, and partially. Appeals to the historical record can be shaped to prove any number of assertions. This claim should not be read as relativist; it is merely meant to highlight the political nature of both the multicultural and the liberal agenda and the selective appeals that are made.

While much of multicultural historiography seems to be propelled by a perpetual 'cataloguing the failures of the previous generation,' as John Gerring points out, it 'is not enough merely to describe....'[52] As Gerring's remarks reiterate, appeals to the historical record involve facts and values, a distinction within historiography comparable to that between fact and law within law. Rather than fact and law, historians work with fact and interpretation. Gerring's point that 'this historiographic debate is not resolvable by an appeal to facts, for the facts themselves can be ordered in too many ways' suggests that the debate is as much ideational as it is empirical, although the two shift continuously between the foreground and the background in these debates.[53] While there is often (eventually) agreement about what the facts *are*, there is much less agreement about what the facts *mean*.

The debate between liberals and multiculturalists is not factual but political. Multiculturalists have a quarrel with liberalism and often posit their 'interrogations' of liberalism and 'liberal theories of justice' as a process that 'unearths their partial nature.'[54] The archeological metaphor is interesting, but surely, the dig did not take too long. Does it really constitute an insight to find out that liberalism is partisan? Conservatives have argued against liberals throughout the twentieth century, liberals against conservatives. Politics *is* partisan. The frequent use of the term 'contested' in much of multicultural (and postmodern) writing suggests that these authors have only recently discovered the political, a field where 'positioning' and 'contesting' have always been the norm. Debates over and compromises about social policy have not been petty disagreements. Was the Civil War an exercise in the denial of racial diversity? Were Justice John Marshall Harlan's dissent to *Plessy* or Justice Frank Murphy's dissent to *Korematsu v. United States* (1944)[55] storms in a monolithic teacup? Obviously, the NAACP's Legal Defense and Education Fund did not think so in pursuing litigation as a course for remedy to the injustices of segregation in public education. As Laurence Tribe points out, the Supreme Court's application of strict scrutiny, beginning in the postwar era, to 'state classification by race, national origin, or, in some cases, alien status or illegitimacy' and its often finding those classifications to be suspect were that tribunal's reaction to 'a long history of prejudice against non-citizens and against illegitimate as well as against racial and national minorities – a history of continuing subordination.'[56] Importantly, the Court did not need to adopt multiculturalism's view of American history or reject the political ideals embedded in American exceptionalism in order to hand down decisions that overturned discriminatory laws.

As Appleby describes them, American exceptionalism and American national identity were a national delusion that lasted for over two hundred years until they were shattered by the avalanche of empirical evidence produced by social history since the 1960s. That the breadth of American historiography was not as wide as it became is obvious. As Appleby correctly asserts in another context, the democratization of academia in the postwar era has had positive effects in widening the subject area of American history through the growth of social history is fortunate.[57] This essay does not argue with Appleby's desire for a wider range of historical scholarship that tells stories long untold or told untruly. However, it rejects the notion that American exceptionalism hampered (or hampers) such scholarship. That is, it rejects the notion that American exceptionalism has only served to inhibit alternative historical narratives, and it argues instead that aspects of American society and culture generally identified with American exceptionalism have ultimately made the burgeoning of narratives possible by creating a political and legal framework within which different narratives could be produced, distributed, and consumed. Rather than attacking American historiography, it would seem more fruitful to look forward and continue broadening the scope of history.

Rather than becoming an obstacle to inclusive understandings of American society and culture and American history, these ideals would eventually contribute to the rights revolution of the twentieth century. Liberal ideals – as are most political generalities – are declared applicable to everyone. The universality of the claim has made it possible for groups other than those who originally asserted it to make it their own. Regardless of the understanding of the phrase 'All men are created equal' by those who signed the Declaration of Independence, the universality of the proposition makes it difficult for those who claim equality for themselves to argue that the claim is not universal. Thus, when groups to whom the claim was originally argued not to apply, such as African Americans in the United States, argue that it does apply to them, then those who originally had hegemonic control over the application of the generality are faced with a conundrum: either explicitly redefine equality in less than universal terms or admit that the universality applies to African Americans and other minorities and women. Either exclusion or universality has to give. Judicial review provided individuals and groups the possibility of challenging exclusionary conceptions of liberal ideals and demanding that their beliefs that the ideals were their ideals too be taken seriously and respected.

Judicial review has provided that opportunity because the political ideals expressed in the Constitution, especially the Bill of Rights, do not advance foreclosure and exclusion. The foreclosure that took place with regard to Native Americans, African slaves, and women could have taken place under any number of governments or national identity formations and a more oppressive political system could have easily been devised. Granted, seen through the lens of liberty and equality as broadly understood today, the denial of freedom and equality that took place in the eighteenth and nineteenth centuries (and the twentieth century, for that matter) were (and are) despicable. But it is against liberal ideals of freedom and equality that racism and sexism are measured and found deplorable. That the understanding of freedom, equality, and community that dominated mainstream public discourse during the early years of the Republic were not as enlightened as they are today, or that the understanding of freedom, equality, and community throughout the rights revolution of the last half of the twentieth century, or that the understanding of freedom, equality, and community today is contentious, does not detract from the importance of the ideals of American exceptionalism as elements of American national identity.

Having been unique to the United States for over 150 years, judicial review has helped distinguish American society and culture from other countries' societies and cultures by allowing individuals to challenge the state's conception of fundamental rights with their own understanding of those rights. It has been argued many times that the 'American Constitution is of exceptional importance, both because of its bold innovations and its universal impact.'[58] A similar, though perhaps less audacious claim has been made here for judicial review and its role in the expansion of rights awareness within the United States. Because Appleby's argument with American exceptionalism is also informed by the comparative critique, it is worth considering briefly how American judicial review has been influential abroad in the postwar era.

As Caenegem notes, 'the American innovation has had no success in Britain, where the sovereignty of Parliament is a sacred dogma and the judiciary expressly declared itself incompetent to examine the compatibility of Acts of Parliament with the Constitution or the fundamental principles of the common law.'[59] Judicial review was also widely rejected on the Continent because of the European civil law tradition that also viewed the parliament as the only source of the law, including constitutional law. Under the theory of separation of powers that shaped most European governments, 'the role of the independent judiciary was to interpret the legislature's will and to administer the law *as written*.'[60] Since the end of World War Two, though, American judicial review has 'been imitated in Europe, *inter alia*, through the creation of constitutional courts.'[61] The impact of the American constitutionalism and judicial review on contemporary understandings of the rule of law and its relationship to constitutionalism internationally, as Louis Henkin and other many other legal scholars have emphasized, is evident in the influence of American constitutional thought in shaping human rights instruments outside the United States following the Second World War:

Americans were prominent among the architects and builders of international human rights, and American constitutionalism was a principal inspiration and model for them. As a result, most of the Universal Declaration of Human Rights, and later the International Covenant on Civil and Political Rights, are in their essence American constitutional rights projected around the world.[62]

The American institution of judicial review has spread throughout Europe as the result of 'a synthesis of three separate concepts: the supremacy of certain higher principles, the need to reduce even the higher law to written form, and the employment of the judiciary as a tool for enforcing the constitution against ordinary legislation.'[63] As Cappelletti further notes, this 'union of concepts first occurred in the United States, but it has since come to be considered by many as essential to the rule of law anywhere.'[64] Since 1959, European human rights jurisprudence, developed through the decisions of the European Court of Human Rights, has supported individual challenges to legislative supremacy.

It is in this regard worth emphasizing the large role played by the Supreme Court through its use of judicial review, in particular its role in carving out an expansive understanding of what are internationally recognized as *human rights*, but are generally known as *constitutional rights* in the United States, a usage that reflects the embedding of those rights in the United States long before their entrenchment in Europe. As Louis Henkin has noted, 'Americans are aware of their rights, as if in their blood. We live our rights in our lives, daily.... Human rights, by contrast, have only recently entered our common consciousness....'[65] The difference in American and European terminology reflects the manner in which judicial review fostered – albeit exceedingly slowly in the eighteenth and nineteenth centuries, at least in terms of individual political and civil rights – a unique national identity in the United States. Judicial review is, then, not the only innovative American contribution to constitutional theory and government, but it perhaps comes closest to being exceptional, given its long history in the United States and its rejection by European governments until the postwar era.[66]

Given the importance of the Constitution in American society and culture, rather than being fragile bonds, 'language, law, and institutional history' have been extremely important in forging a national identity among the citizens of the United States and judicial review in particular has played a crucial role.[67] It is exceptional but not odd that political issues become legal ones in the American legal system, given that constitutional issues are both political and legal issues since, as John Harrison notes, the Supremacy Clause 'also makes clear that the Constitution itself is not a purely political, but also a legal, phenomenon.'[68] Evidence of the continuing importance of the institution of judicial review and of the United States Supreme Court in particular in exercising the right to review the constitutionality of legislation was evident when the returns in Florida in the 2000 United States presidential election were so close that an automatic recount was triggered and the court cases soon began. The presidential contestants turned to state and federal courts and eventually to the United States Supreme Court to determine how the process should play out. CNN/*USA Today*/Gallup conducted a poll on December 10 to find out whether Americans would accept a Supreme Court decision that determined the outcome of the election. Seventy-three percent of those polled said they would accept the Supreme Court's decision as a 'legitimate outcome no matter which candidate it favors.' Only nineteen percent disagreed. That poll also found that a majority of Americans believed that the 'U.S. Supreme Court is the best institution to make the final decision on who will be the next president.'[69] By contrast, commentary from abroad revealed that most Europeans were perplexed by the involvement of the courts in a political process. Commentary also focused on the election problems of the country that is presumed to be the exemplification of democracy: America had not lived up to its ideals. It is difficult to imagine that critique hurled at any other nation. But, then, everyone expects the United States to be different.

## Notes

1. 309 U.S. 227 (1940).
2. Laurence Veysey, 'The Autonomy of American History Reconsidered,' *American Quarterly*, 31 (1979): 455–56.
3. See Veysey, 455–77; Carl N. Degler, 'In Pursuit of an American History,' *American Historical Review*, 92, Supplement (1987): 1–12; Ian Tyrrell, 'American Exceptionalism in an Age of International History,' *American Historical Review*, 96 (1991): 1031–55; Michael Kammen, 'The Problem of American Exceptionalism, a Reconsideration,' *American Quarterly*, 45 (1993): 1–43. Comparisons along international lines bring the question of what qualifies as exceptional to the foreground. International comparisons generally lead to two sorts of conclusions: first, the United States is not *that* different statistically speaking, or second, the United States is *no longer* different. The latter is particularly interesting because of the manner in which it

downplays the significance of a century or two of institutional practice. This is clearly the case with Mary Ann Glendon's argument against the significance of judicial review discussed below.

4. Joyce Appleby, 'Recovering America's Historic Diversity: Beyond Exceptionalism,' *Journal of American History*, 79 (1992): 419–31.

5. Appleby, 426.

6. Appleby, 420. There are numerous examples of this move, but two of Veysey's claims are representative. First, he suggests that individualism had its origins in 'new ideas that had floated westward across the Atlantic.' Second, he describes the romanticism of nineteenth-century American literature as 'a novel mode of perception that was of course European in origin' (Veysey, 461). On this view, the United States was, presumably, the victim of European cultural imperialism.

7. Appleby, 420.

8. Historical scholarship supports many of Appleby's points concerning the divisions that trumped national unity during the Revolutionary era and the period of the early republic. Edmund S. Morgan, *The Birth of the Republic, 1763–89* (Chicago: University of Chicago Press, 1956); John M. Murrin, 'A Roof Without Walls: The Dilemma of American National Identity,' *Beyond Confederation: Origins of the Constitution and American National Identity*, ed. Richard R. Beeman, Stephen Botein, and Edward Carlos Carter (Chapel Hill: University of North Carolina Press, 1987), 333–48; Rogers M. Smith, *Civic Ideals: Conflicting Visions of Citizenship in U.S. History* (New Haven: Yale University Press, 1997).

9. Appleby, 421. She deftly characterizes 'language, law, and institutional history' as fragile but does not indicate why bonds such as law and institutional history are not resilient.

10. For representations of the political diversity at the Convention that would have important implications for judicial review, see, for example, John Harrison, 'The Constitutional Origins and Implications of Judicial Review,' *Virginia Law Review*, 84 (1998): 353.

11. Appleby, 422. For a different perspective, which draws on an examination of voluntary organizations at the trans-local, sub-national, and national levels, see Theda Skocpol, Marshall Ganz, and Ziad Munson, 'A Nation of Organizers: The Institutional Origins of Civic Voluntarism in the United States,' *American Political Science Review*, 94 (2000): 527–46. In 'A Nation of Organizers,' the view emerges of a gradual development of shared attitudes, values, and beliefs that inspired the creation of a wide variety of voluntary organizations. Skocpol, Ganz, and Munson list the American Revolution, the Constitutional debates, and evangelical religious movements as early examples of national behavior. They further argue that the trend toward nationally organized voluntary organizations came into its own between the 1820s and 1840s, as political parties matured and numerous organizations such as American Temperance Society, the American

Anti-Slavery Society, and the General Union for Promoting the Observance of the Christian Sabbath emerged as politically active forces (529–31).

12. Donald S. Lutz, 'Religious Dimensions in the Development of American Constitutionalism,' *Emory Law Journal*, 39 (1990): 27–28.

13. Kermit Hall, William M. Wiecek, and Paul Finkelman, eds, *American Legal History: Cases and Materials*, 2nd ed. (New York: Oxford University Press, 1996). For a closer examination of the early American understanding of higher law, see Edward S. Corwin, 'The 'Higher Law' Background of American Constitutional Law,' *Harvard Law Review*, 42 (1928–29): 149–185.

14. Daniel J. Boorstin, *The Americans: The Colonial Experience* (New York: Random House, 1958), 27.

15. Hall, Wiecek, and Finkelman. For greater detail of the debates across the Atlantic over the rights of the colonists, see John Phillip Reid, *Constitutional History of the American Revolution: The Authority of Rights* (Madison: University of Wisconsin Press, 1986), 114–23, for a discussion of the relationship between migration to the colonies and the retention of the common law and individual rights.

16. Gordon S. Wood, *The Creation of the American Republic, 1776–1787* (1969; New York: Norton, 1993), 260.

17. Lutz, 24.

18. Lutz, 27.

19. Leonard W. Levy, 'Judicial Review, History, and Democracy,' *Judicial Review and the Supreme Court: Selected Essays*, Ed. Leonard W. Levy (New York: Harper and Row, 1967), 91–142.

20. 8 Coke 113b (1610).

21. R. C. van Caenegem, *An Historical Introduction to Western Constitutional Law* (Cambridge: Cambridge University Press, 1995), 160.

22. Quoted in Levy, 3. Any discussion of judicial review in the United States must acknowledge the concept's detractors. Some Americans have rejected it forthright as undemocratic; others have rejected some instances (or patterns) of its use in practice, preferring judicial restraint to judicial activism, for example. Judicial review has had both its supporters and its detractors on and off the Court throughout American history. Numerous debates have surrounded the grounding of judicial review, its countermajoritarian role in a democracy, and the extent of its effectiveness. The literature is voluminous – and far from homogenous; as Daniel J. Solove succinctly notes, the countermajoritarian protection of individual rights by the courts through judicial review 'is a conundrum that has plagued statesmen and jurists since the inception of the American republic' ('The Darkest Domain: Deference, Judicial Review, and the Bill of Rights,' *Iowa Law Review*, 84 [1999]: 967).

23. Quoted in Levy, 4.

24. Levy, 10.

25. Levy, 11.

26. Levy, 11.

27. 1 Cranch 137 (1803).
28. This essay does not attempt to answer 'the classic, indeed hoary question that lies at the heart of the master narrative of American constitutional history: how do we explain the origins of the doctrine of judicial review of legislation' (Jack N. Rakove, 'The Origins of Judicial Review: A Plea for New Contexts,' *Stanford Law Review*, 49 [1997]: 1034).
29. Ellen E. Sward, 'Values, Ideology, and the Evolution of the Adversary System,' *Indiana Law Journal*, 64 (1989): 323, n. 115.
30. Sward, 324 (endnote omitted).
31. Mary Ann Glendon, *Rights Talk: The Impoverishment of Political Discourse* (New York: Free Press, 1991), 163.
32. 198 U.S. 45 (1905).
33. Solove, 966. For a brief review of the positions legal scholars have taken on judicial review and its countermajoritarian protection of minority rights, see Michael J. Klarman, 'Rethinking the Civil Rights and Civil Liberties Revolutions,' *Virginia Law Review*, 82 (1996): 3–6 (and accompanying endnotes). As noted above, the outcome of judicial review in particular Supreme Court decisions does not always support values that are consistent with the liberal values championed by American exceptionalism as an element of national identity. It is not necessary for the argument advanced here that the outcome of constitutional rights litigation be liberal since it is the institution of judicial review and its effect on national identity that is important. Thus, it does not effect the argument advanced here that conservative Justices have used judicial review to restrict freedom of expression or equal protection. What is crucial to the role of judicial review as an element of American exceptionalism is that the possibility to address perceived infringements on individual rights institutionalized the turn to the courts as an institution within government that could redress those infringements. In any case, according to *The Supreme Court Compendium: Data, Decisions, and Developments*, just under half of Supreme Court decisions between the 1946 and 1994 terms were 'liberal.' The high during the period for decisions concerning civil liberties was the Warren Court (67.7 percent) while the low was the Rehnquist Court (43.1 percent) (Lee Epstein, 'Direction of Court Decisions by Issue Area and Chief Justice, 1946–1994 Terms,' tables 3–7; Lee Epstein, Jeffrey A. Segal, Harold J. Spaeth, and Thomas G. Walker, eds, *Supreme Court Compendium: Data, Decisions, and Developments*, 2nd ed. [Washington, DC: Congressional Quarterly, 1996], 213).
34. Solove, 966.
35. Solove, 967.
36. Robert Post, 'Democracy, Popular Sovereignty, and Judicial Review,' *California Law Review*, 86 (1998): 441, endnotes omitted.
37. 347 U.S. 483 (1954).
38. 358 U.S. 1 (1958).
39. *Gideon v. Wainwright*, 372 U.S. 335 (1963).
40. 292 U.S. 313 (1934).

41. 505 U.S. 833 (1992).

42. Post, 441, endnotes omitted.

43. S. E. Finer, Vernon Bogdanor, and Bernard Rudden, *Comparing Constitutions* (Oxford: Clarendon, 1995), 15.

44. Wood, 260.

45. 319 U.S. 624 (1943).

46. Appleby, 430.

47. Joyce Appleby, Lynn Hunt, and Margaret Jacob, 'Response,' *Journal of the History of Ideas*, 56 (1995): 679.

48. David A. Hollinger, 'National Culture and Communities of Descent,' *Reviews in American History*, 26 (1998): 316–17.

49. 163 U.S. 537 (1896).

50. 83 U.S. 130 (1872).

51. Appleby, 'Beyond Exceptionalism,' 429–30.

52. John Gerring, 'The Perils of Particularism: Political History after Hartz,' *Journal of Policy History*, 11 (1999): 319.

53. Gerring, 315.

54. Colin Harvey, 'Governing after the Rights Revolution,' *Journal of Law and Society*, 27 (2000): 71.

55. 323 U.S. 214 (1944).

56. Laurence H. Tribe, *American Constitutional Law*, 2nd ed. (Mineola, NY: Foundation Press, 1988), 1558.

57. Appleby, along with Lynn Hunt and Margaret Jacob in a joint response to their *Telling the Truth About History* (1994), argues this point: Appleby, Hunt, and Jacob, 'Response,' 679.

58. Caenegem, 150.

59. Caenegem, 159. T. R. S. Allan's discussion of the conflicts between democracy and judicial review in the British context is suggestive of how exceptional the American tradition of judicial review is by comparison ('Legislative Supremacy and the Rule of Law: Democracy and Constitutionalism,' *Cambridge Law Journal*, 44 [1985]: 111–43).

60. Donald P. Kommers, 'Judicial Review: Its Influence Abroad,' *Annals of the American Academy of Political and Social Science*, 428 (1976): 54.

61. Caenegem, 159.

62. Louis Henkin, 'Rights: American and Human,' *Columbia Law Review*, 79 (1979): 415.

63. Mauro Cappelletti, *The Judicial Process in Comparative Perspective* (Oxford: Clarendon, 1989), 131–32.

64. Cappelletti, 131–32.

65. Henkin, 405.

66. Judicial review stands up well under the scrutiny of comparative critiques. Within the field of constitutional jurisprudence, the number of studies comparing American constitutional experience and those of other countries has grown since the end of the 1990s. For an overview, see the introduction to

Mark V. Tushnet, 'The Possibilities of Comparative Constitutional Law,' *Yale Law Journal*, 108 (1999): 1225–310.

67. Equally important, although an issue that Appleby does not address, were the contentions debated out in terms of federalism and states' rights. Those debates do not lend much support to the view that the Framers, let alone the citizens of the thirteen states, understood their collective past to have been homogenous (or even that they were in possession of a collective past). Similarly, debates over slavery suggest that not all involved in writing or ratifying the Constitution conceived of African slaves as an 'invisible other.'

68. Harrison, 365.

69. Jeffrey M. Jones, 'Public Willing to Accept Supreme Court as Final Arbiter of Election Dispute,' *Gallup Online* (2000), Gallup Organization, http://www.gallup.com.

# Returns

# The Problem of American Exceptionalism: A Reconsideration[1]

*Michael Kammen*

> National consciousness, which is not nationalism, is the only thing that will give us an international dimension.
>
> Frantz Fanon, The Wretched of the Earth (1966)

Several new and important publications have appeared recently concerning a subject that has engaged many of us for decades – one that we discuss with colleagues and advanced students on a regular basis. I am inclined to suspect that we continue to do so largely because the issue remains so intriguing. One striking feature of the latest contributions is that they differ so radically among themselves. The most visibly polarized are Ian Tyrrell's 'American Exceptionalism in an Age of International History' (which repudiates American exceptionalism) and a collection of essays edited by Byron Shafer entitled *Is America Different? A New Look at American Exceptionalism* (which reaffirms the notion). Moreover, I have noticed two other quite recent contributions that reinforce American exceptionalism as a historical phenomenon from diametrically opposite perspectives: management and labor, plus a third work that examines urban development in four 'fragment' societies of Great Britain.[2]

Understandably, my initial response was to wonder about the dramatic discrepancy, particularly in view of the fact that Tyrrell is a historian while most of the rest are political scientists, sociologists, authorities on management, economics, religion, and education. An admittedly impressionistic pattern began to occur to me that is curious, indeed, because it seems the reverse of what one might expect. For about a quarter of a century following World War II, while tough-minded social scientists became

*Marks of Distinction: American Exceptionalism Revisited*, ed. Dale Carter, *The Dolphin* 32, pp. 285–334. © 2001 by Aarhus University Press, Denmark. ISBN 87 7288 383 9; ISSN 0106 4487.

increasingly wary of national character studies in general and American exceptionalism in particular, professional historians of diverse ideological persuasions (including Daniel J. Boorstin, David M. Potter, Frank Tannenbaum, Carl Degler, John Higham, and myself *inter alia*) continued to make inquiries and ventured generalizations about such slippery subjects. Subsequently, however, and for more than a decade now, such historians as Laurence Veysey, C. Vann Woodward, Eric Foner, Sean Wilentz, Akira Iriye, and Ian Tyrrell have expressed profound skepticism and have made American exceptionalism extremely unfashionable in their guild, whereas prominent social scientists such as Daniel Bell, Seymour Martin Lipset, Alex Inkeles, Sanford M. Jacoby, Samuel P. Huntington, Mona Harrington, John P. Roche, Peter Temin, Aaron Wildavsky, and Richard Rose have comfortably resuscitated and reaffirmed the whole gnarly matter and have done so largely on the basis of empirical studies.[3]

As a humanistic historian who has never been a card-carrying social scientist, my impulse would ordinarily be supportive of the currently skeptical historians. Yet in this instance, respecting this particular topic, I find the social scientists more persuasive – perhaps because they are, in fact, heavily reinforced by recent historical scholarship, as I hope to demonstrate below.

Before doing so, however, I want to address a few of the broader procedural and conceptual issues that have been raised in the most recent literature. The call for an internationalized historiography voiced by Tyrrell, Iriye and others has been accompanied by a curious tendency to disparage or even discount the work of comparative history, especially if it happens to highlight differences rather than similarities. I find that tendency strange as well as sad because we waited so long for comparative history to really develop; and when it did, as it turned out, differences appeared to preponderate. Scholars such as Peter Kolchin and Alfred D. Chandler, whose work I regard as superb, had no problem with that outcome, yet the transnational enthusiasts seem to be morally or ideologically disposed to minimize all those irritating yet illuminating differences.

Surprisingly, few scholars have noted an inclination (less than a decade old) to believe that looking at subnational units of social organization might actually help us to get a better handle on the problem of American exceptionalism. I have in mind, for example, Richard Oestreicher's fine study of the working class in late nineteenth-century Detroit, which concedes that the dynamics of class formation and consciousness varied from one American city to another; or James McPherson's interesting suggestion that prior to the Civil War it was the North, rather than the South that was 'exceptional,' that is, a deviation from what the United States traditionally had been and valued; or Carl Becker's droll assertion that if the United States was exceptional, Kansas was distinctive within it![4]

What develops, then, from reading such studies end to end? Perhaps a realization that because of American heterogeneity we have not had a singular mode or pattern of exceptionalism. Rather, we have had a configuration of situations that are not static (see McPherson on regional exceptionalism), and consequently they reveal why it is both difficult and dangerous to conclude that the United States as a whole, over an extended period of time, is different from all other cultures with respect to some particular criterion.

Therefore, the next step in this necessarily intensive process may well be the internationalization of history *pari passu* the comparative history of American cities and regions, American unions and voluntary associations, American patterns of internal migration and mobility, American modes of advertising and expressions of taste, or even the geographic configuration (distribution) of syndicated columnists. That kind of domestic comparative history will have to be diachronic as well as synchronic in order to establish nuances of change over time.

I hope it will not seem banal if I suggest that international history ought to be accompanied by comparative 'local history' that seeks to develop typologies; for Walt Whitman's words, 'I am large, I contain multitudes, ' have become far more telling in the generations since he wrote those lines in *Song of Myself.*

The implications of local, national, and international history for our apprehension of American exceptionalism (not to mention their inter-connectedness) become clearer when we notice that new societies in the nineteenth century looked to the United States as a prototype – though not necessarily a paragon – because they viewed it as the first, the largest, and the most advanced among freshly emerging yet diverse cultures. As one writer for *The Australian* phrased it in 1831, the United States was commonly considered 'a model for all new countries and New South Wales (hereafter) in particular.' Living in France during the 1950s prompted James Baldwin to wonder, 'What does it mean to be an American?, ' and by the time he returned home the alienated Baldwin believed passionately in American exceptionalism and even used that now despised word 'unique.'[5]

When we pursue the interconnectedness of micro and macro scales of historical analysis, we achieve considerable illumination from two important comparative studies of management and labor. Starting with the latter, we find Gary Marks (a political scientist) wanting to explain the historical absence of a major labor party in the United States, noting the remarkable range of diversity in unionism *within* and *across* western societies, and concluding that the absence of a European-style labor party resulted from the 'unique character of American unionism.' He insists upon the need for systematic understanding of the political orientations of particular unions, and quotes a tailor who spoke at the Denver convention of the American Federation of Labor late in 1894: 'We have in this country conditions that do not exist in Great Britain. We have the "spoil" system which is something almost unknown in Great Britain and on account of it we cannot afford to try at this time to start a political party as an adjunct with their unions.'[6]

Marks observes that the United States was the only Western society in which workers could participate in politics prior to the institutionalization of unions and socialist political parties. He notices the persistent temptation to influence the two major political parties by participating in coalitions. He calls attention to the critical importance of closed unionism for understanding

American exceptionalism. Nowhere else, Marks argues, was the 'grip of craft unions on the union movement as strong or as durable' as it was in the United States from the 1890s onward. Following his in-depth case studies and systematic comparisons, Marks concludes that structural aspects of American politics posed much greater obstacles to a potential labor party than the British political system did. Marks also finds that while some American socialists may have been even more radical than their German counterparts, 'the context in which American socialists acted made their strategies particularly sectarian. Whereas German socialists played a vital role in creating the Free Union movement, American socialists from the late 1880s had to respond to the establishment of an independent union movement along economistic craft lines.'[7]

When we shift our attention from labor to management, the most current scholarship strongly supports an exceptionalist position also, and even contends that the comparative weakness of unionism in the United States must be attributed to the distinctive values and preferences of American managers, which caused them to be more hostile to unionism than managers in other nations. Sanford M. Jacoby, who teaches at UCLA's Graduate School of Management, argues that business in the United States has historically enjoyed an unusual degree of political power, and that in recent decades there has even been an increase in the extent of illegal employer resistance to unions. Jacoby insists that American employers 'faced a different set of incentives and had more substantial resources to resist unionization than was true of employers elsewhere. These included economic and political factors not usually considered in either mainstream or Marxist analyses, such as the size and structure of firms and the state's role in the industrial relations system, which was more variable and complex than instrumental theories would have it.'[8]

Jacoby demonstrates startling discrepancies between French, British, and American companies in terms of their respective approaches to long-range investment decisions. He attributes these differences to significant national variations in management education, in attitudes toward risk, in corporate career structures, and in tax laws. Not only did American managers have greater incentives to be hostile, according to Jacoby they also had available a wider range of political and ideological resources with which to implement that hostility. Labor in the United States had a more difficult time achieving employer recognition than labor elsewhere, because American employers had greater economic covert resources and overt. with which to carry out anti-union campaigns, both covert and overt. Finally, in Jacoby's view, what made the American situation highly unusual was not only the absence of a positive industrial relations policy, but also the government's willingness to stand aside during violent labor disputes, or even to mobilize the state's repressive means on behalf of employers.[9]

So, what I wish to offer is an impressionistic tally, a reckoning as it were, in which the impact of critical essays that have been appearing since the mid-1970s is weighed against the substantive scholarship that has emerged in the wake of those essays. Where do we actually stand? Is there a gap between the newly orthodox homilies that we assign our students and the unsettling implications of solid work recently produced by judicious and conscientious practitioners?

To answer those questions I shall proceed in four stages: first, a section devoted to the cultural and historical origins of American exceptionalism, included here, in part, because the full story is not familiar to everyone, and in part because the background of our problem is inseparable from its foreground – by which I mean the state of the art today. Second, I shall notice the critics of American exceptionalism and their resonance over time. It is noteworthy, I believe, that the critics are not necessarily unAmerican or even anti-American, just as the advocates of exceptionalist positions have not inevitably been spread-eagle nationalists. Third, I shall look at what has actually happened to the exceptionalist position in this age of careful, cosmopolitan comparisons. Has mindless self-deception merely given way to a sophisticated surfeit of national similarities? And fourth, what lessons can we learn by weighing the diagnostic against the intractably descriptive, the prescriptive against serious products of in-depth scholarship over the past dozen years?

## The Historical and Cultural Origins of American Exceptionalism

When critics of American exceptionalism – the notion that the United States has had a unique destiny and history, or more modestly, a history with highly distinctive features or an unusual trajectory – identify those writers responsible for such objectionable myopia, their usual suspects date from the generation and circumstances directly following World War II: the Cold War, the consensus school of historians (exemplified by Daniel J. Boorstin and Louis Hartz), and ideological stimuli that shaped the American Studies enterprise. They commonly fail to recognize that American exceptionalism is as old as the nation itself and, equally important, has played an integral part in the society's sense of its own identity. Noah Webster provides a familiar case in point, but we should not overlook Samuel Latham Mitchill (1764-1831), a physician whose passion it became to promote a particular feeling of American identity that would be manifest in government and politics, literature and science, medicine and society. There were also people, such as William Findley of western Pennsylvania, who decided even before the eighteenth century ended that Americans had 'formed a character peculiar to themselves, and in some respects distinct from that of other nations.'[10]

Throughout the nineteenth century, imaginative writers and historians, popular orators and clergy joined a chorus that continually chanted an ode to the nation's special mission and readiness to fulfill it. Nick Salvatore has correctly argued that awareness of the republican tradition as a legacy of the American Revolution contributed significantly to a strong sense of exceptionalism, one that became pervasive in the popular culture.[11] However astute Tocqueville may have been in observing and explaining American distinctiveness, we should note that his 'informants,' such as Alexander Everett and Jared Sparks, insisted over and over again that the uniqueness of the United States could only be understood in terms of 'our origins.' A Bostonian reminded Tocqueville that 'those who would like to imitate us should remember that there are no precedents for our history.' Lest all of that be casually dismissed as predictable super-patriotism, we should keep in mind that Patrice Higonnet's recent study of *The Origins of French and American Republicanism* contrasts the individualistic character of American society with the persistence of corporatism in France.[12]

What is especially striking in the literature written about the United States by foreign observers is that the emphasis upon exceptionalism is so persistent and so powerfully felt. 'The position of America is quite exceptional,' Tocqueville wrote; and in 1851 Friedrich Engels warned Joseph Weydemeyer (his friend and Karl Marx's co-worker) about 'the special American conditions: the ease with which the surplus population is drained off to the farms, the necessarily rapid and rapidly growing prosperity of the country, which makes bourgeois conditions look like a beau ideal to them, and so forth.' If it is noteworthy that most of Marx's co-workers who came to the United States after 1848 soon abandoned socialism, it is equally important that explanations that were offered for American exceptionalism by the likes of Francis Lieber, Hermann E. von Holst, James Bryce, H. G. Wells, G. K. Chesterton, and Hilaire Belloc tended to be complementary rather than redundant or contradictory.[13] The same is true of more scholarly writers since World War II whose concerns have ranged from the vision and venturesome nature of American businessmen to the comparative fluidity of our class structure.[14]

Curiously, although foreign observers have hardly been indifferent to scenery, environment, and natural resources in the United States, they have been less disposed than American writers to invoke those phenomena in attempting to account for major contrasts. The author of an 1818 essay on 'National Poetry' found a literary imperative in 'our country's being beautiful and sublime and picturesque,' while a modem scholar (known for his iconoclastic revisionism) has asserted that American farmers were distinctively confident about their ability to conquer nature and adverse agricultural conditions, and that they were markedly successful in doing so.[15]

Environmental explanations for the special circumstances in North America date back to the colonial period, especially the eighteenth century, when it became virtually a cliché to call, for example, Virginia or Pennsylvania, the 'best poor man's Country in the World.' Who could have imagined such a temperate climate, such fertile land, such fecund harvests? That mythos would eventually reinforce the early New England presumption that America was predestined to be a New Jerusalem, a site specially favored by God – perhaps the very place that he had chosen to initiate the millennial Kingdom of Christ. Jonathan Edwards firmly believed that America had a unique spiritual destiny and that the millennium would begin in New England – all of which had unintended, secular implications for national self-confidence during the Revolutionary era and the young republic.[16] Other New Englanders would embroider vague yet earnest variations on that theme, even in times of crisis. Hence the assertion by James Russell Lowell in 1864 that 'America is something without precedent,' and hence the will to believe that artistic expression in the United States would be place-specific and therefore distinctive, not merely in its subject matter, but in its manner of expression.[17]

During the half-century following World War I, proponents of American exceptionalism who felt a particular affection or concern for the arts often explained their position in terms of economic organization, or a fluid social structure, or sometimes the sheer determination of creative people to differentiate their work from modes of artistic expression produced elsewhere. Such statements, however vague and naive they may seem to us, were heartfelt and widely noticed. In 1936, for example, Bernard DeVoto supported Gilbert Seldes's assertion that 'the mode of production of material life in the United States has been so different from what it has been anywhere else that the social and political life here is conditioned in a unique, characteristic form and function.'[18] These kinds of sentiments came from cosmopolitan expatriates like Gertrude Stein (when she returned to the

United States following a thirty-five year absence), as well as from hopeful home-bodies who either extolled native voices that already sounded distinctive (Thornton Wilder) or abstract expressionism that *would* be different by design (Clement Greenberg).[19]

There has been a curious tendency, by the way, to assume that prominent Americanists of the Progressive era were provincials whose limited perspectives can be explained accordingly. Frederick Jackson Turner, for example, was indeed a patriotic exceptionalist; yet he travelled through Europe in 1900, read a considerable amount about contemporary Europe, and discussed European history at great length with his colleague, Charles Homer Haskins. Turner's exceptionalism did *not* result from intellectual narrowness or ignorance. Similarly, when Lewis Mumford spent almost a year in Great Britain in 1920 he developed a desire to preserve 'the valuable part of the American heritage.' Five years later, after he gave lectures in Geneva, Switzerland, his commitment to exceptionalism grew even stronger and he found in nineteenth-century American culture a fascinating wealth of native traditions in the arts. Charles and Mary Beard wrote *The Rise of American Civilization* during the mid–1920s following twenty-five years of extensive travel in western Europe and Asia. When Mumford reviewed their book in *The New Republic,* he noted the Beards's penchant for making comparisons.[20]

Exceptionalism did not necessarily equate with chauvinism. Harsh critics of American culture liked to use hyperbole in order to highlight just how phenomenally mired in mediocrity the arts and intellectual life in the United States had become. H. L. Mencken is perhaps the most memorable example, but J. E. Spingarn comes to mind in literary criticism and Thomas Craven in the realm of art. 'If the nations of Europe are agreed on any one thing,' Craven complained in 1932, 'it is that America is a pretty distinct place – peculiar, individual, unique, characterized by certain vile traits and low habits.'[21]

Beginning in the 1930s, however, a symbolic quest for the 'meaning of America' seemed to top the agenda of diverse writers: critics, historians of literature and culture, serious journalists, and even such watchdogs of the film industry as Will Hays. Gilbert Seldes began his *Mainland* in 1936 with a declaration that it was 'an attempt to discover what America means; not so much what it means to me, as what it can mean in the world.'[22] Jacques Barzun would echo those sentiments, virtually verbatim, in *God's Country and Mine* (1954). When Henry Lute wrote his widely noticed editorial about the 'American Century' in *Life Magazine* (February 1941), he also linked the 'meaning of America' to 'the meaning of our time.' Later that same year the novelist James Boyd published a series of radio broadcasts that he had arranged for CBS under the title *The Free Company Presents ... a collection of plays about the meaning of America.*[23]

The notion that America had a palpable meaning persisted for more than two decades beyond 1941, and Luce publications played a major part in perpetuating the quest as a lofty goal. By the later 1960s, however, the war in Vietnam had become so bitterly divisive that the editor-in-chief of *Time, Inc.,* proclaimed an unprecedented situation: the country had lost a working consensus 'as to what we think America means.' More than twenty years after that, moreover, when multiculturalism in secondary education became a subject of intense debate and partisanship, the editor of the *Journal of American History* observed that 'the debate is really about the meaning of America.'[24]

This spasmodic yet sustained discourse about the meaning of America, recurrent for more than sixty years now, may seem to ebb and flow; but from time to time it spills over into a pool that is still murkier: the meaning of Americanism. Two points are notable here. First, those who invoke that phrase have invariably been exceptionalists; and second, the invocation is intended to have ideological force, a point that I shall return to at the conclusion of this essay. 'To analyze combinations of character that only our national life produces,' a New Englander wrote in 1870, 'to portray dramatic situations that belong to a clearer social atmosphere, – this is the higher Americanism.' More than half a century later, in 1934, Leon Samson discussed the concept while explaining the peculiar potency of American exceptionalism: 'When we examine the meaning of Americanism, we discover that Americanism is to the American not a tradition or a territory ... but a doctrine – what socialism is to a socialist.'[25]

Irving Howe, a committed socialist with an abiding concern about the persistent power of American exceptionalism, has remarked that it took 'primarily an ideological or a mythic form, a devotion to the idea that this country could be exempt from the historical burdens that had overwhelmed Europe.' Consequently, Howe does not reject the emotional reality of exceptionalism, and he explores its affective force as an ideological surrogate in a society not given to lucidly articulated ideological effusions. Howe's analysis is one of the most insightful that has appeared, yet it is incomplete in the sense that it is negative because it rationalizes exceptionalism as the celebration of an absence, namely, historical burdens. I am persuaded that the 'meaning of America' and of 'Americanism' have also had affirmative ideological content, exemplified by this representative extract from a speech given by Harry Overstreet, a philosopher, in 1937: 'It is the high distinction of America to have been the first nation in civilized history to welcome different cultures and to give them free scope to participate in the building of a new nation.'[26]

It is that kind of cosmic claim that has been featured so aggressively when Americans have attempted to explain the meaning of America. The historical narrative of nativism may suggest just how hollow such rhetoric can be. But we are not concerned here with authentic narratives. We are trying to catch hold of recurring rhetoric as a cultural reality and potent force.

### Critics of American Exceptionalism and Their Resonance

Disdain for American exceptionalism first appeared in sustained fashion in 1975. It has not been monolithic, however, and at least five fairly discrete phases can be identified. One finds common ground and overlap, to be sure, but also disagreement and inconsistencies among the critics. Although space does not permit in-depth summaries, it is at least possible to identify some of the leading participants and indicate their points of departure.

First, essays appeared in the mid–1970s that clearly derived from circumstances involving the crisis of political morality: a national fall from grace in the wake of Watergate and, more importantly, humiliation in and about Vietnam. In 'The End of American Exceptionalism,' Daniel Bell acknowledged that the United States had had a unique history but that it was initially based upon a belief in moral superiority and subsequently upon sheer power. Now that illusions about the former had been shattered, and the latter had been rendered nugatory, all that remained of American exceptionalism, according to Bell, was the 'constitutional system, with a comity that has been undergirded by history.' He closed with the speculative hope that the United States would remain aware of the 'moral complexity of history.' Less than a year later Alexander E. Campbell, Professor of American History at Birmingham in England, argued that the United States had lost its claim to national purpose, that 'most Americans are conscious of sharing problems which are world-wide rather than peculiar to themselves,' and. that the country had ceased to be a 'great experiment' or the last best hope of earth.[27] The American Adam had given way to a helpless, tarnished Gulliver.

The next move, which still seems to me the pivotal one, involved the appearance in 1979 of Laurence Veysey's compelling essay titled 'The Autonomy of American History Reconsidered.' Veysey was hardly insensitive to the same stimuli that had provoked Bell and Campbell, but his revisionism also arose from academic and scholarly concerns: namely, that excessive attention to contrasts flatly distorted historical realities; that industrialism and modernism had created some pervasive international patterns that historians had neglected at their peril; that the new social history mandated much more attention to transnational themes – such as mobility studies, which clearly demolished the customary claims for American distinctiveness in that regard. 'The sobering demystification of America,' Veysey wrote, 'the new awareness that we are but one fractional (and internally fractionated) unit in a polyglot world, and that social history is composed of a vast number of separate and distinct pieces, like a mosaic that seldom stops at international boundary lines, has enabled students of American social evolution to view their subject with fewer blinders than before.'[28]

Phase three of the emerging critique appeared in 1984 when Eric Foner and Sean Wilentz, swiftly joined by other historians of the working class, sought in various ways to address and redefine the persistent line of inquiry first introduced by Werner Sombart in 1906: 'Why is there no socialism in the United States?' Because the responses of these historians are wide-ranging and probe deeply, there is considerable danger in compressing a brief summary; but their principal points include the following. Socialism failed to produce a successful political and class transformation in many other countries, not only in the United States; the absence of a powerful social democratic party here does not mean that American workers passively accepted the status quo; a vigorous tradition of radical protest has, in fact, existed in the United States ever since the later 1820s if not from Tom Paine's time in Philadelphia; the republican ideology provided meaning and direction for artisans and mechanics as well as the elite; and ethnicity has not been an insuperable barrier to working class cooperation for political objectives.[29]

Phase four emerged as a familiar choir during the mid- and later 1980s, but the most strident soloist may well have been William C. Spengemann, whose *Mirror for Americanists* relentlessly argued against the distinctiveness of American literature and mocked the mindless assumptions, implicit or explicit, of those guilty of thoughtless chauvinism. 'Although our feelings of cultural uniqueness persuade us that American literature is different,' Spengemann observed, 'our cultural paranoia forces us to prove that American literature is just as good as European literature, in exactly the same ways, and hence to concentrate our efforts upon the very works that, in measuring up to transnational standards, may well be our least distinctive productions. ' It is my impression, however, that Spengemann's position has met with proportionately less support from literary critics than the views of Veysey, Foner, and others have received from their colleagues in history.[30]

Phase five, which is the most diffuse and least cohesive of my groupings, concerns colonial as well as postcolonial societies and their systems of thought. Thus Jack P. Greene argued in 1988, following John M. Murrin and others, that 'the central cultural impulse among the colonists was not to identify and find ways to express and to celebrate what was distinctively American about themselves and their societies but, insofar as possible, to eliminate these distinctions so that they might – with more credibility – think of themselves and their societies – and be thought of by the people in Britain – as demonstrably British.' For apparently ideological reasons, resting mainly upon his conservative hostility to the 'liberal-capitalist [critical] interpretation of the American founding,' J. G. A. Pocock has condemned the Lockean emphasis that runs from Louis Hartz to John Diggins and Isaac Kramnick, and quips that Americans who prefer 'the splendid misery of uniqueness' might be 'happier if they shared their history with other people.'[31]

I would be the first to confess that fault can be found with my five-phase evolution of the critique of American exceptionalism. Aside from the historian's penchant for imposing excessive order upon intractable materials, I wish to call attention to two awkward problems in particular. First, it must be recognized that some of the most prominent critics have placed themselves on record with categorical concessions of distinctiveness – not necessarily the whole works, America entire, but important components thereof. Let's look at four examples.

In 1974 I listened with rapt fascination as David D. Hall sandbagged a generation of exceptionalists, including Hartz, Handlin, Boorstin, Marvin Meyers, and Stanley Elkins, for overdramatizing a stark contrast between orderly societies in the Old World and disorderly ones in the New. Hall's recent innovative book on popular religion in colonial New England, however, acknowledges many determinative distinctions: the circumstances of New England in the seventeenth century were 'not the circumstances to which Europeans were accustomed. The differences are great enough to force us to revise the very sense of "popular religion."' Hall contends that because space was much less consequential than in Europe, ordinary people could more readily ignore the obligations of organized religion, and church membership became a more voluntary matter than in Europe. When Hall turns to relationships between religious ritual and social order, he stresses the contrast between Old World hierarchies of rank and New World emphases upon collective godliness. Without minimizing the European origins of popular religion in the colonies, Hall leaves the reader with a clear sense of important deviations based upon variables that ranged from the environment to social values.[32]

Although Sean Wilentz is customarily regarded as a critic of American exceptionalism, his well-received *Chants Democratic* insists upon 'distinctively American forms of class conflict' that arose from ideological differences over 'fundamental American values' and led to 'a distinctly American trade unionism.' Similarly, an essay published by Eric Foner in 1988 demolishes some of the foolish reasoning that has been used to bolster American exceptionalism, yet acknowledges highly significant variations that occurred in different nations during the age of industrialization, accepts the 'distinctive character of American trade unionism,' and observes that the trajectory of socialist movements in the United States during the first half of the twentieth century varied significantly from their European counterparts.[33]

In the work of social historian Alan Dawley, adjustments have actually moved to and fro. In 1978 he observed that Gramsci's concept of hegemony had been misapplied to the United States because the prevalence here of industrial violence, racism, xenophobia, and reactive ethnic cultures did not, taken together for the later nineteenth and early twentieth centuries, conform to Gramsci's pattern of a dominant social group diffusing its notions of normative relations and realities throughout the culture. 'If there is to be a school of cultural studies in the United States,' Dawley wrote, following the lead of E. P. Thompson, 'it will have to honor the "peculiarities" principle and pay strict attention to special national characteristics.' Ten years later Dawley developed this assertion but with a different spin in a short paper titled 'Farewell to "American Exceptionalism."' There he took a position that I shall return to in my conclusion because it is judicious and has broad applicability. The United States is different but not exceptional, he remarked, not a curiosity in the political history of industrialization. Dawley urged that greater attention be given to variability in national patterns of capitalism, in the timing of capitalist development, in the disposition of social elites displaced by upwardly mobile industrialists, in the structure of state power, and in the diverse composition of various national working classes.[34]

I am *not* trying to imply that critics of American exceptionalism have been wildly inconsistent or mindlessly ambivalent. Rather, I do want to suggest that some of the most subtle among them have adjusted their views as fresh research and theoretical perspectives have emerged, that some have occasionally been misunderstood or misinterpreted, and above all that the best among them have tried very hard to be judicious, to look at all of the pertinent evidence, and to tally up accordingly. Thus Aristide A. Zolberg, who teaches political science at the New School for Social Research, is a comparativist who is quite partial to similarities. He nonetheless recognizes major contrasts between the development of capitalism (and its social consequences) in the United States and in Europe. He finds, for example, a greater degree of integration by American workers in *their* political and social system than occurred in Europe, particularly because of ideological tensions that were generated in Europe during and after World War I.[35]

An overview of the critics and revisionists, however brief, would not be complete without a look at the ideological Left because here, too, simplistic generalizations are not viable. The Old Left along with some progenitors of the New Left tended to believe quite passionately in American exceptionalism. I have in mind Dwight Macdonald, for instance, who wrote in 1959 of Nathanael West's *Miss Lonelyhearts* that is was a 'marvelously pure expression of our special American sort of agony, the horror of aloneness, and of our kind of corruption, that of mass culture.' In the same year C. Wright Mills declared that 'in the United States there is no long-standing traditional establishment of culture on the European model.' Mills also elaborated his belief that persons with white-collar vocations in the United States were decidedly different from their European counterparts.[36]

Connections between the New Left and American exceptionalism are more complicated. Giles Gunn has observed that critical assessments of exceptionalism within American Studies were by no means rooted exclusively in the New Left, yet they did arise during the later 1960s and early 1970s from a feeling of embarrassment with American chauvinism and parochialism, from a growing sense of international interdependence, and from antipathy to the consensus school of historiography.[37] A more scholarly and less ideological grounding for the critique then followed in the later 1970s; what transpired in the subsequent decade leaves one feeling fairly reluctant to generalize about the New Left. Fierce critics of exceptionalism remained vocal, to be sure; but advocates of American working-class distinctiveness, such as Mike Davis, could make a persuasive case for the potency of their belief in exceptionalism.[38]

## Persistent Differentiations in the Age of Comparative Scholarship

Suppose we try to compile a tally, a rough and ready reckoning of major scholarship since 1980 in diverse fields and subdisciplines? The reason for choosing 1980 is not just to be recent and therefore up to date. Veysey's landmark essay appeared in 1979 and within five years, as we have noted, quite a few vigorous voices had spoken in ways that reinforced Veysey's critique. How far did the pendulum really swing after 1980? How much has our vocational vantage point been changed? The answer, based upon a survey of diverse books, is: not a whole lot.

Let's begin at the chronological beginning. *The Peopling of British North America,* by Bernard Bailyn, contends that the dynamics of land speculation 'shaped a relationship between the owners and the workers of the land different from that which prevailed in Europe.' Speculators had to offer very low rental fees in order to get land developed and enhance its value. Bailyn's emphasis upon the contrast between core and periphery, between the metropolis of empire and its marchlands, causes him to highlight the 'distinctive' aspects of the colonial society and culture. That word, the 'd' word, recurs frequently in Bailyn's recent work and represents a clear continuity with his earlier analyses of pre-Revolutionary politics.[39] Similarly, Jon Butler's reinterpretation of the first centuries of American Protestantism seeks to explain, among other things, why religious development in the New World differed so markedly from Britain's.[40]

Comparable conclusions emerge when we look to politics and public life. Leon D. Epstein is impressed by the limits that historical American circumstances have imposed upon the growth of political parties and their clout. 'The distinctiveness of American parties is old and well established,' he explains. 'It is not mainly the product of the last few decades of widely perceived decline. As governing agencies, American parties have nearly always been less cohesive in national policymaking than parties in parliamentary regimes. And as extra-governmental organizations, their strength, where it existed, was traditionally state and local rather than national. Moreover, American parties have ordinarily been without the dues-paying mass memberships characteristic of European parties.' Turning to public policy made manifest in historic pieces of legislation, Harold M. Hyman concludes that American exceptionalism 'is not a busted superstition suitable only for the trash heap of history.' He finds in certain key statutes a pattern of access to socioeconomic mobility and personal fulfillment that is 'unique in the world.'[41]

Recent historians of American literature, especially those whose orientation is more cultural and *con*textual than structural and textual, also tend to be exceptionalists. A notable example is David S. Reynolds's study of 'subversive literature' during the early and mid-nineteenth century. While acknowledging its roots in earlier criminal and Gothic British fiction, Reynolds insists repeatedly, with multiple variations, that 'it took on distinctly American characteristics when reinterpreted by authors who wished to find literary correlatives for the horrific or turbulent aspects of perceived reality in the new republic.' He bolsters his case with numerous expressions by native writers that indicate just how earnestly they sought an American voice and vision. Not once but twice Reynolds quotes Ahab's eulogy for the sinking *Pequod:* 'Its wood could only be American!' (8 and 549).[42]

In addition to numerous utterances of that sort by Herman Melville, Reynolds cites still others by Emerson, Whitman, Bushnell, obscure writers of sensational pulp fiction, and frontier humorists. The author also demonstrates just how many genres and subgenres lacked counterparts elsewhere: the dark adventure style, the irrational mode, and the confidence man as an ironic character type are a few of Reynolds's illustrations. Whether he is examining Crockett almanacs or George Lippard's grim urban melodramas, Reynolds insists that the blend of egalitarianism, frightful situations, and unorthodox literary strategies ('intentional disruptions of linear patterns and wholesale assaults on conventional literary rules,' (198)) is 'at once totally American and totally bizarre' (452). Reynolds has added a considerable dimension and documentary depth to general themes long accessible to students of American literary history.[43]

There has been even greater unanimity among folklorists in assuming that American folk life reflected a distinctive national experience. Nevertheless the scope of what folklorists and historians of folk culture do has broadened during the past twenty-five years. In 1966 Alan Dundes complained that Americanists tended to neglect festivals, folk dance, art, cuisine and related phenomena.[44]

In recent years, however, Mary Ryan has scrutinized the civic parade as a mirror of the nineteenth-century social order in the United States. She concludes that Americans devised a 'distinctive and curious mode of public celebration' in which a sizable portion of the urban population organized into platoons, companies, regiments, ranks and columns, and marched through public thoroughfares. 'This particular type of celebratory performance seems to have been an American invention.' It was also more socially inclusive than its European counterparts. Similarly, David Glassberg's thorough study of American historical pageantry, which focuses on a period more than half a century after Ryan's, finds that civic pageantry provided a uniquely American form of 'social ceremonial' even though it had obvious English models.[45]

If space permitted we could also for American distinctiveness in terms of middle-class values (rooted in 'widespread economic opportunity'), in terms of the 'uniquely American proclivity for joining voluntary groups,' in terms of the functions of symbolic ethnicity and what Mary C. Waters has called 'personally constructed American ethnic communities,' and in the activities and assumptions of philanthropic organizations in relation to the responsibilities that government will and will not undertake.[46] Also, a meticulous study of Thomas A. Edison's reputation in American popular culture concludes that the aspect of American exceptionalism that appeared most often in conjunction with the Edison image 'is that which glories in "American inventive genius," of which Edison is naturally seen as the "incarnation."' The literature is characterized by such phrases as 'we are the most ingenious people in the world' and 'America is the chosen home of invention.'[47]

Other claims for American uniqueness that have appeared in the past decade, however, are less persuasive because little or no evidence is presented to show whether any empirically comparative inquiry has been conducted. This is true of assertions on behalf of environmentalism, historic preservation, the situation of art and artists in the marketplace, and the overall configuration of governmental institutions in the United States.[48]

Marianne Debouzy has tactfully noted the tendency of some American historians to make unwarranted assumptions about working-class people in Europe.[49] I worry about colleagues who are insufficiently empirical and self-critical – who proceed, as Carl Becker once put it, without fear and without research.

This brings me to the crux of this post–1980 reckoning: what happens to American exceptionalism when scholars take seriously the imperative to do comparative work? Laurence Veysey has been saying for twenty years that 'careful comparison lies close to the heart of historical explanation.' His distaste for the negative consequences of nationalism has caused Veysey (and more recently Akira Iriye) to call for trans-national investigations and to assume that, in modern history especially, the quest for comparisons will more likely than not turn up similarities.[50]

Both C. Vann Woodward and Carl Degler, however, like to quote Marc Bloch, who pioneered in calling for comparative work and remarked in 1928 that 'it is often supposed that the method has no other purpose than hunting out resemblances.' Bloch contended that 'correctly understood, the primary interest of the comparative method is, on the contrary, the observation of differences.'[51] In my judgement, comparative scholarship produced in the past decade bears Bloch out – not because researchers preferred differences but simply because their investigations turned up a disproportionate imbalance favoring difference.

Based upon the survey of recent literature that I have made, it is my impression that researchers were not predisposed to find a preponderance of similarities or differences, and certainly that they had no stake in defending or propping up the precarious remains of American exceptionalism. In fact, most of the works that I am about to cite were *undertaken* during the later 1970s and early 1980s, when the very notion of American exceptionalism seemed to be least credible and most unfashionable. Although it may be excessively schematic, I am going to organize the overview that follows in terms of the three categories (or lines of inquiry) that have generated the greatest amount of comparative interest: race relations, class formation and attendant ideologies, and the role of the state in terms of active intervention versus degrees of restraint.[52]

With respect to the history of slavery, emancipation, and race relations, I call to your attention the consistent pattern that appears in four overtly comparative efforts. In *White Supremacy: A Comparative Study in American and South African History* (1981), George M. Fredrickson is ultimately more impressed by differences. Race relations in the United States acquired a highly particular character for several reasons: the geographical setting, the political origins and assumptions of the settlers, the overall population being constituted in a certain way, and because the indigenous peoples could not be readily recruited as a labor force. In Peter Kolchin's extraordinary book, *Unfree Labor: American*

*Slavery and Russian Serfdom* (1987), the author is even more impressed by contrasts than by similarities. Whereas the latter are structural and to some extent causal, the differences are demographic, ethnic or racial, involve degrees of autonomy, more impersonal relations between masters and serfs in Russia (an absence of paternalism there), divergent modes of seeking redress and patterns of resistance, and differences in the ways the two systems of unfreedom were terminated, to mention only some of the contrasts. Ultimately, as Kolchin writes in his conclusion, 'despite many similar features of Russian serfdom and southern slavery, there was a contrast in their viability. By the middle of the nineteenth century, as southern slavery was flourishing as never before, Russian serfdom constituted a bankrupt system widely recognized as on its last legs.... After the 1820s, when southerners were elaborating with increasing frequency and forcefulness their arguments in defense of the "peculiar institution," public defense of serfdom in Russia virtually disappeared.'[53]

In 1969 C. Vann Woodward called the pattern of racial classification in the United States 'unique'; twenty years later he rejected an exceptionalist interpretation of Reconstruction. Instead he urged historians to give 'scrupulous attention to uniquely American conditions, but also to remember that the post-emancipation problem they attack was not unique to America.' Rebecca Scott, effectively sustaining that point, highlights the particularity of geography and environmental patterns, contrasts the goals and political behavior of poor non-slaves in Brazil with the southern United States, and notes the absence of white violence aimed at former slaves in Brazil.[54]

When we turn to social structure, class formation, and attendant ideologies, the dynamics get somewhat more complex yet the outcome is essentially the same. A massive and nuanced study of Buffalo, New York, prior to 1860 demonstrates the development of what David A. Gerber considers a distinctively American situation. Bourgeois businessmen and their allies exercised social and moral authority in such a way that class differences among artisans and other occupational groups were

muted. Moreover, temperance and related reform energies helped
to integrate various strata into a common effort to create a
bourgeois social order.[55]

Although Herbert G. Gutman always insisted that many Old
World cultural traditions persisted in the New, he too believed
that, in Ira Berlin's words, Protestantism and political access
'clarified the special circumstances under which an American
working class came into being. While religion might be central to
the experience of workers on both sides of the Atlantic, there were
still important differences of politics, class composition, and
national domain.' American workers had the vote and became
active in partisan politics long before the Reform Act and Char-
tism began to effect slow changes in nineteenth-century Britain.[56]
Gutman also believed that workers in the United States self-
consciously sought to 'assert their rights as Americans by distinguishing themselves from workers in other countries.' And he
proclaimed the 'unique history' of the American working class by
calling attention to the 'continued reinvigoration of pre-industrial
culture by wave upon wave of new pre-industrial recruits.'
Gutman reached these conclusions precisely *because* he was
familiar with European labor history and admired the work of E.
P. Thompson, Raymond Williams, Sidney Pollard, and Eric
Hobsbawm.[57]

Laurence Veysey suggested in 1979 that the onset of widespread industrialization during the later nineteenth century
meant that nations undergoing the process, and their work forces,
became more alike. But Aristide Zolberg, who is not sympathetic
to conventional notions of exceptionalism, has recently concluded
that the United States grew more distinctive rather than less as a
consequence of undergoing the process. Why? According to
Zolberg, the reason is that American industrial workers 'constituted less of a critical mass in the United States than they did in
Britain or Germany; and there is little doubt that the precocious
development of a large segment of white-collar workers also
contributed to the formation of a more diffuse sense of class
among Americans more generally.' Zolberg points to the development here of a form of capitalism organized around a

segmented labor market, and in a variation of Gutman's view, Zolberg contends that the immigrants contributed to institutionalized segmentation as a 'particularly pronounced feature of American industrial capitalism.' He, too, believes that American workers consciously differentiated between their status as 'labor' and their role as citizens more generally.[58]

Although Werner Sombart's famous query in 1906, 'Why is there no socialism in the United States?' and his own response are no longer compelling, the issue will not disappear and elements of Sombart's answer still surface in scholarship stimulated by his question. Morris Hillquit once complained that the Socialist Party in the United States had to publish its literature in twenty different languages. For a union trying to organize a steel plant in Pittsburgh, where the work force was ethnically diverse, that could be a very serious problem. Hence Mike Davis observes that whereas the western European class struggles of the 1880s and 1890s elicited a web of integrating proletarian institutions, the labor movement in the United States at that time was unable to generate a working-class culture that could overcome ethnic and religious bonds that remained powerful beyond the workplace. By 1910, Davis concludes, the American industrial city had developed a 'strikingly different social physiognomy from that of European factory centers.'[59]

Last though certainly not least, I find increasingly that when scholars function comparatively they are struck, in one way or another, with the state's relatively decentralized or noninterventionist nature, historically, in the United States. Aristide Zolberg makes a persuasive case that the most important 'determinant of variation in the patterns of working-class politics' for the later nineteenth and early twentieth centuries seems to have been whether, 'at the time this class was being brought into being by the development of capitalism, it faced an absolutist or a liberal state.' In the western world prior to World War I, 'the relevant range of variation was defined by the United States as the democratic end of the continuum (at least for the white majority) and Imperial Germany at the other, which may be termed "modernizing absolutism."' Alfred D. Chandler's magisterial study of American business management finds that in Europe,

> the much larger military and governmental establishments were a source for the kind of administrative training that became so essential to the operation of modem industrial, urban, and technologically advanced economies. In Europe, too, the government played a much larger role than it did in the United States in financing, locating, and even operating the transportation and communication infrastructure.... In Europe, public enterprise helped to lay the base for the coming of modem mass production and mass distribution. In the United States this base was designed, constructed, and operated almost wholly by private enterprise.[60]

The role of the state also turns out to be a crucial variable in the comparative history of women, as Kathryn Kish Sklar and others have shown. The state has been a major factor in France, for example, by providing public assistance for migrating single women. In the United States, by contrast, the presumption in favor of limited government created major opportunities for activism and social service by women reformers. The situation in Great Britain fell in between these two 'extremes': a fairly strong state policy implemented by means of voluntarism. Moreover, while prostitution tended to be regulated or licensed by the state in Europe, American morality could not countenance such flagrant tolerance, even in the interests of public health; so we substituted hypocrisy for 'mere' regulation: payoffs to the police as a cover for free enterprise in sexual gratification.[61]

To summarize this section, then, a pronounced increase in comparative work since 1980 by historians of the United States has caused a very marked enhancement in our awareness of differences, but only a modest increase in the frequency and importance of similarities. Even among studies that do not attempt to be comparative in a systematic way, such as books about immigrant communities in the United States, sharp contrasts with group life in the Old World become compellingly noticeable.[62] And authors who choose explicitly to contest the idea of American exceptionalism are nonetheless obliged to acknowledge variations in racial attitudes, in the role of class in popular entertainments and their audiences, and in the uses of leisure.[63] If anything, the outcome in 1993 is very much at odds with the apparent agenda a dozen years ago and what that agenda caused me, for one, to anticipate in the historiographical trends that lay ahead.

### What Have We Learned? Some Reconsiderations

What have we learned? What can be concluded? And where do we go from here? I believe we are obliged to acknowledge the swiftly spreading perception that 'every country is different' and that each society or culture is exceptional in its own way(s). The most enlightened historians, irrespective of their national fields of inquiry or topical concerns, have recently begun making that point with some consistency.[64] This awareness warrants at least a mini-survey because Laurence Veysey insists upon the fundamental similarity of all claims to national distinctiveness – a point with which I cannot agree.[65]

E. P. Thompson inaugurated the 'multi-peculiarity' approach in 1965 when he published an essay critical of structuralist theorists, such as Perry Anderson, who sought to assess and explain the course of British history since the seventeenth century in terms of a Marxist model that regarded the pattern of modern French history as normative. Thompson insisted that 'each national bourgeoisie has its own peculiar nastiness' and argued that the ruling class in eighteenth-century England constituted a 'unique formation.' Subsequently, Linda Colley has contended that class consciousness and national identity were *not* antithetical in Britain between 1750 and 1830, which historians had previously argued must inherently be the case. 'Because British political, military, social and economic conditions were quite unique,' Colley wrote, 'national consciousness here assumed a peculiarly pervasive but also a peculiarly complex form.'[66]

Manifestations of French exceptionalism with varied emphases and concerns – Tocqueville's proposition concerning the implications of a long history of governmental centralization,

Jerrold Seigel's belief in the uniqueness of the French Revolution, the widely shared notion that for geographical and economic reasons France has a split personality – have been propounded by French, American, British, and other scholars of diverse nationalities. Advocates of Russian exceptionalism have emerged from academe as well as from activists and journalists in the political arena.[67]

Turning to a country where the issue of exceptionalism has aroused powerful passions during the past decade, in particular, Gordon Craig informs us that Germans have long been preoccupied with the question: 'What is truly German?' Distinguished historians in Germany, such as Karl Dietrich Bracher, have been committed to exceptionalism for reasons intensely critical of the Reich; and George L. Mosse, who left Germany as a young man, finds distinctiveness in the Enlightenment's failure to sink significant roots in German soil. Consequently, he believes, no German literature founded on revolutionary principles emerged, which provided the opportunity for a twisted national mystique to develop that would solidify national unity – a propensity that evoked a radically destructive response.[68]

The most provocative book in recent years about German exceptionalism, however, *The Peculiarities of German History* by David Blackbourn and Geoff Eley, actually argues just the opposite of what its title would seem to suggest – sort of. The revisionist authors are critical of the widely held belief that liberalism failed to take hold in nineteenth-century Germany, that consequently the bourgeoisie could not develop and play the positive role that it did elsewhere in the West, and that an autocratic, militaristic class of antidemocratic landowners put Germany on its disastrous path to the Third Reich. Without a successful bourgeois revolution in 1848, catastrophe became virtually inevitable: that has been the conventional wisdom.[69] (Here we have a fine illustration of why I disagree with Laurence Veysey. The notion of exceptionalism emerged in Germany to justify social and political failure, whereas it developed in the United States to explain moral and political success.)

If I may reduce a complex and controversial thesis to just a few of its most essential points, Blackbourn and Eley reject any attempt to assess nineteenth-century Germany by some external and abstract standards of liberal democracy. They acknowledge the singularity of British and French history; assert that each national case is different; and suggest that similar results may be produced by different modes of development or patterns of evolution. They believe that the basic characteristics and chronology of capitalist industrial development in Germany and the United States were comparable. They also detect parallel histories of trade union weakness and employer intransigence in the two countries, the latter manifest in ruthless forms of company paternalism.[70]

Blackbourn and Eley have managed, without any apparent attempt at irony, to produce an attack upon the historiography of German exceptionalism that tends, nonetheless, to leave the reader with a profound sense that German history has, indeed, been different if not 'peculiar.' Intentionally or not, their book suits the spirit of Johan Herder's relativism, a social philosophy that acknowledged the existence and importance of national differences while rejecting the assumption that one group's development or customs could be judged by the measure or achievement of another.[71] It is that outlook and set of assumptions, in my opinion, that underpins much that is best in comparative historical inquiry today.

Blackbourn and Eley also believe that the public and moral implications of historical writing have been felt with particular acuteness in Germany. They may very well be right, though similar implications (nuanced in different ways) have also emerged from New Left scholarship in the United States and Great Britain since the later 1960s. Prior to that time, at least in the United States, the quest for the 'meaning of America' that I referred to earlier may have served to give historical writing about the United States an upbeat rather than a critical moral dimension. Surely, understanding the past in moral terms is considered desirable in many societies, yet I am not aware of any other that has been preoccupied with its own meaning, in a moral sense, for such a long time as ours. Given the persistence of American present-mindedness for several centuries, and given the Emersonian notion of the past as a burden to be shed, perhaps the 'meaning of America' (as a quest) seized the imagination of people who lacked a secure sense of history. The 'meaning of America,' so rich with moralistic implications for the future, and for people not fortunate enough to be Americans, perhaps served as a surrogate for history.[72]

Because a few scholars who are interested in this whole issue (including Dorothy Ross and Ian Tyrrell) have begun to acknowledge that the fervent belief in national exceptionalism has a political and cultural history that is consequential, perhaps the time is now ripe for some sort of transnational team to undertake a comparative history of various national 'exceptionalisms.'[73] If and when that happens, I suspect that some surprises will emerge involving differences as well as similarities. Students of comparative urban development have noticed cultural, along with political, variables in attempting to explain why cities such as Chicago and Toronto developed in such divergent ways despite similar prospects and possibilities. I must say that I find the cultural explanations (an aggressive future-oriented elite in Chicago versus a more cautious, conservative, genteel elite in Toronto) considerably more persuasive than the political and governmental ones.[74]

Unanticipated outcomes emerge when we look at recent work, for instance, by an astute younger Australian historian who insists upon an *absence* of exceptionalist thought in Australia during the first century of its existence – a very stark contrast to the situation in the United States at the same time. Richard White found that

[i]t was difficult in the nineteenth century to pin down what was distinctive about Australia, apart from its unique flora and fauna. On the one hand, the Australian colonists were busy identifying themselves with wider loyalties, considering themselves primarily as British, or as being one of the new societies, another America. On the other hand there were narrower loyalties competing with the sense of being

distinctively Australian. Politically Australia had no formal existence until Federation: the colonies were separate political entities owing their allegiance directly to Britain.

White acknowledges that while 'some sense of Australian identity' did develop during the nineteenth century, it occurred primarily in the 1890s and then during the Boer War. As late as 1887 the popular *Bulletin* perceived nothing distinctive about the Australian: its editors simply applied that label to a composite that it called 'The Coming Man. ' National identity remained inchoate, perhaps a coming attraction.[75]

The writing of history is commonly affected, even driven, by a sense of moral mission or by ideology. Those kinds of connections are common if not universal. I am inclined to wonder, however, whether the sense of moral mission has not been peculiarly prominent in American culture in a rather perverse way. On the one hand, it appears with amazing frequency and in many guises. On the other, it usually is invoked with a vagueness that encourages misunderstanding, elasticity, distortion, and hypocrisy. Irving Howe, who believes in American exceptionalism as a cultural reality, insists that 'to recognize the power of the American myth of a covenant blessing the new land is simply to recognize a crucial fact in our history.' Who could refuse to acknowledge the sheer force of that myth, despite its vagueness? Then Howe calls our attention to the power of Americanism; and once again one wants to affirm his acuity, but Americanism is even vaguer than that covenant. So we begin to balk.[76]

But important new work, especially in the field of labor history, has provided us with abundant evidence that Americanization as a social construct, as well as political and governmental process, flourished as a result of diverse stimuli for more than half a century following the 1880s. Catherine Collomp, for instance, has observed that in the 1890s and beyond both the American Federation of Labor and the Knights of Labor responded to the menace of mass immigration by stressing their firm allegiance to an American sense of national identity rather than a transnational or even domestic working-class alliance.

Organized labor deliberately emphasized 'its American character,' Collomp notes, 'and becoming an agent in the regulation of
the components of immigration. In this respect citizenship, as an
incorporating value, was a more potent factor than – and directly
in opposition to – working-class identity, an ideology that
reinforced the political and national consensus.' For Samuel
Gompers, trade union membership became a surrogate form of
American citizenship and, wherever appropriate, a prologue to it.
Collomp concludes with a strong affirmation of American
exceptionalism in the labor movement at the turn of the century,
because the constricted scope of what Gompers perceived as a
'legitimate working class' only reinforced a sense of union elitism,
thereby creating, as she puts it, 'a wider gap between skilled and
unskilled workers than in other countries.'[77]

In the decades that followed, government, visible intellectuals,
unions, and large business firms all reinforced these powerful
pressures for 'Americanization,' a quadripartite ideological
phalanx that had no counterpart elsewhere in the world. Three
examples will have to suffice. First, between 1902 and 1909
Woodrow Wilson used diverse occasions to articulate his favorite
speech, 'What It Means to Be an American,' a theme that he
continued to voice later throughout his presidency. Then, in her
extraordinary book titled *Making a New Deal: Industrial Workers in
Chicago, 1919–1939*, Lizabeth Cohen describes the Americanization programs privately developed and maintained by employers
in Chicago during the 1920s.[78]

Finally, we have an illuminating recent book by Gary Gerstle
called *Working-class Americanism: The Politics of Labor in a Textile
City, 1914–1960*. Its subject is the Independent Textile Union of
Woonsocket, Rhode Island, arguably the most powerful textile
workers' union in New England. Its *dramatis personae* are Franco-
Belgian socialists and French-Canadian Catholics who came to
Woonsocket to work in the woolen mills. Its dynamic emerges as
leaders of both ethnic groups, but the Belgians especially, are able
to fashion a critique of capitalism by using the traditional political
discourse that conservative Americanizers had devised at the turn
of the century – the rhetoric of Americanism.[79]

Gerstle shrewdly observes that a national obsession with 'Americanism' occurred during the 1920s and 1930s. Although he concedes that its meaning was vague, he looks at various texts, including transcripts of interviews, and finds four basic elements in the invocation of Americanism: nationalistic, democratic, progressive, and traditionalist. Consequently these elements of discourse could and did sustain various visions of politics. Among them, radicals and ethnics could present their socialist and communitarian ideals in the language favored by old-line Americans. They would thereby gain acceptability and achieve much of a difficult agenda. To Americanize did not necessarily mean to assimilate or accept the status quo. It did mean adapting Yankee discourse in ways that makes 'Americanism' seem even more vague on the surface; yet Gerstle describes particular people in particular situations using particular texts.[80] The role of ideology therefore becomes palpable in ways that it does not in Clifford Geertz's famous essay concerning 'Ideology as a Cultural System.'[81] And, *mirabile dictu*, because class and ethnicity are centrally involved, the links between ideology and American exceptionalism become considerably clearer than they once were.

Friedrich Engels turns out to have been remarkably prophetic. He forecast the tactics that American exceptionalism as a nativistic ideology would mandate. For success in politics, he pleaded, American socialists 'will have to doff every remnant of foreign garb. They will have to become out and out American.'[82] That is exactly what happened in Woonsocket, Rhode Island. When Marx and Engels actually examined particular cases, or situations, they too tended to sound like exceptionalists!

Curiously enough, however, leaders and members of the Independent Textile Union did not really disguise or fully shed their ethnic origins; rather, they simply *added* historical Americanism to their identities. Without entirely abandoning their traditional cultural life, they explicitly identified with George Washington and Abraham Lincoln. They emphasized the constitutional rights and political opportunities of American citizens. They frequently referred to 'our forefathers.'[83] Americanism mostly meant addition, but not much in the way of subtraction.

The creation of compound identities has been a highly significant aspect of Americanization as a social process.

The value of books like *Working-class Americanism* lies in the way that they serve notice: cultural values and political discourse need not be vague or disembodied variables when we try to illuminate the particularities and peculiarities of life in the United States. They also connect with earlier studies that have been the objects of harsh criticism by skeptics of American exceptionalism. Henry Nash Smith's *Virgin Land*, for instance, needs to be re-examined and mined for material that demonstrates a greater degree of realism about political rhetoric in the United States than we ordinarily acknowledge. In 1860 Senator Louis T. Wigfall of Texas attacked Andrew Johnson's expansionism with these words: 'The Senator from Tennessee supposes that we have a sort of blatherskiting Americanism that is going to spread over whole continent, and cross the Pacific ... and that, in the area of freedom, we are going to take in the whole world, and everybody is going to benefit us.'[84] One of these days, someone will write a cultural history of Americanism, both the benign and the blatherskiting varieties. That will make a major contribution to our understanding of American exceptionalism because the author will want to ask what sorts of comparable discourse have occurred elsewhere.[85]

We are aware that the problem of American exceptionalism is a matter of considerable concern to sociologists (like Daniel Bell), to political scientists (like Seymour Martin Lipset), to lawyers, to literary historians and critics, and to students of public policy whose work I have not been able to explore here.[86] Although I see much that is valuable in what they have done, I also find most of it deficient in chronological specificity, lacking in sensitivity to change over time. I am persuaded that this is where historians can and should make a particular contribution. Gary Gerstle, for example, does an excellent job of showing the gradual process in Woonsocket whereby the French-Canadian workers shifted from extolling only their traditional heroes (early French explorers, generals who fought valiantly at Quebec, and *habitants)* to admiring the heroes of their adopted land as well. In 1937, none of the floats in an annual parade dramatized the familiar themes from French-Canadian history; and by 1939 the dominant refrain was 'Unionism is the spirit of Americanism.'[87] These shifts occurred in increments – units of time and of a cultural process that the historian's vocation is best suited to analyze.

Perhaps the schematization that follows, which is offered heuristically yet hesitantly, has at least three features that recommend its consideration. First, it takes change over time into account without seeking to be too chronologically precise when realism dictates only rough approximations. Second, it derives from cultural perceptions and from ideology, which have been emphasized as essential factors in the preceding pages. And third, it takes into account the inevitable presence of contradictory impulses, of yea-sayers and nay-sayers. It does not presume the existence of consensus about any system of belief, any situation, or any prospect as it appeared to historical participants. It offers a way of thinking about the elusive meaning of America as it was perceived at different times, yet acknowledges the existence of those who cried foul, sham, and hypocrisy.

During the century that followed 1775, the model of republicanism received adherence from people representing all classes of Americans and from newly arrived immigrants as well.[88] Nevertheless, democracy was not so widespread as its devotees believed, even though political participation may have been more accessible than anywhere else in all of human history. Free enterprise and capitalism flourished, but at a high cost in terms of human exploitation and wasted resources.

For three generations following 1875 the United States became a model, even an archetype, of democratic capitalism triumphant – to many – and yet the epitome of aggressive imperialism fueled by capitalist excess to many others.[89] The former may overestimate the accomplishments of the Progressive movement, the New Deal, and the Great Society legislation of the 1960s; but the latter unfairly demean those reformist impulses and the high standard of living achieved by large numbers of Americans.

In the decades following 1965 America entered a prolonged phase in which it resembled Gulliver: powerful yet incapable of achieving its basic objectives; willful yet indecisive; influential in an inconsistent and seemingly rudderless manner; undisciplined and increasingly plagued by gross materialism and consumerism. Others, however, would point to numerous innovations and achievements: in civil rights for minorities, new opportunities for women in the workplace; dramatic breakthroughs in science, health care, and applied technology; and ultimately, an apparent vindication for free enterprise in the political and economic collapse of communist states.[90]

If this national trajectory is distinctive, it is also burdened by dualistic tendencies and perceptions. If it is comparable in certain respects to what happened elsewhere – to Great Britain in phase two, for instance – it is quite different in phase one or three or both. It takes into account how Americans have perceived themselves, how foreigners and immigrants have perceived the United States, and how we have responded to their perceptions, admiring as well as unflattering.[91]

Where do we stand, then, in describing cultural developments and patterns in the United States? The words 'unique' and 'exceptional' must be used with extreme caution because both imply the existence of a norm that describes most or all other industrialized nations – a norm from which we alone deviate and to which, perhaps, we are somehow superior. The word 'different' seems to me both acceptable and accurate because the United States is different. Such usage does not deny that other societies are different, too; but it follows the fundamental assumption, voiced by Carl Degler and others, that Americans 'differ in some important ways from people of other nations.'[92]

It seems reasonable to assert that while the United States has retained a great many differences, over time those differences have gradually become notably less exceptional. Some might even choose to argue that the 'burden' of exceptionalism (i.e., profound difference) has perhaps passed to Japan. The rather lengthy historical period in which the concept of American exceptionalism carried a double meaning – one or both of which seemed compellingly persuasive – is now, I believe, over. The concept nonetheless retains its special importance for those of us who seek to understand the *historical* dynamics of American culture and values.

Finally, as for the 'meaning' of America, I respond positively to Degler's suggestion that we pose the question: What has it meant, historically, to be an American or to have lived for an extended period of time in the United States? Answers to that kind of question, surely, will refresh our perennial interest in the meaning of America, particularly if we expand the question to read: What has it meant, historically, to be an American, and how have American perceptions of their experience compared with the process of self-recognition and self-deception in other societies?

The notion (or even notions) of exceptionalism is only one among various meanings that Americans can derive from and attach to their experiences as a nation – even when exceptionalism serves as a kind of compendium of other meanings, a summation that almost inevitably stimulates some sense of societal distinct-iveness once the nation itself is identified as the primary locus and focus of national identity. Precisely because that same opportunity for summation is available to *other* self-reflexive cultures, some variant of exceptionalism has to be expected of all such collective introspection. Consequently, a crucial component in the comparative analysis of cultures becomes the comparative analysis of exceptionalism as a cultural phenomenon. Perhaps the next item on one or another agenda, therefore, will be the ques-tion: how exceptional *was* (past tense) American exceptionalism? I will venture a one-word hunch: Very.

## Notes

This paper was presented on April 3, 1992, at the annual meeting of the Organization of American Historians in Chicago. I am grateful to my desig-nated critics – Marianne Debouzy, Akira Iriye, and Rebecca Scott – for their thoughtful comments on that occasion. I also thank Stuart M. Blumin, David Brion Davis, John Higham, R. Laurence Moore, Richard Polenberg, Nick Salvatore, and Laurence Veysey for their constructive criticisms. Needless to say, I have not been able to satisfy all their suggestions.

1.  This paper was originally published in *American Quarterly*, 45 (1993): 1–43, and is reproduced here by kind permission of the author, the editors of the journal and Johns Hopkins University Press.

2.  Ian Tyrrell, 'American Exceptionalism in an Age of International History,' with a critique by Michael McGerr and a rejoinder by Tyrrell, *American Historical Review*, 96 (1991): 1031–72; Byron Shafer, ed., *Is America Different? A New Look at American Exceptionalism* (Oxford: Clarendon, 1991); Sanford M. Jacoby, ed., *Masters to Managers: Historical and Comparative Perspectives on American Employers* (New York: Columbia University Press, 1991), esp. chap. 8 by Jacoby: 'American Exceptionalism Revisited: The Importance of Management'; Gary Marks, *Unions in Politics: Britain, Germany, and the United States in the Nineteenth and Early Twentieth Centuries* (Princeton: Princeton University Press, 1989), chap. 6, 'American Exceptionalism in Comparative Perspective'; David Hamer, New *Towns in the New World: Images and Perceptions of the Nineteenth-Century Urban Frontier* (New York: Columbia University Press, 1990), a comparative study of New Zealand, Australia, the United States, and Canada.

3.  For some citations of their work, in addition to those mentioned in note 1 above, see Daniel Bell, '"American Exceptionalism" Revisited: the Role of Civil Society,' *The Public Interest*, 95 (1989): 38–56; Mona Harrington, *The Dream of Deliverance in American Politics* (New York: Knopf, 1986), esp. chap. 1, 'The Promise and the Myth'; Samuel P. Huntington, *American Politics: The Promise of Disharmony* (Cambridge, MA: Belknap, 1981), esp. chap. 2, 'The American Creed and National Identity'; Alex Inkeles, 'The American Character,' *The Center Magazine* (November/December, 1983): 25–39; Alan F. J. Artibise, 'Exploring the North-American West: A Comparative Urban Perspective,' *American Review of Canadian Studies*, 14 (1984): 29–43; John P. Roche, 'Immigration and Nationality: A Historical Overview of United States Policy, ' in Uri Ra'anan and Roche, ed., *Ethnic Resurgence in Modern Democratic States: A Multidisciplinary Approach to Human Resources and Conflict* (New York: Pergamon, 1980), 30–76.

4.  Richard J. Oestreicher, *Solidarity and Fragmentation: Working People and Class Consciousness in Detroit, 1875–1900* (Urbana: University of Illinois Press, 1986); Kathleen Neils Conzen, 'Mainstream and Side Channels: The Localization of Immigrant Cultures,' *Journal of American Ethnic History*, 11.1 (Fall 1991): 5–20; James M. McPherson, 'Antebellum Southern Exceptionalism: A New Look at an Old Question,' *Civil War History*, 29 (1983): 230–44; Carl L. Becker, 'Kansas', *Everyman His Own Historian: Essays on History and Politics* (New York: Crofts, 1935), 5, 28.

5.  Quoted in Richard White, *Inventing Australia: Images and Identity, 1688–1980* (Sydney: Allen & Unwin, 1981), 49; James Baldwin, *Nobody Knows My Name: More Notes of a Native Son* (New York: Dial, 1961), 17, 117, 123.

6.  Marks, xiii, xvi, 223 n. 42.

7.  Marks, 210, 212, 217–19, 231–34.

8. Jacoby, 'American Exceptionalism Revisited,' 173–200, esp. 177, 184, 187, 200, and the quotation on p. 199.

9. Jacoby, 'American Exceptionalism Revisited,' 173, 176, 178–79, 182. See also Olivier Zunz, *Making America Corporate, 1870–1920* (Chicago: University of Chicago Press, 1990), which examines the social characteristics and values of people who participated in the formation of corporate bureaucracies.

10. V. P. Bynack, 'Noah Webster's Linguistic Thought and the Idea of an American National Culture,' *Journal of the History of Ideas*, 45 (1984): 99–114; Alan D. Aberbach, 'A Search for an American Identity,' *Canadian Review of American Studies*, 2 (1971): 76–88; William Findley, *History of the Insurrections, in the Four Western Counties of Pennsylvania* (Philadelphia, 1796), vi. See also Arthur H. Shaffer, *To Be an American: David Ramsay and the Making of the American Consciousness* (Columbia: University of South Carolina Press, 1991).

11. See Michael Kammen, *A Season of Youth: The American Revolution and the Historical Imagination* (New York: Knopf, 1978), 7–9, 24; Henry Adams, *History of the United States during the Administrations of Thomas Jefferson and James Madison* (New York, 1889), vol. 1, chap. 6, 'American Ideals'; James Chace, 'Dreams of Perfectibility: American Exceptionalism and the Search for a Moral Foreign Policy,' *America in Theory*, ed. Leslie Berlowitz, et al. (New York: Oxford University Press, 1988), 249–61; Nick Salvatore, 'Some Thoughts on Class and Citizenship in America in the Late Nineteenth Century,' *In the Shadow of the Statue of Liberty: Immigrants, Workers and Citizens in the American Republic, 1880–1920*, ed. Marianne Debouzy (Saint-Denis: Presses universitaires de Vincennes, 1988), 226–27.

12. James T. Schleifer, *The Making of Tocqueville's Democracy in America* (Chapel Hill: University of North Carolina Press, 1980), 50, 58–59; Patrice Higonnet, *Sister Republics: The Origins of French and American Republicanism* (Cambridge, MA: Harvard University Press, 1988), 5.

13. R. Laurence Moore, *European Socialists and the American Promised Land* (New York: Oxford University Press, 1970), 4–5; Daniel Bell, *The Winding Passage: Essays and Sociological Journeys, 1960–1980* (Cambridge, MA: Abt Books, 1980), 256; Robert P. Frankel, 'British Observers of America, 1890–1950' (Ph.D. diss., Harvard University, 1989), 152, 261, 274, 286–87, 298–308.

14. F. R. Leavis, 'The Americanness of American Literature' (1952), *Van Wyck Brooks: The Critic and His Critics*, ed. William Wasserstrom (Port Washington, NY: Kennikat, 1979), 157–67; Edmund Wilson, *Patriotic Gore: Studies in the Literature of the American Civil War* (New York: Oxford University Press, 1962), 491; Denis W. Brogan, 'The Character of American Life,' *American History – British Historians: A Cross-Cultural Approach to the American Experience*, ed. David H. Burton (Chicago: Nelson–Hall, 1976), 11, 14, 20; Christopher Thorne, *Border Crossings: Studies in International History* (Oxford: Blackwell, 1988), 5; Stuart M. Blumin, *The Emergence of the Middle Class: Social Experience in the American City, 1760–1900* (New York: Cambridge University Press, 1989), 293 (citing a contrast made by Jurgen Kocka).

15. [John Knapp], 'National Poetry,' *North American Review*, 8 (1819), 169–76; Robert G. Athearn, *The Mythic West in Twentieth-Century America* (Lawrence: University Press of Kansas, 1986), 81. See also Roderick Nash, *Wilderness and the American Mind*, 3rd ed. (New Haven: Yale University Press, 1982), 261.

16. T. H. Breen, ed., *Shaping Southern Society: The Colonial Experience* (New York: Oxford University Press, 1976), 131; James Lemon, *The Best Poor Man's Country: A Geographical Study of Early Southeastern Pennsylvania* (Baltimore: Johns Hopkins, 1972); Sacvan Bercovitch, *The Puritan Origins of the American Self* (New Haven: Yale University Press, 1975), esp. chap. 3.

17. James Russell Lowell, 'The Rebellion: Its Causes and Consequences,' *North American Review*, 99 (1864): 254; Robert R. Hubach, 'Three Uncollected St. Louis Interviews of Walt Whitman,' *American Literature*, 14 (1942): 144–45; Michael Kammen, *Meadows of Memory: Images of Time and Tradition in American Art and Culture* (Austin: University of Texas Press, 1992), xiii, 133–34, 160–62; James H. Duff, et al., *An American Vision: Three Generations of Wyeth Art* (Boston: Little, Brown, 1987), 80, 84.

18. Bernard DeVoto reviewed Seldes, *Mainland* (New York, 1936) in *The Saturday Review*, 3 October 1936: 7; and see Gilbert Seldes, *Mainland* (New York: Scribner's, 1936), 415; Seldes, *The Public Arts* (New York: Simon and Shuster, 1956): 284–85. See also John A. Kouwenhoven, *The Beer Can by the Highway: Essays on What's 'American' about America* (Garden City, NY: Doubleday, 1961), a collection of pieces written mostly during the 1950s.

19. Gertrude Stein, *Four in America* (New Haven: Yale University Press, 1947), xv-xvi; Thornton Wilder, 'Toward an American Language,' *Atlantic Monthly*, July 1952: 29–37; and Clement Greenberg, '"American-Type" Painting,' in William Phillips and Philip Rahv, ed., *The Partisan Review Anthology* (New York: Holt, Rinehart, and Winston, 1962), 165–78.

20. Carl L. Becker, 'Frederick Jackson Turner,' *Everyman His Own Historian*, 216–17; Turner to Haskins, 6 May 1925, Haskins Papers, box 17, Mudd Library, Princeton University; Donald L. Miller, *Lewis Mumford: A Life* (New York: Weidenfeld & Nicolson, 1989), 132, 231–32; Ellen Nore, *Charles A. Beard: An Intellectual Biography* (Carbondale: Southern Illinois University Press, 1983), 124, and chaps. 8–9 generally.

21. William H. Nolte, ed., *H. L. Mencken's Smart Set Criticism* (Washington, DC: Regnery Gateway, 1987), 3; J. E. Spingam, 'Criticism in the United States,' Irving Babbitt, et al., *Criticism in America: Its Function and Status* (New York: Harcourt, Brace, 1924), 292–93; Thomas Craven, 'American Men of Art,' *Scribner's Magazine*, November 1932: 262- 63.

22. Seldes, *Mainland*, 6. Seldes asserted that the meaning of America was not simply part of the meaning of Europe (8), a point that echoed John Crowe Ransom's concern for 'the meaning of European history' and 'Europeanism.' See Twelve Southerners, *I'll Take My Stand: The South and the Agrarian Tradition* (New York: Harper, 1930), 4–5.

23. Bell, *The Winding Passage*, 254; Ralph G. Martin, *Henry and Clare: An Intimate Portrait of the Lutes* (New York: Putnam's, 1991), 172. See also Neal Gabler, *An Empire of Their Own: How the Jews Invented Hollywood* (New York: Crown, 1988), 1; David A. Hollinger, *In the American Province: Studies in the History and Historiography of Ideas* (Bloomington: Indiana University Press, 1985), 162–64.

24. Kouwenhoven, 30–31; Allen F. Davis, 'The Politics of American Studies,' *American Quarterly*, 42 (1990): 360, 370; Karen J. Winkler, 'Organization of American Historians Backs Teaching of Non-Western Culture and Diversity in Schools,' *The Chronicle of Higher Education*, 6 February 1991: A7.

25. Thomas Wentworth Higginson, 'Americanism in Literature,' *The Atlantic*, 25 (January 1870): 63; Leon Samson, 'Americanism as Surrogate Socialism,' in John Laslett and Seymour Martin Lipset, eds, *Failure of a Dream? Essays in the History of American Socialism* (Garden City, NY: Anchor, 1974), 426; Roy Rosenzweig, '"United Action Means Victory": Militant Americanism on Film,' *Labor History*, 24 (1983): 274–88.

26. Irving Howe, *Socialism and America* (San Diego: Harcourt Brace Jovanovich, 1985), 133–34; 'American Culture Is Called Unique,' *New York Times*, 26 April 1937: 3. For an extraordinary echo of Overstreet in 1992, see Lewis H. Lapham (the editor), 'Who and What is American?' *Harper's*, January, 1992: 49.

27. Daniel Bell, 'The End of American Exceptionalism,' *The Public Interest*, 41 (1975): 193–224, reprinted in Bell, *The Winding Passage*, 245–71; Campbell, 'The American Past As Destiny,' in Burton, ed., *American History – British Historians*, 51–72, esp. 64–66. Contrast Bell's position in 1975 with his exceptionalist emphasis in *The End of Ideology: On the Exhaustion of Political Ideas in the Fifties* (New York: Collier, 1961), Part I generally and esp. 113 and 310.

28. Laurence Veysey, 'The Autonomy of American History Reconsidered,' *American Quarterly*, 31 (1979): 455–77, esp. 458. It should be noted that Seymour Martin Lipset and Reinhard Bendix, *Social Mobility in Industrial Society* (Berkeley: University of California Press, 1959) sought to show that all industrial societies have had approximately the same rates of mobility. Therefore the notion of a uniquely 'open' American society cannot explain why our political history has been different, that is, no significant socialist persuasion. See also David A. Hollinger's complaint that historians of the United States 'remain too concerned ... with the uniqueness of American history and not enough with the place of American intellectual history in the history of the West....' In John Higham and Paul K. Conkin (eds), *New Directions in American Intellectual History* (Baltimore: Johns Hopkins University Press, 1979), 63.

29. Sean Wilentz, *Chants Democratic: New York City and the Rise of the American Working Class, 1788–1850* (New York: Oxford University Press, 1984); Wilentz, 'Against Exceptionalism: Class Consciousness and the American Labor Movement, 1790–1920,' *International Labor and Working Class History*,

26 (1984): 1–24; Eric Foner, 'Why Is There No Socialism in the United States?' *History Workshop Journal*, 17 (1984): 74–76.

30. William C. Spengemann, *A Mirror For Americanists: Reflections on the Idea of American Literature* (Hanover, NH: Dartmouth College–University Press of New England, 1989), esp. p. 13. For the opposite perspective, see George Watson (an Australian), 'The Americanness of American Poetry,' *Virginia Quarterly Review*, 65 (1989): 81–93; Jeffrey H. Richards, *Theater Enough: American Culture and the Metaphor of the World Stage, 1607-1789* (Durham, NC: Duke University Press, 1991), esp. xii, 179, 182–83.

31. Jack P. Greene, *Pursuits of Happiness: The Social Development of Early Modern British Colonies and the Formation of American Culture* (Chapel Hill: University of North Carolina Press, 1988), 175; J. G. A. Pocock, 'Between Gog and Magog: The Republican Thesis and the *Ideologia Americana*,' *Journal of the History of Ideas*, 48 (1987): 325.

32. Hall lectured at Cornell on April 3, 1974. Cf. Hall, *Worlds of Wonder, Days of Judgement: Popular Religious Belief in Early New England* (New York: Knopf, 1989), esp. 4–6, 18, 212. For an early critique of exceptionalism from the perspective of American religion, see Winthrop S. Hudson, 'How American is Religion in America?' in Jerald C. Brauer, ed., *Reinterpretation in American Church History* (Chicago: University of Chicago Press, 1968), 153–67, esp. 156, 166–67.

33. Wilentz, *Chants Democratic*, esp. 142, 156–57, 238; Foner, 'Why Is There No Socialism in the United States?', *Why Is There No Socialism in the United States?*, ed. Jean Heffer and Jeanine Rovet (Paris: Éditions de l'école des hautes études en sciences sociales, 1988), 61, 63–64.

34. Alan Dawley, 'E. P. Thompson and the Peculiarities of the Americans,' *Radical History Review*, 19 (1978–79): 33–59, esp. 34–35, 56–57; Dawley, 'Farewell to "American Exceptionalism,"' Heffer and Rovet, 311–15. In his recent book, *Struggles for Justice: Social Responsibility and the Liberal State* (Cambridge, MA: Belknap, 1991), 10-11, Dawley presents his most strident attack upon American exceptionalism.

35. Zolberg, 'The Roots of American Exceptionalism,' Heffer and Rovet, 105–06; Zolberg, 'How Many Exceptionalisms?' *Working-Class Formation: Nineteenth-Century Patterns in Western Europe and the United States*, ed. Ira Katznelson and Zolberg (Princeton: Princeton University Press, 1986), 427–28, 454–55.

36. Dwight Macdonald, *Discriminations: Essays and Afterthoughts, 1938–1974* (New York: Grossman, 1974), 255; Macdonald, 'The String Untuned', *Against the American Grain* (New York: Random House, 1962), 315; *Power, Politics, and People: The Collected Essays of C. Wright Mills*, ed. Irving Horowitz (New York: Oxford University Press, 1963), 228; and Mills, *White Collar: The American Middle Classes* (New York: Oxford University Press, 1951), xi, 3–4.

37. Giles Gunn, *The Culture of Criticism and the Criticism of Culture* (New York: Oxford University Press, 1987), 161–62; Marian J. Morton, *The Terrors of*

*Ideological Politics: Liberal Historians in a Conservative Mood* (Cleveland: Press of Case Western Reserve University, 1972).

38. Mike Davis, *Prisoners of the American Dream: Politics and Economy in the History of the US Working Class* (London: Verso, 1986); Myra Jehlen, *American Incarnation: The Individual, the Nation, and the Continent* (Cambridge, MA: Harvard University Press, 1986).

39. Bernard Bailyn, *The Peopling of British North America: An Introduction* (New York: Knopf, 1986), 60, 81–83, 85, 114, 118, 123; Bailyn, *The Origins of American Politics* (New York: Knopf, 1968), 92, 96.

40. Jon Butler, *Awash in a Sea of Faith: Christianizing the American People* (Cambridge, MA: Harvard University Press, 1990), esp. 162–63, 174, 212. See also Leonard W. Levy, *Original Intent and the Framers' Constitution* (New York: Macmillan, 1988), 193; Nathan Hatch, *The Democratization of American Christianity* (New Haven: Yale University Press, 1989), 210.

41. Leon D. Epstein, *Political Parties in the American Mold* (Madison: University of Wisconsin Press, 1986), 3- 4; Harold M. Hyman, *American Singularity: The 1787 Northwest Ordinance, the 1862 Homestead and Merrill Acts, and the 1944 G. I. Bill* (Athens: University of Georgia Press, 1986), 11, 13. The roster of American writers who have been perfectly sanguine about using the word 'unique' is diverse and spans many decades. It includes Randoph Boume in 'Trans-National America' (1916), Gilbert Seldes in *Mainland* (1936) and *The Public Arts* (1956), Daniel Bell in some of the essays collected in *The End of Ideology* (1962), James Baldwin in some of the pieces collected in *Nobody Knows My Name* (1961), and Gary Marks in *Unions in Politics* (1989), xvi.

42. David S. Reynolds, *Beneath the American Renaissance: The Subversive Imagination in the Age of Emerson and Melville* (New York: Knopf, 1988), 8, 170, 198–99, 340, 442, 452, 460.

43. Reynolds, 190, 203, 277, 291, 364, 445, 448–49, 489–90, 496. For some of Reynolds's predecessors, see Leo Marx, 'The Vernacular Tradition in American Literature,' *Studies in American Culture*, ed. Joseph J. Kwiat and Mary C. Turpie (Minneapolis: University of Minnesota Press, 1960), 109–22; Roy Harvey Pearce, *The Continuity of American Poetry* (Princeton: Princeton University Press, 1961), 379 n. 4; and Leslie Fiedler, *The Return of the Vanishing American* (New York: Stein and Day, 1968), Preface, n.p.

44. Jerrold Hirsch, 'Folklore in the Making: B. A. Botkin,' *Journal of American Folklore*, 100 (1987): 6–7; Bert Feintuch, ed., *The Conservation of Culture: Folklorists and the Public Sector* (Lexington: University Press of Kentucky, 1988), 55; Alan Dundes, 'The American Concept of Folklore,' *Journal of the Folklore Institute*, 3 (1966): 237.

45. Mary Ryan, 'The American Parade: Representations of the Nineteenth-Century Social Order,' *The New Cultural History*, ed. Lynn Hunt (Berkeley: University of California Press, 1989), 132, 134; Kathleen Neils Conzen, 'Ethnicity as Festive Culture: Nineteenth-Century German Americans on Parade,' *The Invention of Ethnicity*, ed. Werner Sollors (New York: Oxford University Press, 1989), 44–76; David Glassberg, *American Historical*

*Pageantry: The Uses of Tradition in the Early Twentieth Century* (Chapel Hill: University of North Carolina Press, 1990), 111, 149–50.

46. Loren Baritz, *The Good Life: The Meaning of Success for the American Middle Class* (New York: Knopf, 1989), xi-xii; Mary C. Waters, *Ethnic Options: Choosing Identities in America* (Berkeley: University of California Press, 1990), 148, 166; Robert Anthony Orsi, *The Madonna of 115th Street: Faith and Community in Italian Harlem, 1880–1950* (New Haven: Yale University Press, 1985); Barry D. Karl and Stanley N. Katz, 'Foundations and Ruling Class Elites,' *Daedalus*, 116 (1987): 36–39.

47. Wyn Wachhorst, *Thomas Alva Edison: An American Myth* (Cambridge, MA: MIT Press, 1981), 120. In Nathan Reingold, *Science, American Style* (New Brunswick, NJ: Rutgers University Press, 1991), the author explicitly rejects 'any assumption of American singularity' (17), in an essay prepared in 1976, yet titles another essay 'Science and Technology in the American Idiom' (1970), and still another one 'European Models and American Realities' (1987). The introduction to this volume does not indicate that a well-modulated emphasis upon exceptionalism characterizes several of the essays. *Yankee Enterprise: The Rise of the American System of Manufactures*, ed. Otto Mayr and Robert C. Post (Washington, DC: Smithsonian Institution Press, 1981) offers essays initially presented at a 1978 symposium held at the National Museum of American History. Although the editors acknowledge that many of the phenomena discussed had Old World origins, they find 'these circumstances' to have been 'anomalous' there, 'while in America, by contrast, techniques of quantity production – and extension of the techniques to an ever broader range of products – became fundamentals in the nation's social and economic history' (xi). Although the contributors to the volume vary in their emphases, all agree that foreign visitors to the United States believed that they were witnessing a new and different system in terms of its component elements. In the closing essay Neil Harris asserts the following: 'If the American experience was not unique, it did offer, so far as historians of consumption are concerned, special circumstances' (190).

48. Lee Clark Mitchell, *Witnesses to a Vanishing America: The Nineteenth-Century Response* (Princeton: Princeton University Press, 1981), 20–21; Barbara J. Howe, 'Women in Historic Preservation: The Legacy of Ann Pamela Cunningham,' *The Public Historian*, 12 (1990): 34; Daniel J. Czitrom, *Media and the American Mind from Morse to McLuhan* (Chapel Hill: University of North Carolina Press, 1982), 31, 58, 113, 191; Stephen E. Weil, *Rethinking the Museum and Other Meditations* (Washington, DC: Smithsonian Institution Press, 1990), 143; Richard E. Neustadt and Ernest May, *Thinking in Time: The Uses of History for Decision-Makers* (New York: Free Press, 1986), xv.

49. Marianne Debouzy, 'La classe ouvrière américaine: recherches et problèmes,' *Le Mouvement social*, 102 (1978): 3–7.

50. See Laurence R. Veysey, *The Communal Experience: Anarchist and Mystical Counter-Cultures in America* (New York: Harper & Row, 1973), 7; and see his

critical response to Carl Degler's presidential address, 'In Pursuit of an American History,' in *American Historical Review*, 92 (1987): 1081–82; and Iriye, 'The Internationalization of History,' *American Historical Review*, 94 (1989): 1–10, esp. 3–4.

51. C. Vann Woodward, *The Future of the Past* (New York: Oxford University Press, 1989), 81, 168–69; Carl Degler, 'Comparative History: An Essay Review,' *Journal of Southern History*, 34 (1968): 427. Rebecca J. Scott has also remarked of the comparative method that it has 'certain obvious advantages for the highlighting of crucial differences....' Scott, 'Exploring the Meaning of Freedom: Postemancipation Societies in Comparative Perspective,' in Scott, et. al., *The Abolition of Slavery and the Aftermath of Emancipation in Brazil* (Durham, NC: Duke University Press, 1988), 2.

52. There is actually a fourth category that is quite important and revealing because it, too, generally reinforces a sense of American distinctiveness. I have in mind a cluster of highly empirical works that compare selected issues and themes in three societies that one might expect to be more alike than they are like any others. See, for example, Seymour Martin Lipset, *Continental Divide: The Values and Institutions of the United States and Canada* (New York: Routledge, 1990); Richard M. Merelman, *Partial Visions: Culture and Politics in Britain, Canada, and the United States* (Madison: University of Wisconsin Press, 1991); Walter Kendrick, *The Secret Museum: Pornography in Modern Culture* (New York: Viking, 1987), 135, 142–43, 150, 158–59; and Howard M. Leichter, *Free to be Foolish: Politics and Health Promotion in the United States and Great Britain* (Princeton: Princeton University Press, 1991), esp. 5, 211. John Harmon McElroy, *Finding Freedom: America's Distinctive Cultural Formation* (Carbondale: Southern Illinois University Press, 1989), builds on comparisons between the United States, Brazil, Canada, and Spanish America.

53. For the relentless litany of differences, see Peter Kolchin, *Unfree Labor: American Slavery and Russian Serfdom* (Cambridge, MA: Belknap, 1987), xii, 43, 45–46, 50–51, 57–58, 78, 83, 85, 98, 117, 140, 148–49, 155–58, 169, 178, 218–19, 222, 234–35, 239, 276–78, 290, 352, 355–57, 361–62, 374–75, the quotation on 362.

54. Woodward, 44, 198–99; Scott, 'Exploring the Meaning of Freedom: Postemancipation Societies in Comparative Perspective,' Scott, et. al., *Abolition of Slavery*, 2, 5, 6, 9, 19. See also Scott, 'Comparing Emancipations: A Review Essay,' *Journal of Social History*, 20 (1987): 565–83.

55. Gerber, *The Making of an American Pluralism: Buffalo, New York, 1825–60* (Urbana: University of Illinois Press, 1989), esp. chaps. 3, 4, 5, and 9.

56. When contrasting British and American conditions, David Montgomery suggested that the most effective deterrent during the pre-Civil War era to the maturation of class consciousness and creation of a labor party in the United States was the 'ease with which American working men entered elective office': Montgomery, *Beyond Equality: Labor and the Radical Republicans, 1862–1872* (New York: Knopf, 1967), 215.

57. Ira Berlin, 'Herbert G. Gutman and the American Working Class,' in Gutman, *Power and Culture: Essays on the American Working Class*, ed. Berlin (New York: Pantheon, 1987), 25, 28, 29, 34, 36, and 198.

58. Veysey, 467, 469, 477; Aristide Zolberg, 'The Roots of American Exceptionalism,' Heffer and Rovet, 110, 112–14.

59. Irving Howe, *Socialism and America* (San Diego: Harcourt Brace Jovanovich, 1985), 128–29; Davis, *Prisoners of the American Dream*, 41, 43.

60. Zolberg, 'The Roots of American Exceptionalism,' 114–15; Chandler, *The Visible Hand: The Managerial Revolution in American Business* (Cambridge: Belknap, MA, 1977), 64, 93, and the quotation on 205. See also Alfred D. Chandler, Jr., *Scale and Scope: The Dynamics of Industrial Capitalism* (Cambridge, MA: Belknap, 1990), which highlights differences among the business systems that developed in the United States, Great Britain, and Germany, ca. 1880 to 1940; and also, Howe, *Socialism and America*, 121–22, and especially Richard Rose, 'How Exceptional Is the American Political Economy?' *Political Science Quarterly*, 104 (Spring, 1989): 91–115.

61. Kathryn K. Sklar, 'A Call for Comparisons,' *American Historical Review*, 95 (October, 1990): 1109–14, esp. 1111; Carl N. Degler, *At Odds: Women and the Family in America from the Revolution to the Present* (New York: Oxford University Press, 1980), 290. See also Elizabeth H. Pleck, 'Women's History: Gender as a Category of Historical Analysis,' *Ordinary People and Everyday Life: Perspectives on the New Social History*, ed. James B. Gardner and George R. Adams (Nashville: American Assoc. for State and Local History, 1983), 52–53. Donald Meyer, *Sex and Power: The Rise of Women in America, Russia, Sweden, and Italy* (Middletown, CT: Wesleyan University Press, 1987), strongly emphasizes distinctive national patterns derived from cultural differences. He believes that under the impact of democratic capitalism in the nineteenth century, only in the United States did a separate sphere of behavior and activity emerge for women. That 'separate sphere' in America would be crucial in providing a stimulus for the growth of a feminist movement and for individual self-realization. Meyer's rejection of any universal explanation for the subordination of women, and his insistence upon national particularity, disturbed some prominent reviewers of the book. Meyer acknowledges on pp. xxv-xxvi that his project reinforces the penchant for American exceptionalism.

62. See, for example, Orsi, 55, 95, 107–12. Orsi also happens to make the intriguing point that during the decades, ca. 1890–1910, the Vatican regarded Catholicism in the United States as deviant and problematic. At stake, in key respects, was a conflict between the Marian Catholicism advocated by Pope Leo XIII and a form of modernism supported by the Irish clergy in the United States who tended to be assimilationist (See Orsi, 62–63).

63. Richard Waterhouse, *From Minstrel Show to Vaudeville: The Australian Popular Stage, 1788–1914* (Kensington, NSW: New South Wales University Press,

1990), xi, xiii, 14–16, 28, 38, 139–41; Ian Tyrrell's response to Michael McGerr, *American Historical Review*, 96 (1991): 1068–70; John Agnew, *The United States in the World-Economy: A Regional Geography* (Cambridge: Cambridge University Press, 1987), 15.

64. See, for example, Dorothy Ross, *The Origins of American Social Science* (New York: Cambridge University Press, 1991), xvii; John Rickard, *Australia: A Cultural History* (London: Longman, 1988), xi; Charles S. Maier, *The Unmasterable Past: History, Holocaust, and German National Identity* (Cambridge, MA: Harvard University Press, 1988), 108; Dawley, 'Farewell to "American Exceptionalism,"' in Heffer and Rovet, 312.

65. Veysey's letter to the Editor, *American Historical Review*, 92 (1987): 1081–82.

66. E. P. Thompson, 'The Peculiarities of the English,' *The Socialist Register 1965*, ed. Ralph Miliband and John Saville (New York: Monthly Review Press, 1965), 311–59, esp. 323, 329–30; Linda Colley, 'Whose Nation? Class and National Consciousness in Britain, 1750–1830,' *Past and Present*, 113 (1986): 97–117. For additional statements of British exceptionalism, see Gareth Stedman Jones, *Languages of Class: Studies in English Working Class History, 1832–1982* (Cambridge: Cambridge University Press, 1983), 2, 4; Paul Fussell, *The Great War and Modern Memory* (New York: Oxford University Press, 1975), 232–35, 245–46.

67. Jerrold Seigel, 'Politics, Memory, Illusion: Marx and the French Revolution,' *The French Revolution and the Creation of Modern Political Culture*, ed. François Furet and Mona Ozouf, vol. 3: *The Transformation of Political Culture, 1789–1848* (Oxford: Pergamon, 1989), 636; Theodore Zeldin, *France, 1848–1945: Politics and Anger* (1974; New York: Oxford University Press, 1979), 1–2; Roger Chartier, *Cultural History: Between Practices and Representations* (Ithaca, NY: Cornell University Press, 1988), chap. 8; James H. Billington, *The Icon and the Axe: An Interpretive History of Russian Culture* (New York: Knopf, 1966); George Seldes, *Witness to a Century: Encounters with the Noted, the Notorious, and the Three SOBs* (New York: Ballantine, 1987), 285.

68. Gordon A. Craig, *The Germans* (New York: Putnam, 1982), 25, 184; George L. Mosse, *Masses and Man: Nationalist and Fascist Perceptions of Reality* (New York: Fertig, 1980), 21–51.

69. Blackbourn and Eley, *The Peculiarities of German History: Bourgeois Society and Politics in Nineteenth-Century Germany* (New York: Oxford University Press, 1984; first pub. in Germany in 1980), 1–35, 41–42.

70. Blackbourn and Eley, 45–46, 83–84, 89, 123, 133.

71. Isaiah Berlin, *Vico and Herder: Two Studies in the History of Ideas* (New York: Viking, 1976), 145, 153.

72. Both Ian Tyrrell and Michael McGerr acknowledge this in 'American Exceptionalism in an Age of International History,' *American Historical Review*, 96 (1991): 1049, 1063, and 1066. See also Huntington, 36; Harrington, 8–9, 14; and Michael Kammen, *Mystic Chords of Memory: The Transformation of Tradition in American Culture* (New York: Knopf, 1991), esp. chaps. 2 and 3.

73. The closest thing that we have at present is Aristide R. Zolberg's long essay 'How Many Exceptionalisms?' Katznelson and Zolberg, 397–455. See also the essays in Peter Boerner, ed., *Concepts of National Identity: An Interdisciplinary Dialogue* (Baden-Baden: Nomos, 1986); and Richard O. Curry and Lawrence B. Goodheart, ed., *American Chameleon: Individualism in Trans-National Context* (Kent, OH: Kent State University Press, 1991), esp. 3, 10–19, which vigorously reaffirms American exceptionalism based upon extended comparisons with Great Britain, France, and Germany.

74. See (for the cultural explanations) William A. White, 'Tradition and Urban Development: A Contrast of Chicago and Toronto in the Nineteenth Century,' *The Old Northwest*, 8 (1982): 245–72; and (for the political) David Hamer, *New Towns in the New World: Images and Perceptions of the Nineteenth-Century Urban Frontier* (New York: Columbia University Press, 1991), esp. 231–32, a comparison of New Zealand, Australia, the United States, and Canada.

75. White, *Inventing Australia*, 63, 64, 81, 83, and the long quotation on 63. See also Hamer, *New Towns*, 226, 228–29; John Carroll, ed., *Intruders in the Bush: The Australian Quest for Identity* (Melbourne: Oxford University Press, 1982), esp. chap. 14, 'National Identity'; and William M. Johnston, 'A National without Qualities: Austria and Its Quest for a National Identity,' Boerner, 177–86.

76. Chace, 'Dreams of Perfectibility: American Exceptionalism and the Search for a Moral Foreign Policy,' Berlowitz, 249–61; Howe, *Socialism and America*, 136, 138–39. For the formation and role of a comparable myth in Dutch history, see Simon Schama, *The Embarrassment of Riches: An Interpretation of Dutch Culture in the Golden Age* (New York: Knopf, 1987), 7–8, 24, 54, 82, 125, 256, 283, 285, 287. Cf. the interesting poem by Douglas Le Pan, 'The Country without a Mythology,' *The Book of Canadian Poetry*, ed. A. J. M. Smith, 3rd ed. (Chicago: University of Chicago Press, 1957), 422–23.

77. Catherine Collomp, 'Unions, Civics, and National Identity: Organized Labor's Reaction to Immigration, 1881–1897,' *Labor History*, 29 (1988): 450–74. Collomp's point is strongly supported by Zolberg, 'How Many Exceptionalisms?' Katznelson and Zolberg, 427–28; and by Marks, 210, 212.

78. For examples of Wilson's many speeches, see *The Papers of Woodrow Wilson*, ed. Arthur S. Link, 69 vols (Princeton, 1966–94), 12: 265; 14: 365–78; 15: 160, 165, 168, 16: 285–86, 340–41; 18: 550; 19: 112; Lizabeth Cohen, *Making a New Deal: Industrial Workers in Chicago, 1919–1930* (Cambridge: Cambridge University Press, 1990), 165 and 432 note 14. It is interesting and noteworthy that 'Americanisation' became a pejorative phrase in British public discourse during the nineteenth century.

79. Gerstle, *Working-class Americanism: The Politics of Labor in a Textile City, 1914–1960* (Cambridge: Cambridge University Press, 1989), chaps. 1, 2.

80. Gerstle, 6–8, 12, chaps. 5, 9. See also Thomas Gobel, 'Becoming American: Ethnic Workers and the Rise of the CIO,' *Labor History*, 29 (1988): 173–98, esp. 198.

81. Clifford Geertz, *The Interpretation of Cultures: Selected Essays* (New York: Basic Books, 1973), chap. 8.

82. Quoted in Howe, *Socialism and America*, 107.

83. Gerstle, 178, 179, 182, 187.

84. Henry Nash Smith, *Virgin Land: The American West as Symbol and Myth* (1950: Cambridge, MA: Harvard University Press, 1970), 150.

85. In 1899 the Pope explicitly condemned the special heresy of 'Americanism,' by which he meant democracy and its traditions. In 1918 Van Wyck Brooks referred to Americanism pejoratively because 'the world' equated it with 'the worship of size, mass, quantity, and numbers.' Thirty-five years later Edmund Wilson defined Americanism as an affection for and partiality toward the United States. He then suggested that 'it has been made to serve some very bad causes, and is now a word to avoid.' See Sigmund Skard, *The American Myth and the European Mind: American Studies in Europe, 1776–1960* (Philadelphia: University of Pennsylvania Press, 1961), 53–54; Van Wyck Brooks, *Three Essays on America* (New York: Dutton, 1934), 127; Edmund Wilson, 'The United States,' in Wilson, *A Piece of My Mind: Reflections at Sixty* (New York: Farrar, Strauss and Cudahy, 1956), 32–35.

86. See Sheila Jasanoff, 'American Exceptionalism and the Political Acknowledgment of Risk,' *Daedalus*, 119.4 (Fall 1990): 61–81; Mary Ann Glendon, *Rights Talk: The Impoverishment of Political Discourse* (New York: Free Press, 1991); Anthony Lewis, 'Justice Black and the First Amendment,' *Alabama* Law *Review*, 38 (1986–87): 289–306.

87. Gerstle, 187, 195, 218. Aristide Zolberg points out that the labor movement in the United States was not so different from Europe in 1886 or 1936, but very different in 1956. 'The Roots of American Exceptionalism,' Heffer and Rovet, 101.

88. See, for example, Gordon S. Wood, *The Creation of the American Republic, 1776–1787* (Chapel Hill: University of North Carolina Press, 1969), ix and chap. 2, 'Republicanism'; Daniel T. Rodgers, 'Republicanism: The Career of a Concept,' *Journal of American History*, 79 (1992–93): 11–38; Ross, 23–30; Rudolph Vecoli, '"Free Country": The American Republic Viewed by the Italian Left, 1880–1920,' *In the Shadow of the Statue of Liberty*, ed. Debouzy, 35–36.

89. Vecoli, 37–53; Olivier Zunz, *Making America Corporate, 1870–1920* (Chicago: University of Chicago Press, 1990), a work that responds to the question: How did corporate capitalism succeed in creating a new work culture and new living patterns? Also Barry D. Karl, *The Uneasy State: The United States from 1915 to 1945* (Chicago: University of Chicago Press, 1983); and for reasons peculiar to their region and sensibility, unregenerate southern spokesmen also found this phasing both plausible and lamentable. See John Crowe Ransom's essay in Twelve Southerners, 17.

90. See Godfrey Hodgson, *America in Our Time* (Garden City, NY: Doubleday, 1976); Stanley Hoffman, *Gulliver's Troubles: Or, The Setting of American Foreign Policy* (New York: McGraw-Hill, 1968); Studs Terkel, *The Great Divide: Second Thoughts on the American Dream* (New York: Pantheon, 1988).

91. See Daniel T. Rodgers, *Contested Truths: Keywords in American Politics Since Independence* (New York: Basic Books, 1987), esp. chap. 1, and 91; Rob Kroes ed., *High Brow Meets Low Brow: American Culture as an Intellectual Concern* (Amsterdam: Free University Press, 1988), esp. 145; and John Lukacs, 'American History: The Terminological Problem,' *American Scholar*, 61 (1992): 17–32.

92. Carl Degler, 'In Pursuit of an American History,' 1–12 esp. 2, 4, 7. See also Miles Orvell, *The Real Thing: Imitation and Authenticity in American Culture, 1880–1940* (Chapel Hill: University of North Carolina Press, 1989), xxv–xxvi, 4; James Guimond, *American Photography and the American Dream* (Chapel Hill: University of North Carolina Press, 1991), 12, 103.

# Notes on Contributors

**Joyce Appleby** has since 1981 been Professor of American History at University of California, Los Angeles. The Harmsworth Professor of American History at Oxford University in 1990/91, and a former president of both the Organization of American Historians and the American Historical Association, her publications include *Inheriting the Revolution: The First Generation of Americans* (2000), *Capitalism and a New Social Order: The Republican Version of the 1790s* (1984), *Liberalism and Republicanism in the Historical Imagination* (1992); *Telling the Truth About History* (1994, with Lynn Hunt and Margaret Jacob); and (as editor) *Recollections of the Early Republic: Selected Autobiographies* (1997).

**Peter W. Bardaglio** is Interim Vice President and Academic Dean and Professor of History at Goucher College in Baltimore, Maryland, where he has been a member of the faculty since 1983. Educated at Brown University and Stanford, he held the Elizabeth Conolly Todd Distinguished Professorship at Goucher from 1995 to 2000 and was the Jessie Ball duPont fellow at the National Humanities Center in Research Triangle Park, North Carolina for the academic year 1999–2000. His book *Reconstructing the Household: Families, Sex, and the Law in the Nineteenth-Century South* (University of North Carolina Press, 1995), was awarded the 1996 James Rawley Prize from the Organization of American Historians for the best book published on the history of race relations in the United States.

**Thomas Byers** is Professor of American Literature at the Department of English, and Director of the Commonwealth Center for the Humanities and Society at the University of Louisville, Kentucky. During the Fall 1997 semester, Professor Byers was Visiting Fulbright Professor at the Department of English and Center for Gender Studies, University of Aarhus. His research fields include American literature, film and gender studies, and his publications include *What I Cannot Say: Self, Word and World in Whitman, Stevens and Merwin* (1989).

**Dale Carter** is Associate Professor of American Studies at the Department of English, University of Aarhus, Denmark; and Director of the American Studies Center Aarhus. Educated at the University of Warwick, the Institute of American Studies and King's College, University of London, his publications include *The Final Frontier: the Rise and Fall of the American Rocket State* (1988), and (as editor), *War and Cold War in American Foreign Policy, 1942–1962* (2001), *Blood on the Nash Ambassador: Investigations in American Culture* (1989), by Eric Mottram, and *Cracking the Ike Age: Aspects of Fifties America* (1992).

**Inger Hunnerup Dalsgaard** is Assistant Professor of American Studies at the Department of English, University of Aarhus, Denmark. She holds a *Cand. Mag.* degree in English and Religious Studies from the University of Aarhus and a Ph.D. in American Studies from King's College, University of London, where she completed a thesis entitled *The Fabrication of America: Myths of Technology in American Literature and Culture*. A former visiting researcher at the Massachusetts Institute of Technology, she has given papers at academic conferences in the United States, Europe and Scandinavia, and has published a number of scholarly articles on the works of Thomas Pynchon, Herman Melville, Mary Shelley and others. Her teaching and research interests include technology and culture, Asian-American Studies, and postmodernism.

**Eric Guthey** has been a DANVIS Postdoctoral Fellow at Odense University, as well as a Research Fellow in the Society of Scholars, Visiting Assistant Professor of Law, History and Communication in the School of Business Administration, and Faculty Associate in the Program in American Cultures at the University of Michigan, Ann Arbor. Educated at Emory University, he is currently Associate Professor of American Studies at the Copenhagen Business School, and the author of *Ted Turner/Media Legend/*

*Market Realities*, to be published by the University of California Press.

**John Halsey** is Assistant Professor of Sociology at the State University of New York, Brockport. Educated at the University of East Anglia and Exeter University, he has since 1977 been based in London, where he is Resident Director of SUNY Brockport's European Studies Program at Brunel University. Among his publications are 'Teaching Sociology in an Overseas Program,' *Teaching Sociology*, 18 (1990) and 'The Impact of Local Management on School Management Style,' *Local Government Policy Making*, 19 (1993). He has also co-authored a number of review articles with Bruce Leslie. His main research interests involves Anglo-American comparisons, especially in the field of education.

**Michael Kammen** is Professor of History and Culture at the Department of History, Cornell University. His published works include *In the Past Lane: Historical Perspectives on American Culture* (1997); *Mystic Chords of Memory: The Transformation of Tradition in American Culture* (1991), *Selvages and Biases: The Fabric of History in American Culture* (1987), *A Machine That Would Go of Itself: The Constitution in American Culture* (1986); *People of Paradox: An Inquiry Concerning the Origins of American Civilization* (1973); and *American Culture, American Tastes: Social Change and the Twentieth Century* (1999). A former President of the Organization of American Historians, his awards have included the Pulitzer Prize (1973), the Francis Parkman Prize (1987), the Henry Adams Prize (1987), and the National Book Award of the Popular Culture Association (1996).

**W. Bruce Leslie** is Professor of History and Director of Graduate Studies at the Department of History, State University of New York, Brockport, and during 1996/97 was Visiting Fulbright Professor at the Department of English, University of Aarhus. The author of *Gentlemen and Scholars: College and Community in the 'Age of the University,' 1865–1917* (1993), as well as numerous articles on the history of American education, he was educated at

Princeton and Johns Hopkins universities. In addition to serving currently on the Scandinavian Fulbright Selection Board and the Editorial Board of the *History of Higher Education Annual*, Professor Leslie is researching a case study of mass higher education, to be published as *Breaking the Mold: State University College at Brockport Since World War II*.

**James Mendelsohn** has in recent years been an associate of the W. E. B. Du Bois Institute for Afro-American Research at Harvard University. Educated at Amherst College and Washington University. Professor Mendelsohn has taught at Boston University as well as secondary schools in St. Louis. During the 1995/96 academic year he was Visiting Fulbright Professor at the University of Tübingen in Germany. His teaching and research interests focus on American literature and African-American Studies.

**David E. Nye** has since 1992 been Professor of American Studies at the Department of History and Center for American Studies, University of Southern Denmark, Odense. Educated at Amherst College and the University of Minnesota, his books include *Electrifying America: Social Meanings of a New Technology, 1880–1940* (1990), *American Technological Sublime* (1994), *Narratives and Spaces: Technology and the Construction of American Culture* (1998), and *Consuming Power: A Social History of American Energies* (1997). He has also published *Contemporary American Society*, 4th ed (2001) and (as editor) *Technologies of Landscape: From Reaping to Recycling* (2000). His current project is *Second Creation*, a book on American technological foundation stories. He has been a visiting fellow at Harvard, MIT, Cambridge University, and the Netherlands Institute for Advanced Study. His awards include The Abel Wolman Award (1991) and The Dexter Prize (1993).

**Jody W. Pennington** is Acting Associate Professor at the Department of English, University of Aarhus, Denmark, where he teaches Media and Cultural Studies as well as American Studies. Educated at Georgia Southwestern College and the University of Aarhus, he has published articles and presented papers on various aspects of film and popular music, as well as American constitutional law. He has recently been awarded his doctorate for a thesis entitled *Margins in the Mainstream: Changes in Sexual Behavior, in the Representation of Nudity and Sexual Behavior in Popular Film, and in Mainstream Public Discourse between 1965 and 1980.*

**Helle Porsdam** is Associate Professor of American Studies at the Center for American Studies, University of Southern Denmark, Odense. Educated at the University of Copenhagen and Yale University, she was an ACLS Visiting Scholar and a Liberal Arts Fellow at the Harvard Law School in 1992–93, and returned there during the Fall of 2000 as a Liberal Arts Fellow. Professor Porsdam's research interests include law and American culture, American intellectual history, and literature, about which she has published widely. Her most recent publication is *Legally Speaking: Contemporary American Culture and the Law* (1999). She is currently involved in a research project on Danish legalization as a form of Americanization.